Fluent in Fantasy

Genreflecting Advisory Series

Diana Tixier Herald, Series Editor

Genreflecting: A Guide to Reading Interests in Genre Fiction, 4th Edition.
By Diana Tixier Herald.

Teen Genreflecting.
By Diana Tixier Herald.

Romance Fiction: A Guide to the Genre.
By Kristin Ramsdell.

Fluent in Fantasy: A Guide to Reading Interests.
By Diana Tixier Herald.

Now Read This: A Guide to Mainstream Fiction, 1978-1998.
By Nancy Pearl. With assistance from Martha Knappe and Chris Higashi.

Hooked on Horror: A Guide to Reading Interests in Horror Fiction.
By Anthony J. Fonseca and June Michele Pulliam.

Junior Genreflecting: A Guide to Good Reads and Series Fiction for Children.
By Bridget Dealy Volz, Lynda Blackburn Welborn, and Cheryl Perkins Scheer.

Fluent in Fantasy

A Guide to Reading Interests

Diana Tixier Herald

1999
Libraries Unlimited, Inc.
Englewood, Colorado

To Harriett and Bill Banks for their constant encouragement and support.

Copyright © 1999 Libraries Unlimited, Inc.
All Rights Reserved
Printed in the United States of America

Illustrations that are from NoveList (of the CARL Corporation) are used with permission.

Libraries Unlimited, Inc.
P.O. Box 6633
Englewood, CO 80155-6633
1-800-237-6124
www.lu.com

Library of Congress Cataloging-in-Publication Data

Herald, Diana Tixier.
   Fluent in fantasy: a guide to reading interests / Diana Tixier Herald.
   ix, 260 p, 19x26 cm. -- (Genreflecting advisory series)
   Includes bibliographical references and indexes.
   ISBN 1-56308-655-7
   1. Fantastic fiction--Bibliography. 2. Best books. 3. Books and reading--United States. I. Title. II. Series.
   Z5917.F3H47 1999
   [PN3435]
   016.80883'8766--dc21   99-10204
                                                                      CIP

Contents

Acknowledgments

I wish to thank all the fantasy fans who have taken the time to share their favorite authors and titles with me in libraries, on the Internet, at bookstores, and in schools both in the United States and abroad. Special thanks go to Bonnie Kunzel and Nathan Herald who always recommend wonderful titles and know more about fantasy books than anyone else I've ever met. Samuel Lubell has also provided valuable insights. Matt Loy coordinated the Battle of the Books that resulted in the YALSA-BK Best Fantasy for YA List (Appendix B). The list is published in this book with the permission of the Young Adult Library Services Association, a division of the American Library Association.

Authors of fiction are my true heroes because they have filled my life with magic and wonder.

Grateful acknowledgment is made for permission to reprint the following copyrighted material:

To David Hartwell for his definition of fantasy in the introduction to *Masterpieces of Fantasy and Enchantment* (St. Martin's Press, 1988).

I am grateful to NoveList for their permission to use images and concepts of images from their program throughout the Genreflecting Advisory Series. NoveList is the electronic readers advisory resource from CARL Corporation that provides subject and genre access to thousands of fiction titles for readers of all ages, and contains numerous annotations from the Genreflecting Advisory Series. For more information about NoveList, contact (888) 439-2275, or visit http://www.carl.org/novelist. ©1998 CARL Corporation.

And last but not least acknowledgment is made for the great contribution the late Betty Rosenberg made to fans of fiction with her first rule of reading: "Never apologize for your reading tastes."

Chapter 1

Introduction

Fantasy conjures up many images. The enchantment of magic and the seductiveness of heroic figures are part of the appeal. Elven lords in sylvan palaces. Swashbuckling, brawny heroes wielding enormous swords. Guardian angels lurking over a young harpist. Beautiful princesses held captive by mysterious wizards. Girls changing shape and flying away as crows. A world so different from our own that ordinary folk can make enormous changes. Fantasy can be an escape, a journey to mysterious and exotic worlds, or just an entertaining way to while away some spare time.

As a fiction genre, fantasy has greatly expanded and evolved in the past 30 years. It has influenced all forms of media including film, computer games, and comics. Nondevotees of the genre have turned many fantasy novels into best-sellers, including *Dinotopia, The Mists of Avalon,* and Jean Auel's Earth's Children series. Fantasy aficionados have been responsible for a proliferation of fan clubs, newsletters, e-mail lists, and Internet news groups.

The roots of fantasy reach far into the earliest human civilizations with folktales and fables of talking animals, legends of great heroes, and fanciful fairy tales full of magic and mystery.

What Is Fantasy?

It seems that everyone in the world has his or her own definition of fantasy. The way individuals think about and categorize fantasy also varies widely. Whatever it is and whatever it includes, it is widely popular, and many readers have passionate feelings about it. Any time an attempt is made to codify a "true" definition of fantasy, there will be dissent.

In this guide, I consider written fantasy, mostly novels but also some shorter works. Some works that many people might define as fantasy are not included here. The selection is an attempt to define this beloved genre. For some other definitions, consider the following options. According to *The Encyclopedia of Fantasy* (Clute and Grant 1997):

> A fantasy text is a self-coherent narrative. When set in this world, it tells a story which is impossible in the world as we perceive it; when set in an otherworld, that otherworld will be impossible, though stories set there may be possible in its terms.

Manlove's definition from *Modern Fantasy* (1975) is quite different from the preceding definition, perhaps demonstrating the changes that have occurred in the field in the past couple of decades:

> A fiction evoking wonder and containing a substantial and irreducible element of supernatural or impossible worlds, beings or objects with which the reader or the characters within the story become on at least partly familiar terms.

Fantasy Literature: A Core Collection and Reference Guide, by Marshall B. Tymn, Kenneth J. Zahorski, and Robert H. Boyer (1979), defines it as follows:

> Fantasy, as a literary genre, is composed of works in which nonrational phenomena play a significant part. That is, they are works in which events occur, or places or creatures exist, that could not occur or exist according to rational standards or scientific explanations. The nonrational phenomena of fantasy simply do not fall within human experience or accord with natural laws as we know them. Thus history as we know it does not record that someone pulled a sword from a stone, or that someone forged a ring of power to control nine other rings of lesser power in Middle Earth. If such events or places are recorded, we regard the source not as history or as realistic fiction, but as fantasy.

The presence of nonrational phenomena, then, is the principal criterion for distinguishing fantasy from history or from other types of literature.

Award-winning fantasy editors David G. Hartwell and Kathryn Cramer define fantasy in the introduction to *Masterpieces of Fantasy and Enchantment* (1988):

> Fantasy stories take the reader clearly out of the world of consensus reality. Sometimes we begin in the "real" world, but it quickly becomes evident that behind the veil of real things and people another world exists, rich and strange

and magical. The most easily categorized fantasy works are defined by their specifically magical nature, whether they take place in an imaginary medieval landscape, fairyland, or a contemporary metropolis such as New York City or Seattle: magic works. Someone in the story can do magic, has supernatural powers, or is a supernatural creature. While this is the dominant mode, it has never been exclusively the case. The more general case is that fantasy fiction contains and depends upon the intrusion of at least one clearly fantastic element or event into the real world (such as Mark Twain's echo salesman in "The Canvasser's Tale" and Margaret St. Clair's goddess in "The Goddess on the Street Corner"); or, at the other extreme, one real person onto an utterly fantastic landscape (e.g., Alice falling into Wonderland, Dorothy in Oz). In either case we have an entry into the fantastic world through setting or character that we recognize as familiar and comforting in the face of the strange and often disturbingly unfamiliar.

Tom Shippey, in the introduction to *The Oxford Book of Fantasy Stories* (1994), uses the following definition:

> Fantasy literature, in its broadest definition which includes everything from "Cinderella" to *Beowulf* to Stephen Donaldson, is literature which makes deliberate use of something known to be impossible.

Fantasy always tells a tale. No matter how literary a fantasy may be or how surrealistic, the fact that there is a plot, that something happens, is integral to a work being fantasy. Fantasy is the stuff of myth, of flights of fancy, folklore, fairy tales, and magic.

It is nearly impossible to define fantasy in today's world without considering science fiction. Both genres are published by the same companies, edited by the same editors, and featured in the same magazines and on the same newsgroups and e-mail lists. Libraries often shelve fantasy and science fiction together, as do bookstores. Readers and even the writers don't always agree into which genre a specific work falls.

Orson Scott Card, the only author ever to have won back-to-back Hugo and Nebula awards for his Ender Wiggins series, considers many of his works that are frequently described as science fiction to be fantasy. He quips that rivets in the cover illustration are indicative of science fiction, while foliage indicates fantasy.

The idea of fantasy may conjure up visions of children's fairy tales or of dragons and unicorns or sword-wielding heroes and sorcerers, but fantasy can encompass much more. Fantasy can take place in the prehistoric past, as in the books of Jean Auel, William Sarabande, and W. Michael and Kathleen Gear. It can take place in a future so distant that Earth's roots make a mythical past and witches rule, as in Andre Norton's Witch World series, or dragons fly, as in Anne McCaffrey's Pern series. Fantasy can be set in the here and now, where the worlds of the mundane and the magical intertwine, as in the works of Charles de Lint, Emma Bull, and Will Shetterly. Fantasy involves powers or beings outside the realm of what our civilizations consider real.

In the interest of helping as many people as possible find the books they want to read, the broadest definition of fantasy is used here. The titles in this volume include works containing magic and mythical creatures. Works set in a mythical past or a world out of time are also included. This brings in some books that the authors consider to be science fiction (Anne McCaffrey's Pern books most notably) but that readers continue to include in their lists of favorite fantasy.

Fantasy does have rules. It has conventions and traditions. The rules in a fantasy world are not the same as those that exist in the everyday world most of us inhabit, but still the rules are there. For a fantasy world to exist, thrive, and live, it must be internally consistent even if it is not consistent with the world as we know it.

Fantasy is filled with magic, not always deliberately invoked magic, but nonetheless magic as the mundane world would perceive it. It is peopled by individuals like us but often also by those we do not encounter on an everyday basis. Creatures of myth and legend, unicorns, dragons, chimera, harpies, vampires, ghosts, and others roam the halls of fantasy. Professions not known in our contemporary world flourish. Hedgewitches, necromancers, warlocks, magicians, enchanters, and heroes perform their duties amidst settings that may look like our world or may be lavishly fantastic or primitively austere.

One of the most interesting observations about fantasy is that it has appeal to a larger age range than other genres. The authors do not write for adults or for teens but for fantasy readers. This leads to some interesting placements of books in library collections. In some libraries, Meredith Ann Pierce's Dark Angel trilogy starts in the children's department, moves to the teen section with the second volume, and by the third volume is in the adult collection. Adults read C. S. Lewis's Chronicles of Narnia and Lloyd Alexander's Prydain Chronicles, while some children read T. H. White's *Once and Future King*. Ageism doesn't exist in fantasy. This may be in part because until the 1970s fantasy was considered a genre for children, even though adults secretly continued to love the Oz books and other tales of fantasy found in the children's sections of libraries and bookstores. It is interesting to note that in the late 1960s a big deal was made of fantasy for adults. The Ballantine Adult Fantasy series was aimed at adults rather than at children. Currently publishers for both young adults and adults publish books that are enjoyed by a wide range of ages.

Importance of Fantasy

Fantasy takes us out of our world and places us in worlds where anything can happen, as long as it is internally consistent to that world. It can be pure escapism, taking us away from our day-to-day problems to a place where magic can move mountains. The ancients knew the importance of fantasy, the power of the imagination. They used fantasy to convey and pass on to new generations the principles, values, and truths they felt were important. Psychologists such as Carl Jung and Bruno Bettelheim have written about the power of fairy tales. Jayne Ann Krentz, the best-selling romance novelist, has talked about genre fiction as being heroic fiction, stories that present characters who are stronger, smarter, and braver than most people in real life. They face obstacles more formidable than any we usually face and triumph over them. Perhaps fantasy is the genre that most fits what Krentz was talking about, for through fantasy we can journey to a world where we are more beautiful, heroic, and honorable than in our everyday lives.

As humans we need stories, we thrive on them. Every culture has a storytelling tradition. Fantasy can also be a medium for conveying truths in a way that makes them more real than an ordinary telling could. There is something about the portrayal of the holocaust in Jane Yolen's *Briar Rose* that makes the horror more real at a visceral level than true life accounts do.

The following quote refers specifically to Vonda N. McIntyre's *Sun and Moon,* but it describes the importance of fantasy. "Her imaginings enliven her history with wonder, but, as in the best fantasy, they serve less to dazzle by their inventiveness than to illuminate brilliantly real-world truths—here, humanity's responses, base and noble, when confronting the unknown."—*Publishers Weekly*, July 28, 1997.

Where Is Fantasy Going?

Recent trends in fantasy indicate that a divergence is taking place between the adventure tale and the literary tale. While the adventure-based fantasy is growing fully realized worlds rich with history, language, politics, and involved genealogies, the literary fantasy is moving toward mainstream fiction as mainstream fiction more readily embraces magic realism. The trend in adventure fantasy is toward epic sagas, using multiple volumes to develop the worlds and magic and heroism to demonstrate the character of the populations. Literary fantasy is usually contained between the covers of individual works, although they sometimes are related. While not in a strict sense a shared world, the fantasy worlds created by such literary writers as Charles de Lint and Terri Windling bear a commonality that enlarges their boundaries. The animal people and other beliefs found in Native American legends are playing a larger role in fantasy writing. The magic in literary fantasy takes place on a smaller, more personal scale than in adventure fantasy.

Scope and Purpose

The purpose of this volume is to help readers find the books they want to read and to help booksellers and librarians help their clients find those books. It is designed as a guide that can be taken into the stacks. It groups books together that may be enjoyed by the same reader so that person can find the next book he or she wants to read at a glance. The titles selected for this book have been gleaned from many sources. Some came from talking with library users, bookstore shoppers, and fantasy readers on the Internet and from the author's fourteen years' experience as a readers' advisor in public libraries and as a bookseller. Other titles listed were gathered from lists of favorite fantasy titles found in books, on the Internet, and in magazines. Bestseller lists, review journals, and magazines featuring fantasy were used. The listings are not intended to be all inclusive of recently published fantasy but rather to list the works most likely to have been read by library users and the titles of similar books that should be readily available. The books listed were first published from sometime in the nineteenth century up to 1998.

Selection of Titles

The publications included in this volume were selected from titles, authors, and series that are found in public libraries, requested by library patrons, award winners, and are favored in reader polls. The purpose of grouping by subgenre is to facilitate readers finding similar books that they may enjoy. Further access points are provided by descriptors which are indexed in the subject index. The subgenres were determined by observing fantasy readers' tastes in libraries and bookstores.

Selected titles are annotated to provide a flavor of the subgenre. Not all titles are annotated, especially in series, to keep this volume compact enough for easily taking to the stacks in pursuit of books.

Publisher information, with the exception of anthologies, is not included, because book-length fantasy is often reprinted by different publishers. It is not uncommon to find a hardcover edition, a trade paperback, and a mass market paperback of the same title, all published by different houses. ISBN numbers change rapidly, especially in paperback editions, so they also are not included. Publication dates are included only on items of historical significance. The international nature of fantasy fandom makes for varied publication dates from country to country. It is not uncommon for short stories or novellas to be rewritten into novel-length works, further clouding the dating issue.

Organization of the Book

The first section of this volume attempts to define fantasy, to tell why it is important, and to direct users (librarians, educators, booksellers, fans, and writers) to resources with additional information on fantasy literature. It also provides the reader with a historical overview of the genre and information on how to use this guide.

Part 2 defines the many and varied subgenres of fantasy and provides annotations and lists of titles demonstrative of each type. It is not meant to be all inclusive, but rather to provide examples and starting places. Most titles do fit into several subgenres. For some annotations, keywords printed in indented, italic type are provided to help readers search the subject index to find other related headings. Award-winning titles are denoted by a ♀. Books popular with young adults but not necessarily published for them are denoted by a ⊄. Books that have a subject heading of "younger readers" may be of particular interest for middle or junior high school readers, but they are also enjoyed by adults. Books released in 1998 are denoted by a ☜. (See the example on page 7.) Each subgenre chapter ends with "D's Picks," a listing of some of this author's personal favorites. Inclusion in "D's Picks" is a personal recommendation only, in answer to the question "Which books do you like?"

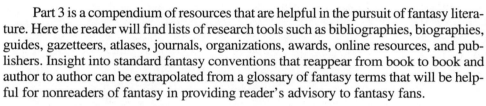

Bishop, Michael

 Unicorn Mountain. The problems of dying unicorns in an other dimension and the AIDS epidemic in our world intersect. 1989 Mythopoeic Award Winner.

Parallel Worlds • AIDS.

Coville, Bruce

YA Unicorn Chronicles.

Parallel Worlds • Dragons • Younger Readers.

Into the Land of Unicorns.

NEW A Glory of Unicorns.

Part 3 is a compendium of resources that are helpful in the pursuit of fantasy literature. Here the reader will find lists of research tools such as bibliographies, biographies, guides, gazetteers, atlases, journals, organizations, awards, online resources, and publishers. Insight into standard fantasy conventions that reappear from book to book and author to author can be extrapolated from a glossary of fantasy terms that will be helpful for nonreaders of fantasy in providing reader's advisory to fantasy fans.

The appendixes give readers a guide to some of the terminology common in fantasy fiction and list titles recommended for young adults.

Reviews and Resources for Librarians

Because fantasy and science fiction (SF) are so inextricably linked, the resources for both genres tend to have a huge overlap. Standard library review sources such as *Library Journal* and *Booklist* do a commendable job on the small quantity of fantasy that they review. *Kirkus* reviewers seem to like very little fantasy and frequently give scathing reviews to books that go on to become beloved favorites of fantasy readers. *VOYA* is one of the best library market review resources because it covers many paperback originals not reviewed elsewhere. Genre-specific review journals such as *Locus* and *Science Fiction Chronicle* devote much more space to fantasy and science fiction and therefore can review many more titles. Magazines such as *Asimov's Science Fiction Magazine, Magazine of Fantasy and Science Fiction*, *Realms of Fantasy,* and *Marion Zimmer Bradley's Fantasy Magazine* also feature reviews.

It is important in fantasy as with most genre fiction to be aware of what is currently being published in paperback. Many of the most popular authors and series start out in that format and after achieving popularity and a following in paperback are then published in hardcover.

Browse the science fiction sections of bookstores, where fantasy is shelved. Many popular fantasy authors are published by game companies (such as TSR) and are never reviewed in the journals read by librarians, possibly because game marketing people don't always recognize the library market.

Ask library fantasy readers what they like. A great question is "What fantasy authors do you like that you haven't found in our library?"

Online resources also offer information for the fantasy reader's advisor. Some of the publishers who list new releases on their Web sites even provide sample chapters. Online resources such as science fiction and fantasy databases, publishers' Web sites, organizational Web sites, and review sites are listed in Chapter 20. All online sites listed in this guide can be reached by hyperlinks that are regularly checked and updated at http://www.sff.net/people/dherald.

SF Weekly (www.scifi.com/sfw/ [all Web sites in this chapter accessed Nov. 30, 1998]) is an online publication that discusses news of the science fiction and fantasy world including reviews of books and movies.

Amazon.com (http://www.amazon.com), a large online bookseller, features many lists and reviews from professional journals as well as reader comments on fantasy titles. Mysterious Galaxy (http://www.mystgalaxy.com/mainrev.html) features reviews of selected titles. Mark V. Ziesing Bookseller (http://www.bigchar.com/ziesing/fantasy.htm) is one of the few online booksellers that lists fantasy separately from science fiction. His sometimes outrageous comments are always entertaining and often right on the mark. BookPages (http://amazon. co.uk), a British site, includes fantasy with science fiction and is an excellent source of books published in Great Britain. While it is difficult to sift the fantasy from the science fiction, the annotations may make it worth the effort. A Canadian fantasy bookseller is White Dwarf books (http://www.deadwrite.com). Dangerous Visions (http://www. readsf.com/index~main.html) lists fantasy, science fiction, and horror (all lumped together) by publication date, with one-line annotations. DreamHaven Books (http://www.visi.com/~dreamhvn/) provides much of the same information. Future Fantasy (http://futfan.com) also offers a list of books recommended in *Locus*. It and other online bookstores that do not offer reviews of the books can be helpful in discerning if a reader's favorite author has anything new.

The Nature of Fantasy Readers

Keep in mind that this section contains sweeping generalizations and should be understood not to refer to every fantasy reader, because of course all readers are individuals. Fantasy readers often latch onto the genre at a younger age than do readers of other genres. The teen-aged fans of fantasy, and even precocious child fans, read the same books as senior citizen and adult fans. The reader of Robert Jordan's Wheel of Time series is as likely to be fourteen as forty-one. The reader of C. S. Lewis's Chronicles of Narnia could be ten or a hundred. This is not true of other genres: adult readers of romance are unlikely to read YA romance novels and adult readers of suspense are not in the habit of hunting down the newest R. L. Stine book.

Fantasy readers are not intimidated by sheer volume. Indeed, it sometimes seems that they select their books by the pound. Thick books in lengthy series are common and perhaps even the norm in fantasy.

Adolescent males who tend to read less than people in other groups are curiously often attracted to fantasy. Because of this, fantasy is responsible for turning many young men into avid readers.

The appeal of fantasy knows no boundaries of age or gender. The readers are those who choose to see the magic in possibilities and are eager for good new titles to read. The multiculturalism of fantasy brings beings as divergent as elves, dwarves, dragons, and humans together in a way that makes minor variations of skin color or hair texture totally insignificant.

Chapter 2

Overview of the Genre

The world of fantasy can be a confusing place for individuals unfamiliar with the conventions and history of the genre. Avid fantasy readers have their own language, the language that is spoken in fantasy fiction. Readers new to the genre may be helped by knowing about these conventions and reader's advisors in both libraries and bookstores will better be able to help their clientele if they have an understanding of some of the common terms and elements frequently found in the genre and the history of the field.

Fantasy Conventions

The conventions of fantasy are many and an understanding of them is often necessary to derive full enjoyment from a book. Most readers pick these up over months or years of reading fantasy. They are the unofficial rules of the fantasy genre. Many of the current conventions in fantasy date back to Tolkien's masterwork, *The Lord of the Rings,* but the history of others is lost in the mists of time. A list of definitions of some of the most common fantasy conventions is provided in Appendix A.

History of the Fantasy Genre

If fantasy is defined as tales of magic and wonder, the roots of the genre reach into the depths of the past to the oldest tales we know. *Gilgamesh, The Odyssey,* and *Beowulf,* among the oldest of written tales, could also be considered to be the oldest of fantasy. The fairy tales written by Charles Perrault in seventeenth-century France and by the Brothers Grimm in nineteenth-century Germany are the stories many think of as the underpinnings of fantasy. The "sanitizing" of these stories for children has led to the misconception that fantasy is a children's genre.

There are three major schools of thought regarding the history of fantasy. One holds that all stories written before the eighteenth century were fantasy, because science as we know it did not exist. Another school of thought traces the origins of fantasy to the popularity of fairy tales in the eighteenth century. The last major school of thought places the origins of fantasy with the one writer who is universally credited with being the originator of modern fantasy, J. R. R. Tolkien. He was a member of a group formed in the 1930s called the "Inklings," which also included C. S. Lewis.

To throw another theory into the mix, Robert Silverberg, in his introduction to *The Fantasy Hall of Fame: The Definitive Collection of the Best Modern Fantasy Chosen by the Members of the Science Fiction and Fantasy Writers of America,* attributes the beginning of the genre to John W. Campbell in 1939, with the inception of the magazine *Unknown.* That is the cutoff date used by the Science Fiction and Fantasy Writers of America when voting on the best modern fantasy to include in their Fantasy Hall of Fame. The fifteen authors receiving the most votes are indicative of who the writers themselves consider the greatest of their number. The top fifteen authors selected (in order of ranking) were:

Fritz Leiber

Shirley Jackson

Theodore Sturgeon

Avram Davidson

Peter S. Beagle

Ray Bradbury

Ursula K. Le Guin

Roger Zelazny

James Tiptree, Jr.

J. G. Ballard

Philip K. Dick

Harlan Ellison

Jorge Luis Borges

Robert Bloch

Terry Bisson

Although fantasy as a marketing genre began in the late 1960s, it really took off in the 1970s. In 1992 the Science Fiction Writers of America added "Fantasy" to the title of their organization, recognizing the importance of the genre and the close relationship of the two speculative fiction genres.

Opinions on the history of fantasy as a genre are often found in the introductions of fantasy anthologies and sometimes in essays contained therein. The beautifully written introduction to Patti Perret's *The Faces of Fantasy,* written by fantasy author, editor, and expert Terri Windling, is also a terrific introduction to the history of the fantasy genre.

Early Fantasy Authors

As the best of things are built on a solid foundation, the world of fantasy has several early writers who provide this foundation. The following list of authors is not intended for scholars of fantasy fiction but rather for the reader of fantasy who is likely to be using the public library. For readers who consider Tolkien the originator of fantasy, the following could be considered as precursors.

L. Frank Baum. *The Wonderful Wizard of Oz,* published in 1900, and the subsequent books in the series are set in a parallel world reached by a Kansas tornado (see Chapter 10). They involve a quest quite similar to those later found in sword and sorcery books (see Chapter 3).

Lewis Carroll. *Alice's Adventures in Wonderland* (1865) and *Through the Looking-Glass and What Alice Found There* (1871) feature a parallel world reached originally through a rabbit hole leading to a surrealistic land.

Lord Dunsany. The prolific Edward John Moreton Drax Plunkett, Eighteenth Lord of Dunsany, is credited with creating much of the basis for modern fantasy. His oeuvre is long and varied, but *The King of Elfland's Daughter* (1924) (see Chapter 8 for modern tales of Faerie) is a work that still sparks interest in fantasy fans.

E. R. Eddison. *The Worm Ouroboros* (1922) is often cited and is therefore important in the history of fantasy but fans who enjoy the conflict of good versus evil will not find it in this alternate world, which is filled with battles for battling's sake.

H. Rider Haggard. *King Solomon's Mines* (1885) is the prototype of the heroic lost world fantasy.

Rudyard Kipling. *The Jungle Book* (1894) is a prototype for animal fantasy (Chapter 7). *Puck of Pook's Hill* (1906) is a collection of stories with an emphasis on Faerie (Chapter 8).

H. P. Lovecraft. Known for his Cthulhu mythos, Lovecraft's dark fantasy (Chapter 16) has had his greatest influence on authors of horror fantasy.

George MacDonald. *Lilith* (1895) is a journey into a parallel world.

William Morris. *The Well at the World's End* (1896). In an alternate world (see Chapter 10), a young prince goes on a quest, experiencing many adventures.

Mervyn Peake. Gormenghast trilogy: *Titus Groan, Gormenghast,* and *Titus Alone.* In an ancient, crumbling, enormous castle, Titus's life is strictly circumscribed. Many fans believe this is the best fantasy series ever written.

Evangeline Walton. Mabinogion quartet: *The Virgin and the Swine* (also published as *The Island of the Mighty*) (1936), *The Children of Llyr, The Song of Rhiannon,* and *The Prince of Annwn.* These books are based on Welsh legends.

An online resource listing many early fantasy authors and their fantasy titles is on the World Wide Web at http://www. mcs. net/~finn/fant/authors/erlyindex.html (accessed Nov. 30, 1998).

It lists the sixty or so Ballantine Adult Fantasies edited by Lin Carter in the late 1960s and early 1970s. It is interesting to see which books Carter and editor Betty Ballantine considered classics of fantasy.

Readers interested in early writers of fantasy may also want to find *Classic Fantasy Writers,* edited by Harold Bloom (1994). The writers included are L. Frank Baum, William Beckford, James Branch Cabell, Lewis Carroll, Lord Dunsany, Kenneth Grahame, H. Rider Haggard, Lafcadio Hearn, Rudyard Kipling, Andrew Lang, George MacDonald, William Morris, Beatrix Potter, and Oscar Wilde.

The recognition of modern fantasy as a genre can be considered to have started in 1975 with the first World Fantasy Convention and the first World Fantasy Awards. It can also be traced back to 1971 when publishers first started labeling some of their books "Fantasy."

One interesting way to look at the evolution of fantasy as a modern genre is by looking at which authors have won the World Fantasy Life Achievement Awards, first awarded in 1975:

1975   Robert Bloch

1976   Fritz Leiber

1977   Ray Bradbury

1978   Frank Belknap Long

1979   Jorge Luis Borges

1980   Manly Wade Wellman

1981   C. L. Moore

1982   Italo Calvino

1983   Roald Dahl

1984   L. Sprague de Camp, Richard Matheson, E. Hoffman Price, Jack Vance, and Donald Wandrei. (Previous recipients of the award deadlocked the year they voted, creating a five-way tie.)

1985   Theodore Sturgeon

1986   Avram Davidson

1987   Jack Finney

1988   E. F. Bleiler

1989   Evangeline Walton

1990   R. A. Lafferty

1991   Ray Russell

1992   Edd Cartier

1993   Harlan Ellison

1994   Jack Williamson

1995   Ursula K. Le Guin

1996   Gene Wolfe

1997   Madeleine L'Engle

1998   Edward L. Ferman and Andre Norton

Perhaps through the history of fantasy we can gain some inkling of what the future of this genre will bring.

Chapter 3

Sword and Sorcery

According to the *Encyclopedia of Fantasy* (1997), the term *sword and sorcery* was coined in 1961 by Fritz Leiber at the behest of Michael Moorcock to describe the subgenre of fantasy featuring "muscular heroes in violent conflict with a variety of villains, chiefly wizards, witches, evil spirits and other creatures whose powers are—unlike the hero's—supernatural in origin."

This subgenre is often confused with the genre as a whole. Sword and sorcery is usually set in an alternate pastoral or nonindustrialized world, sometimes akin to medieval European kingdoms, where magic is manifest and heroic deeds including swashbuckling feats of derring-do are commonplace. The protagonist usually starts off as an ordinary soul who is caught up in a chain of events leading to encounters with magic and the need to fight or flee.

This world of adventure, in which magic works and heroes and heroines wage epic combat with forces of evil, is one of fantasy's most popular types. These tales feature sorcerers and magicians, large elements of the supernatural, romance, and often a quest with daunting hazards. Many of the authors listed here also appear on science fiction lists. The heroes, and sometimes heroines, of the sword-and-sorcery, magic-filled adventures usually inhabit a world created for them, and typically appear in trilogies or in lengthy open-ended series.

Sword and sorcery could also be divided into two major theme types: those with a moral focus and those without. Most sword and sorcery has at its core the conflict between good and evil. There are some, however, that have as their basis the conflict between strong and stronger. In the Howard books and the Eddison books, it is not so much a matter of might makes right, but rather might triumphant at any cost, never mind what is right.

This is perhaps the largest subgenre of fantasy. It is broken down further into quest, heroic, epic, and magic.

The following series combine all the major themes of sword and sorcery, involving heroic quests and magic in many varied forms.

Brenner, Mayer Alan

Dance of the Gods series.

Catastrophe's Spell.

Spell of Intrigue.

Spell of Fate.

Spell of Apocalypse.

Cooper, Louise

Time Master trilogy. "The forces of Order against the forces of Chaos in the age-old struggle of good versus evil."—Bonnie Kunzel.

Sorcery • Gods • Parallel Worlds.

The Initiate.

The Outcast.

The Master.

Star Ascendant. "The prequel to the Time Master Trilogy in which the new First Magus of the Lords of Chaos is so insanely sadistic that a movement rises to unleash the Lords of Order and reverse the balance of power."—Bonnie Kunzel.

de Camp, L. Sprague

Novaria series.

Humor • Alternate Worlds.

The Goblin Tower. In a country where no bad king can last long, no good king can either, because after ruling for five years the monarch must be beheaded. King Jorian is quite attached to his head, so he decides it is in his best interest to effect a daring escape from the scaffold.

The Clocks of Iraz. An ancient prophecy foretold that the clocks would save Iraz. Jorian knows he must repair them so that he can rescue Queen Estrildis, his wife, from Xylar City, where he is still wanted for a royal beheading.

The Unbeheaded King. Three years after his escape, Jorian has still been unable to rescue his beloved wife from Xylar City, but now he and the aged wizard Karadur are flying through the night in a great copper bathtub powered by a demon. But alas, the best laid plans can go wrong, especially when you put a chair, a dog, and a unicorn into the equation.

The Reluctant King is an omnibus edition of the first three volumes in the series.

The Honorable Barbarian. Jorian is safely retired, so now it is his brother Kerin's turn to get into trouble, and his talent for trouble is considerable.

The Fallible Fiend.

The Incorporated Knight sequence. Co-authored with Catherine Crook de Camp.

The Incorporated Knight. Practical Eudoric Dambertson is well suited to trade, but unfortunately he is a knight in pursuit of a bride and must deal with all the impractical demands of chivalry. To please his future father-in-law and win the hand of his bride he must bring back two square yards of dragon hide, not the easiest of tasks.

The Pixilated Peeress. Sergeant Thorolf's problems are just beginning when he finds the naked countess Yvette hiding behind a bush. She demands that he take her to a wizard for a magical disguise. Unfortunately Doctor Bardi is slightly senile, and his spell to disguise her as a dark, dumpy female turns her into something rather like an octopus.

Duane, Diane

Tale of the Five series.

> *Dragons • Gods.*

The Door into Fire. Herewiss must come to terms with his past and find his inner name to master Flame, the magic that was thought to be long gone from the men of the world, but that he was born with.

The Door into Shadow. "Segnbora absorbs the memory and personality of a dying dragon. To Dragons the past, present, and future all happen at once and what happens in the future can influence the past. When a dragon dies, its soul goes into another dragon, forming a chain going back generations although since each imprinting is weaker, the newest are the strongest."—Samuel Lubell.

The Door into Sunset. "Segnbora tries to win the support of the dragons, Herewiss becomes ambassador to Freelorn's kingdom's usurper, and Freelorn goes disguised in his own kingdom."—Samuel Lubell.

The Door into Starlight. Not yet published. Even though the earlier books in the series are out of print, Duane continues to receive fan mail and inquiries about when *The Door into Starlight* will be published. The series can still be found in many libraries.

Frankos, Steven

Aitchley Corlaiys series.

> *Dragons • Talismans • Quest.*

Beyond Lich Gate.

Cathedral of Thorns.

Legend Reborn. With the sword of the legendary Procursus and the fabled Elixir of Life, Aitchley Corlaiys nears the end of his quest.

King, Stephen

Ⓨ **The Eyes of the Dragon.** "A kingdom is in turmoil as the old king dies and his successor must do battle for the throne. Pitted against an evil wizard and a would-be rival, Prince Peter makes a daring escape and rallies the forces of Good to fight for what is rightfully his. This is a masterpiece of classic dragons-and-magic fantasy that only Stephen King could have written!"—Amazon.com.

> *Dragons • Fairy Tales.*

Lackey, Mercedes

Ⓨ Bardic Voices series. The books that follow are set in the world of Alanda, where Bards have a powerful guild and also powerful magic whether or not they belong to the guild. (The first three were published in an omnibus edition as *The Free Bards.*)

> *Music • Ghosts.*

Lark and the Wren. In a world where music is magical and only practiced by men, Rune, a girl, wins a fiddling contest with a wicked ghost and sets out on a quest to learn more.

The Robin and the Kestrel. Robin makes a visit to Skull Hill, home of the ghost, to recruit him to their cause.

The Eagle and the Nightingale. Nightingale joins forces with T'fyrr, a birdman, to find out why the Human High King is allowing the Church to be overtly hostile to nonhuman people as well as gypsies and Free Bards.

Four & Twenty Blackbirds. Lower-class women have been targeted for magical murder, and are being killed by a three-sided stiletto whose wielder immediately commits suicide.

Detection.

Lackey, Mercedes, and Josepha Sherman

YA **A Cast of Corbies: A Novel of Bardic Choices** is also set in Alanda.

Le Guin, Ursula K.

The Earthsea tetrology. Sparrowhawk goes from callow youth Ged to magician's apprentice. The first three books were written for children, but the entire series is read by adults.

Younger Readers • Dragons.

YA **A Wizard of Earthsea.** Before he was dragonlord and Archmage, Ged was a motherless son who learned some magic and had a great adventure.

YA **The Tombs of Atuan.** Tenar was to spend her whole life at the desolate Place of the Tombs, but when a young wizard comes to the deserts of Atuan seeking to steal a broken ring that was the Tomb's greatest treasure, she is forced to choose between her empty life as a priestess and a power and life she does not know.

YA **The Farthest Shore.** As Ged sets out to confront his own past, magic disappears from other lands and Earthsea will either move into doom or a new age.

AW **YA** **Tehanu.** 1990 Nebula Award Winner. 1991 Locus Poll Winner.

Labyrinths.

Lee, Tanith

The Birthgrave trilogy. Starting off as sword and sorcery with a female protagonist, this series switches to science fantasy by the end of the trilogy, much like Marion Zimmer Bradley's Darkover series. Sex plays a large role.

The Birthgrave.

Vazkor, Son of Vazkor.

Quest for the White Witch.

Science Fantasy • Sexuality.

Leiber, Fritz

Fafhrd and the Gray Mouser series. Possibly the greatest sword and sorcery series ever, featuring massively heroic barbarian Fafhrd and thief, sorcerer, and swordsman the Gray Mouser. Over the years since the first Fafrhd and the Gray Mouser short story was introduced in 1939, the tales have been released in many different editions and combinations. As of 1998 the following were available.

Barbarians • Swordsmen.

AW **Fritz Leiber's Ill Met in Lankhmar** is an omnibus version of *Swords and Deviltry* and *Swords Against Death*. The novella "Ill Met in Lankhmar" won the Hugo Award in 1971.

Fritz Leiber's Lean Times in Lankhmar is an omnibus version of *Swords in the Mist* and *Swords Against Wizardry.*

Fritz Leiber's Return to Lankhmar is an omnibus version of *The Swords of Lankhmar* and *Swords and Ice Magic*.

Lucas, George, and Chris Claremont

Chronicles of the Shadow War. Willow once again goes to the aid of Princess Elora. Set in the same world as the film *Willow*.

Shadow Moon.

Shadow Dawn.

Dragons • Dreams • Film.

Lustbader, Eric Van

Sunset Warrior series. Features sword and sorcery with an Asian martial arts flair that veers into SF now and then.

Martial Arts.

The Sunset Warrior.

Shallows of Night.

Dai-San.

Beneath an Opal Moon.

Dragons on the Sea of Night. Not yet published in the United States (April 1998) but published in Great Britain by HarperCollins under the Voyager imprint.

McKillip, Patricia A.

The Hed trilogy. Great fantasy for all ages.

Shapeshifting • Music • Younger Readers.

🅈🅐 **The Riddle-Master of Hed.** "Morgan, land-ruler of the tiny farming community of Hed, wins the hand of Raederle, the King's daughter, when he risks his life to solve a riddle. But his trip to claim his prize is fraught with peril, including shipwreck, amnesia, shape-changing, and of course the requisite struggle against the forces of evil."—Bonnie Kunzel.

🅈🅐 **Heir of Sea and Fire.** "In spite of reports of his death, Raederle sets out to find Morgan, and when she does, both her magical powers and their relationship blossom."—Bonnie Kunzel.

🅐🅦 🅈🅐 **Harpist in the Wind.** 1980 Locus Poll Winner. "In this concluding volume of the Hed trilogy, shape-changers battle while Morgan uses magic to control earth and air, and his lady, Raederle, does the same for water and fire."—Bonnie Kunzel.

"In the midst of conflict and unrest the Prince of Hed solves the puzzle of his future when he learns to harp the wind, discovers who the shapechangers are, and understands his own relationship to Deth, harpist of the wizard Ohm."—Publisher's catalog copy.

Moorcock, Michael

The Chronicle of Prince Corum and the Silver Hand. Corum is an elfin-like hero fighting chaos in a long distant time. The two trilogies featuring Corum can be considered sequels to the Elric series.

🅐🅦 **The Knight of the Swords.** 1973 August Derleth Award Winner.

The Queen of the Swords.

The King of the Swords. 1974 August Derleth Award Winner.

The Swords Trilogy is an omnibus edition of the first three books that most recently has been published under the title *Corum: The Coming of Chaos* (Eternal Champion, volume 7).

The Bull and the Spear.

The Oak and the Ram.

The Sword and the Stallion.

The Chronicles of Corum contains the second trilogy of the series in an omnibus edition.

Elric of Melniboné series. Features an anti-Conan figure, a weakling albino. Elric has also been adapted as a graphic novel series.

> *Anti-hero • Swordsmen.*

Elric of Melniboné.

The Fortress of the Pearl.

The Sailor on the Seas of Fate.

The Weird of the White Wolf.

The Singing Citadel.

The Sleeping Sorceress (The Vanishing Tower).

The Revenge of the Rose: A Tale of the Albino Prince in the Years of His Wandering.

The Bane of the Black Sword.

Stormbringer.

Hawkmoon series.

The Jewel in the Skull.

Sorcerer's Amulet.

Sword of the Dawn.

The Secret of the Runestaff.

The History of the Runestaff is an omnibus of the first three titles in the series.

Count Brass.

The Champion of Garathorm.

The Quest for Tanelorn.

The Chronicles of Castle Brass is an omnibus edition of the last three titles in the Hawkmoon series. Many of these have been reissued recently by White Wolf Publishing, incorporating them into a huge series combining both fantasy and science fiction written by Moorcock. *Elric: Song of the Black Sword* (Eternal Champion, volume 5) contains *Elric of Melniboné, The Sailor on the Seas of Fate,* and *The Weird of the White Wolf.*

Moore, C. L.

Jirel of Joiry (Black God's Shadow). C. L. Moore, another early woman fantasy writer who hid her gender behind her initials, introduced the first sword and sorcery story to feature a woman. Jirel is a strong warrior woman in a medieval French setting. The stories were originally published in the 1930s.

> *Swordswomen.*

Northwest Smith series of stories have been collected as

Shambleau and Others.

Northwest of Earth.

Scarlet Dream.

Norman, John

Gor series. The first few of the twenty-five novels in the series started out in the tradition of the Barsoom series and Conan series, but quickly degenerated into sadomasochistic and anti-woman sadism. Not recommended reading, but something to know about all the same.

Sexuality • Slavery.

Norton, Andre

Ⓨ Witch World series. The series has been so popular that it has spawned a shared world series, listed in Chapter 15.

Parallel Worlds • Psionic Powers.

Witch World. Simon Tregarth is flung from twentieth-century London into a world filled with high adventure and sorcery. This series is also discussed in Chapter 12.

Web of the Witch World. Simon Tregarth wins a witch-wife and a throne, but his triumphs are precarious as long as Kolder's super-science has a foothold on the planet. Jaelithe, his wife, discovers that she did not lose her power as a sorceress and now must answer a magical summons.

Year of the Unicorn. Thirteen brides are pledged to the Were Riders of the Wastelands by the Lords of High Hallack.

Three Against the Witch World. Simon's wife Jaelithe, a Wise Woman of Estcarp, gives birth to three children, Kyllan, Kemoc, and Kaththea, born to be a warrior, a sage, and a witch.

Warlock of the Witch World. Kemoc has foreseen that the Enemy has a secret ally as Escore mounts its battle against the Shadow.

Sorceress of the Witch World.

The Crystal Gryphon. Kerovan was born with hooves instead of toes and strange colored amber eyes. Promised at age ten to wed Josian, he does not expect to meet her until they are eighteen, but a disaster sends both of them fleeing their homes, with their only link being a small crystal sphere with a gryphon engraved within that brings them together to save their people.

Spell of the Witch World.

The Jargoon Pard.

Gryphon in Glory.

Gryphon's Eyrie (co-authored by A. C. Crispin). Kerovan has received an irresistible call driving him to the mountains to make peace with his heritage.

The Warding of the Witch World. Simon Tregarth leads the planet's heroes in a final war against the Dark in what is labeled as the "last Witch World book."

(The Gregg Press reprint, seven volumes, contains a chronology of the series and maps.)

Norton, Andre, and Mercedes Lackey

The Halfblood Chronicles (annotated in Chapter 7).

⑭ Elvenbane.

⑭ Elvenblood.

Roberson, Jennifer

Sword-Dancers Saga (this is what Roberson calls it) is also sometimes referred to as The Tiger and Del series.

Martial Arts • Romance • Swordsmen • Swordswomen.

Sword-Dancer. Tiger, a male sword-dancer of the South, and Del, a female sword-dancer of the icy North, set out on a quest to rescue her brother, who has been kidnapped by slavers.

Sword-Singer. As Tiger and Del head North so she can face trial by combat, they are pursued by a deadly unseen presence.

Sword-Maker. Tiger faces the Dragon's Lair, a peril far greater than that of the hounds of hoolies he has been using his sword magic to track.

Sword-Breaker. Del and Tiger have been accused of murdering the Southron tribe's messiah, but that could be the least of their problems because Tiger's sword is possessed by the spirit of a dead evil sorcerer.

Sword-Born. Exiled from the North, Del's home, and Southron lands, where Tiger had been raised in slavery, Del and Tiger set out to the island of Skandi to find Tiger's real homeland.

Sword-Sworn. Tiger and Del go into the dangerous lands of the South.

Pirates.

Rosenberg, Joel

⑭ Guardians of the Flame series.

Gaming • Parallel Worlds.

The Sleeping Dragon. Karl and his friends, Wizard and Warrior, game players on Earth, are suddenly transported into a fantasy world where they are forced to play their roles for real and where not all will survive the struggle to find the way home.

The Sword and the Chain. This is volume 2 in the series.

The Silver Crown. The third volume of the series continues the adventures of the game players from Earth who have been transported to a fantasy world.

The Heir Apparent. Karl, who is now Emperor of the fantasy world he and his companions entered some twenty years ago, battles slavers who have threatened the life of his son.

The Warrior Lives. Features more sword and sorcery in a world where the rules of the game may mean the difference between life and death for the players.

The Road to Ehvenor. Karl is dead, but his wife and son continue the battle against the slavers while struggling against the rise of evil magic from the realm of Faerie.

The Road Home. "The heroic adventures of Karl's son continue in this concluding volume of the Guardians of the Flame series, with 18-year-old Jason battling a semi-mythical warrior who has been murdering slave-owners. All's well that ends well in a magical world where a telepathic dragon can fly in and save the day."—Bonnie Kunzel.

Russ, Joanna

Alyx series.

Alyx. "Alyx is a time-traveling sword-wielding mercenary, tough enough to handle any situation thrown at her, one of the first female protagonists to take the lead in an adventure role from a noted feminist author."—Bonnie Kunzel.

Adventures of Alyx.

Swordswomen.

Saberhagen, Fred

⒴ Swords series. Vulcan created twelve swords with the power to slay gods that were lost throughout the world. As with many other popular fantasy series, other writers have chimed in, providing stories of **An Armory of Swords.**

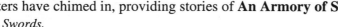

Swords.

The First Book of Swords.

The Second Book of Swords.

The Third Book of Swords.

⒴ Lost Swords series.

The First Book of Lost Swords: Woundhealer's Story.

The Second Book of Lost Swords: Sightblinder's Story.

The Third Book of Lost Swords: Stonecutter's Story.

The Fourth Book of Lost Swords: Farslayer's Story.

The Fifth Book of Lost Swords: Coinspinner's Story.

The Sixth Book of Lost Swords: Mindsword's Story.

The Seventh Book of Lost Swords: Wayfinder's Story. The Sword of Wisdom turns up in the hands of Valdemar, a grower of grapes in search of the perfect woman.

The Last Book of Lost Swords: Shieldbreaker's Story. Prince Mark of Tasavalta maintains peace with the power of the five Swords—Woundhealer, Stonecutter, Dragonslicer, Sightbinder, and Shieldbreaker—but when he goes to a far corner of the kingdom to fight a dragon, the evil Vilkata, the Dark King, invades his kingdom. The only hope is fourteen-year-old Prince Stephen, armed with Shieldbreaker.

Dragons.

Silverberg, Robert

Lord Valentine series (annotated by Bonnie Kunzel).

The Desert of Stolen Dreams.

ⒶⓌ Lord Valentine's Castle. In this work of heroic fantasy, young Valentine joins a troupe of jugglers and travels across Majipoor on a quest to regain the throne. 1981 Locus Poll Winner.

Performers.

ⒶⓌ Majipoor Chronicles. A collection of short pieces that includes "The Desert of Stolen Dreams." 1981 Locus Poll Winner.

Labyrinths • Libraries.

Valentine Pontifex. The concluding volume of what can be considered a trilogy recounts the adventures of Lord Valentine.

> *Dreams • Shapeshifting.*

Mountains of Majipoor. Set 500 years after *Valentine Pontifex,* this takes up the tale of Lord Valentine's descendant Harpirias.

Sorcerers of Majipoor. This is a prequel set 1,000 years before the Lord Valentine trilogy.

Vance, Jack

The Dying Earth series. In a far future world, magic works, but not too well in this series made up mostly of linked or related short stories. Published in book form they are

The Dying Earth.

The Eyes of the Overworld.

Cugel's Saga.

Rhialto the Marvelous.

Watt-Evans, Lawrence

🆈🅐 The Lords of Dûs series (annotated by Bonnie Kunzel).

> *Immortality • Gods.*

The Lure of the Basilisk. The first book of the series features Prince Garth, who must complete several tasks, beginning with the capture of a basilisk, if he hopes to become immortal.

The Seven Altars of Dûsarra. Prince Garth's quest for immortality continues in this second volume of the series. His task this time is to steal seven items that may be located in four different temples.

The Sword of Bheleu. A magical sword is Prince Garth's goal in volume 3.

The Book of Silence. The final volume has Prince Garth seeking an arcane book of magic.

Weis, Margaret, and Tracy Hickman

🆈🅐 Darksword trilogy has become a role-playing game with a guide book, *Darksword Adventures,* that also serves as a guide to the series.

> *Swordsmen • Magic.*

Forging the Darksword. Born without magic, Joram grows to adulthood and joins forces with Saryon to attempt to forge a magic absorbing sword.

Doom of the Darksword. Because Joram was born without magic he cannot inherit the throne of Merilon, but now with the magic absorbing Darksword he returns to claim his birthright.

Triumph of the Darksword. Joram confronts the evil sorcerer Menju and his Technologists in an apocalyptic battle.

🆈🅐 Death Gate Cycle (annotated by Bonnie Kunzel).

> *Labyrinths • Elves • Necromancy • Magic • Dragons • Dwarves • Tattoos.*

Dragon Wing. In this first volume, Hugh the Hand is an assassin who is offered a reprieve by King Stephen, in exchange for the death of the king's ten-year-old son, an assignment that the professional assassin is curiously reluctant to complete.

Elven Star. Pryan, the land of fire, is featured in volume two of the cycle, serving as the setting in which elves, humans, and dwarves battle a race of giants for survival.

Fire Sea. Haplo, a Patryn who derives his strength from the magical sigils covering his body, is on a mission for the Lord of the Nexus that takes him to another of the sundered realms of the Death Gate Cycle.

Serpent Mage. Haplo comes through the Death Gate to the water world of Chelestra in pursuit of his race's most feared enemy, the Sartan Wizard Samah, which is how he gets involved in a deadly struggle against the dragon snakes.

The End of Chaos. Now that the four elemental realms of Sky, Fire, Stone and Sea have been introduced, Haplo returns to Arianos (Sky) to face dragon-like creatures in a struggle for the fate of the four realms.

Into the Labyrinth. Haplo and his companions finally go into the labyrinth in search of the Seventh Gate, located beyond Death itself, all the while aware of the very real danger it poses for their world.

Seventh Gate. Haplo and his companions have reached the Seventh Gate at last, where they are called upon to fight the final battle against the forces of evil for the fate of their world.

Wells, Angus
The Godwars trilogy.

Gods • Quest.

Forbidden Magic. In the wrong hands, a legendary book could lead to the resumption of an ancient war.

Dark Magic.

Wild Magic. A hero is tricked into supporting the wrong wizard, making his mission much more difficult.

Wrede, Patricia C.
Lyra Books. "Lyra is the world of two moons, a world which humans share with magic folk: the ancient Shee, the forest-dwelling Wyrd, and the dread Shadow Born."—Jacket copy.

Shadow Magic.

Daughter of Witches.

The Harp of Imach Thyssel.

Shadows over Lyra. This is an omnibus edition of *Shadow Magic, Daughter of Witches,* and *The Harp of Imach Thyssel.*

Caught in Crystal. Something evil is leaking out of the Twisted Tower. Kayl is told by a sorceress and a wizard that she and her sword may be the only ones able to stop it.

The Raven Ring. Eleret, a young woman of the mountain-dwelling warrior people, the Cilhar, journeys to the city of Ciaron to retrieve the personal effects of her mother, who was killed in the line of duty. Upon arriving in the city she discovers that her mother had with her an heirloom ring that seems to be the focus of several attempts upon Eleret's life. Hooking up with swordsman wizard Daner and thief Karvonen, she unearths a shapeshifter and discovers the motives that could lead to disaster.

Shapeshifting • Tarot.

Zelazny, Roger

Amber series. Amnesiac Corwin seems to be a human but is actually one of the many children of King Oberon of Amber (annotated by Bonnie Kunzel).

Parallel Worlds.

Nine Princes in Amber. An amnesia victim awakens in a hospital on Earth and escapes into another world, where he discovers that he is Corwin, long-lost Prince of Amber. Earth is just one of the countless shadows of Amber, and only someone of royal blood can cross back and forth between these shadows and the real world of Amber.

The Guns of Avalon. In his wandering through Shadow, Prince Corwin devises a scheme to bring gunpowder to Amber.

Sign of the Unicorn. Corwin is befriended by Ganelon, a former enemy.

The Hand of Oberon. Corwin uncovers a threat against Amber that originates in the realm of Chaos.

The Courts of Chaos. The Jewel of Judgment must be brought to Oberon, even if the price is a hell ride across Shadow for Corwin.

Trumps of Doom. 1986 Locus Poll Winner. The focus of the series switches from Corwin to his son Merlin.

Blood of Amber.

Sign of Chaos.

Night of Shadows.

Prince of Chaos.

Quest

A quest, though sometimes accomplished by an individual, usually assembles a group of stalwart companions who set off on a journey and experience wonders and dangers while guarding each others' backs. Members of the party usually represent racial and often species diversity. There is usually someone with magic, someone with leadership abilities, and someone with physical strength. This combination of talents makes the assembled crew greater than the sum of its parts. The archetypal main character has humble beginnings, often as a farmhand, apprentice, or servant and discovers his (usually, but sometimes her) unsuspected talents and hidden ancestry. Quests play a role in many of the epic fantasies that follow.

Anthony, Piers, James Richey Goolsby, and Alan Riggs

Quest for the Fallen Star. A band of travelers is charged with the task of carrying the mightiest weapon ever known to safety in the Holy City of Norivika to preserve the Realm from the rising darkness.

Talismans.

Brown, Mary

Pigs Don't Fly. Losing her home at the death of her mother, the village whore, Somerdai, sets out to find her fortune, assembling a loyal cadre of companions on her travels. Annotated in Chapter 7.

Master of Many Treasures. In this sequel to *Pigs Don't Fly,* Summer finds that love wasn't where she thought. She searches for the love of her life that she let slip away.

> *Dragons • Animals.*

Green, Simon R.

Blue Moon Rising. This is a humorous quest with a feisty princess, a reluctant prince, and a friendly dragon.

> *Humor • Unicorns • Dragons• Swordswomen.*

Martin, George R. R.

Song of Ice and Fire. In a world with little magic, and the climate gone horribly wrong, the Starks of Winterfell may provide the only leaders to save the land.

> *Politics • Environment.*

 A Game of Thrones. 1997 Locus Poll Winner.
A Clash of Kings.

McKiernan, Dennis L.

McKiernan has a suggested reading order at his Web site, http://home.att.net/~dlmck/, where he lists the books both in the order published and the internal chronological order.

> *Tolkien-Like • Elves • Dwarves.*

The Dragonstone. This is set 300 years before the other books in this world. Arin sees horrible visions that a horde of dragons will devastate Mithgar. Valiantly setting out on a mission to block the fulfillment of her prophecy, she finds six extraordinary beings to help her on her quest to find the mighty Dragonstone and stop the devastation from happening.

Iron Tower trilogy.

Dark Tide. The fate of the world may depend on the valor of three of the Warrows (also called Wee Folk)—Tuck, Danner, and Patrel—who are walking Wolf Patrol on their country's borders when Evil Modru sends his vile minions southward.

Shadows of Doom.

Darkest Day. Men, Elves, Dwarves, and Warrows, the Warriors of Light, are massing for the final battle with the Powers of Dark, led by Modru and his lord, the Dark Liege Gryphon.

Silver Call duology.

Trek to Kraggen-Cor. Lord Kian joins arms with Durek the Deathbreaker and his legions of Dwarves, who along with two of the Wee Folk are headed for the high jagged mountains to reclaim the Dwarfian homeland.

The Brega Path. Very Tolkienesque.

The Eye of the Hunter. "Five heroes come together to track down a creature who is half-man, half-demon—and all Lord of Darkness."—Jacket copy.

Voyage of the Fox Rider. Lady Jinnarin and friends set out on a quest to find her mysteriously missing mate and end up combating evil in this tale set far in the distant past of Mithgar.

Modesitt, L. E., Jr.

YA Recluce series.

> *Magic • Epic.*

> **The Magic of Recluce.** On the island country of Recluce, order rules, neatness counts, and potential troublemakers are exiled or sent out on a Dangergeld quest. Lerris is bored with order so is sent away from his land. He comes of age in the midst of the almost hidden war between order and chaos.

> **The Towers of the Sunset.** Creslin sets out on a quest for his true identity after choosing exile over an arranged marriage.

> **The Magic Engineer.** Set prior to *The Magic of Recluce.* Dorrin's fascination with the working of machines and passion for scientific knowledge violate the rules of Order magic.

> **The Order War.** Justen, a young engineer supporting the Black forces of Order, joins with fellow sorcerers to halt the White Wizards of Fairhaven. "Justen must fight both Recluce and Fairhaven, as well as use the highest powers of order and forbidden technology to harness chaos itself in his efforts to halt the conquest of the chaos wizards."—Jacket copy.

> **The Death of Chaos.** Lerris has settled down to life as a carpenter married to Krystal, sub-commander of the autarch's military force. But all is not in order as the Empire of Hamor once again tries to conquer the world. Lerris is forced to strengthen his magical powers or see his world destroyed.

> **Fall of Angels.** This is a prequel to the Recluce books. Nylan, an engineer and builder, is raising a great tower on the plateau known as the Roof of the World, where the women of the Empire of the Legend are to live in exile.

> **Chaos Balance.** The war between chaos and order begins again as Nylan, with his companion, Ayrlyn the healer, and infant son look for a place to lead a peaceful life.

> **The White Order.** Cerryl was orphaned when his father, an amateur magician, was killed by the powerful white mages. After witnessing a renegade magician being destroyed by a white mage, Cerryl is sent to the city of Fairhaven to find his destiny and become a great magician.

Reichert, Mickey Zucker

> **Legend of Nightfall.** Thief, assassin, and much more, Nightfall nonetheless occasionally makes a mistake, and now he must guard and guide a young prince on a quest.

> *Epic • Assassins.*

Silverberg, Robert

> **Kingdoms of the Wall.** Piolar leads forty men and women on the annual quest to scale the "wall" and discover the secret of the gods.

> *Gods • Ghosts.*

Tolkien

J. R. R. Tolkien is the father of modern fantasy. Many books imitate his. Because he is a writer of such importance, it is no surprise that an enormous number of books have been written about him and his works.

Lord of the Rings, credited with being the foundation of modern fantasy, is probably the most widely read fantasy series ever. This is one classic series that everyone doing reader's advisory in fantasy should read. Many of the conventions of fantasy were created by

Tolkien. After Tolkien's death his son Christopher Tolkien continued bringing out books about Middle Earth, its language, and its customs. He is listed as editor on the twelve-volume *History of Middle Earth,* which contains essays, records, and writings about the complex world created by his father.

Tolkien, J. R. R.

⓭ The Hobbit. Bilbo Baggins, a hobbit, goes on a great adventure with a wizard and some dwarves, meeting up with elves and other fantastic beings along the way.

⓭ The Lord of the Rings trilogy.

> *Elves • Dragons • Dwarves • Hobbits • Talismans.*

The Fellowship of the Rings. Frodo Baggins must fight darkness both within and without when he takes up Bilbo's wild wandering ways and embarks on his own adventure.

The Two Towers.

The Return of the King.

⓪ The Silmarillion. Published posthumously and long awaited by his fans, this book fills in some of the background of Middle Earth. 1978 Locus Poll Winner.

Hundreds of books have been written about Tolkien and his fantasy world. There are criticism, festschrifts, biographies, parodies, and even atlases. The following is merely a sampling of what is available.

Beard, Henry N., and Douglas C. Kenney. *Bored of the Rings: A Parody of J. R. R. Tolkien's the Lord of the Rings.* New American Library, 1969.

Blackwelder, Richard E. *A Tolkien Thesaurus,* Garland Reference Library of the Humanities, vol. 1326. Garland, 1990. A concordance to all the minutia in the trilogy.

Chance, Jane. *The Lord of the Rings: The Mythology of Power,* Twayne's Masterwork Studies, no. 99. Twayne, 1992.

Collins, David R. *J. R. R. Tolkien: Master of Fantasy.* First Avenue Editions, 1993. A biography written for children.

Crabbe, Katharyn W. *J. R. R. Tolkien.* Continuum, 1988. A biography.

Curry, Patrick. *Defending Middle-Earth: Tolkien, Myth and Modernity.* St. Martin's Press, 1997.

Day, David. *Tolkien: The Illustrated Encyclopaedia.* Collier Books, 1997.

Duriez, Colin. *The J. R. R. Tolkien Handbook: A Comprehensive Guide to His Life, Writings, and World of Middle-Earth.* Baker Bookhouse, 1992.

Flieger, Verlyn. *A Question of Time: J. R. R. Tolkien's Road to Faerie.* Kent State University Press, 1997.

Fonstad, Karen Wynn. *The Atlas of Middle-Earth.* Houghton Mifflin, 1991.

Foster, Robert. *The Complete Guide to Middle-Earth: From the Hobbit to the Silmarillion.* Ballantine Books, 1978.

Green, William H. *The Hobbit: A Journey into Maturity,* Twayne's Masterwork Studies, no. 149. Twayne, 1995.

Greenberg, Martin H., ed. *After the King: Stories in Honor of J. R. R. Tolkien.* Tor, 1992. Festschrift anthology.

Grotta, Daniel. *The Biography of J. R. R. Tolkien: Architect of Middle Earth.* Courage Books, 1996.

Hammond, Wayne G., and Christina Scull. *J. R. R. Tolkien: Artist & Illustrator.* Houghton Mifflin, 1995.

Hammond, Wayne G., and Douglas A. Anderson. *J. R. R. Tolkien: A Descriptive Bibliography.* Winchester Bibliographies of 20th Century Writers. St. Paul's Bibliographies, 1993.

Johnson, Judith A. *J. R. R. Tolkien: Six Decades of Criticism,* Bibliographies and Indexes in World Literature, no. 6. Greenwood, 1986.

Moseley, Charles. *J R R Tolkien: Conversation With.* University Press of Mississippi, 1997.

Neimark, Anne E. *Myth Maker: J. R. R. Tolkien.* Harcourt Brace, 1996. A biography written for children.

Noel, Ruth S. *The Languages of Tolkien's Middle Earth.* Houghton Mifflin, 1980.

Realms of Tolkien: Images of Middle-Earth by J. R. R. Tolkien. HarperPrism, 1996. Illustrators interpret Tolkien's words.

Ryan, John S. *Shaping of Middle-Earth's Maker: Influences on the Life and Literature of J R R Tolkien.* American Tolkien Society, 1992.

Salu, Mary, and. Robert Farrell, eds. *J. R. R. Tolkien: Scholar and Storyteller; Essays in Memoriam.* Cornell University Press, 1979.

Stevens, David, Carol D. Stevens, and Roger C. Schlobin. *J. R. R. Tolkien: The Art of the Myth-Maker,* The Milford Series Popular Writers of Today, vol. 56. Borgo Press, 1993.

Epic

The epic fantasy takes place over the course of several generations. Throughout the course of time magic and the fortunes of the characters may wax and wane. Often the humble become royal. Frequently a quest starts the series, heroics are definitely involved, and magic plays a role. Epic fantasy frequently involves political intrigue and warfare in a non-industrialized setting.

Brooks, Terry

Shannara series. Shea Ohmsford and a band of stalwart companions set out to find the magic sword that will help defeat an evil warlock lord. Obviously modeled on Tolkien's *Lord of the Rings,* Brooks's series nonetheless has proven to be fantastically popular, perhaps in part because of the sense of adventure with which he infuses his works. The Heritage of Shannara series takes place 300 years after the first series and features quests embarked upon by descendants of the original heroes as they try to save the world in the midst of diminishing magic.

Tolkien-Like • Elves • Dwarves.

The Sword of Shannara. Half-human half-elf, Shea discovers that the Warlock Lord lives and will destroy the world unless stopped.

The Elfstones of Shannara. Only the Elfstones of Shannara can stop the Reaper, who will surely be followed soon by hordes of demons as the spell of Forbidding fails along with Ellerys, the dying tree of Elven magic.

The Wishsong of Shannara. Brin may be the only one who can open a way to the Ildatch, the book of evil spells that is sending Mord Wraiths to destroy humankind.

The Scions of Shannara. The Dwarves are enslaved in the East, and in the West the Elves have disappeared. The totalitarian Federation controls all of the Southland.

The Druid of Shannara. The shade of Allanon appears to Walker and commands him to find the lost city of Paranor and recreate the Order of Druids that had been disbanded for 300 years.

The Elf Queen of Shannara.

The Talismans of Shannara.

The First King of Shannara is a prequel set 500 years before *The Sword of Shannara*, adding the background of the adventures of the last Druid, Bremen, as he battles the evil Warlock Lord.

Cherryh, C. J.

Fortress in the Eye of Time. The old gods are gone and the old towers fallen to ruin, but one old one uses the Old Magic to make a shaping in the form of a young man, whom he sends out to right the wrongs of a long-forgotten wizard war.

Fortress of Eagles. Cefwyn, the king, wants a united Ylesuin and peace the land has never known. His only friend is Tristen, created by a now dead wizard. A sword that says Truth on one side and Illusion on the other rests, gathering dust in a corner of Tristen's room as Cefwyn plans for a war that will bring his plans to pass or ruin them all.

Magic.

Cook, Glen

The Black Company. A company of mercenaries massacre and use magic in the service of whoever hires them for good or for evil.

Mercenaries • Magic.

The Black Company.

Shadows Linger.

The White Rose.

The Silver Spike.

Shadow Games.

Dreams of Steel.

Bleak Seasons.

Cook, Hugh

Wizard War series, also called The Chronicles of an Age of Darkness. Many U.S. public libraries have the British editions (with title variations) even though Roc published the series in the United States.

> **Wizard War. (The Wizards and the Warriors).**
>
> **The Questing Hero. (The Wordsmiths and the Warguild).**
>
> **The Hero's Return. (The Women and the Warlords).**
>
> **The Oracle. (The Walrus and the Warwolf).**
>
> **Lords of the Sword.**
>
> **The Wicked and the Witless.**
>
> **The Wishstone and the Wonderworkers.**
>
> **The Wazir and the Witch.**
>
> **The Werewolf and the Wormlord.**
>
> **The Worshippers and the Way.**
>
> **The Witchlord and the Weaponmaster.**
>
> **NEW** **When Heroes Return.**

Eddings, David, and Leigh Eddings

(Even though Leigh is not listed as co-author of the early books, it has been reported that she is.) These two are among the most popular of recent fantasy authors. There is a newsgroup devoted to their works: alt.fan.eddings.

YA Belgariad series. Seven of the titles in this series have made it to the *Publishers Weekly* Bestseller List in the 1990s.

> *Magic • Quest • Gods.*
>
> **Pawn of Prophecy.** Garion, an orphaned farm boy, starts a quest in search of his destiny as foretold in a 7,000-year-old prophecy.
>
> **Queen of Sorcery.** Garion discovers that his aunt Pol is really the Sorceress Polgara and his grandfather is Belgarath, the Eternal Man.
>
> **Magician's Gambit.** Ce'Nedra, Imperial Princess of Tolnedra, knows, as does everyone, that the tales of the Orb are just silly legends, but why then is she setting out on a quest to recover the Orb with, of all people, Garion, who she finds unbelievably attractive even though he is only a farm boy.
>
> **Castle of Wizardry.** The Orb has been regained, but now the questors must return through perils to reach Riva by Erastide, where Garion and Ce'Nedra will find a surprising future.
>
> **Enchanter's End Game.** Garion, now the king, must still face the evil god Torak.

YA Mallorean series.

> **Guardians of the West.**
>
> **King of the Murgos.** Garion and Ce'Nedra join up with Belgarath and Polgara in quest of their infant son, who has been kidnapped and is being held by Zandramas, who acquired the Dark Prophecy when Torak was slain.
>
> **Demon Lord of Karanda.**
>
> **Sorceress of Darshiva.**

The Seeress of Kell. Time is running out for Garion and his companions to recover his son. If they can't get to him in time, Zandramas will use him in a rite to raise the Dark Prophecy and gain eternal dominion over the world. The only way they can find him in time is with the help of the Seeress of Kell.

Belgarath the Sorcerer is a companion volume that should be read after the first ten books and *Polgara the Sorceress*. Belgarath the Sorcerer is the lone witness to the time when the gods walked the land. He is called the Ancient One and the Old Wolf, but once he was a boy and a young man.

Immortality.

 Ellenium series. Sparhawk searches for a way to save the queen from a deadly enchantment.

The Diamond Throne.

The Ruby Knight. Queen Ehlana has been poisoned and frozen in crystal. Sparhawk must find the Bhelliom, a jewel that has been lost for 500 years, to save her.

The Sapphire Rose.

 Tamuli series. While Sparhawk is on a quest for a magic stone, Sparhawk's wife Queen Ehlana is kidnapped.

Domes of Fire.

The Shining Ones. The Shining Ones, glowing beings whose mere touch can melt human beings, are the most dreaded of all the monsters that terrorize Tamuli.

The Hidden City. "Ravening destruction stalked all the lands"—Jacket copy. Sparhawk has fought the foul god Cyrgon and won, only to find that his beloved wife has been kidnapped by Cyrgon's minions.

Farland, David

The Runelords series.

NEW **The Runelords.** Young Prince Gavon, a Runelord prince who has received endowments of strength and perception, is traveling in disguise with his warrior-guard Borenson, on a quest for the hand of Iome, the daughter of King Sylvarresta. Discovering assassins heading for Sylvarresta, Gavon and Borenson must race to save their world from monstrous evil.

Magic • War.

Feist, Raymond E.

Riftwar series. Pug's journey toward wizardry and Tomas's toward heroism are just part of all the conflicts involving the worlds of Midkemia and Kelewan. The Serpentwar Saga is set in the same world.

Magic • Parallel Worlds.

 Magician. *Magician* is most frequently available in two volumes as *Magician: Apprentice* and *Magician: Master*. Orphaned Pug goes to the Kingdom of the Isles to study with master magician Kulgan, where he wins a place at court and the heart of a princess.

Silverthorn.

A Darkness at Sethanon.

Prince of the Blood.

The King's Buccaneer. The Riftwar over and the Kingdom of the Isles thriving, Prince Arutha sends his son Nicholas to rustic Castle Crydee, where an unexpected attack resulting in murder and the abduction of two young women sets Nicholas on the trail of an enemy connected to dark magical forces.

Pirates.

Serpentwar Saga. This series continues the adventures of Pug.

Politics • War • Magic.

Shadow of a Dark Queen.

Rise of a Merchant Prince.

Rage of a Demon King.

NEW **Shards of a Broken Crown.**

Hobb, Robin

The Farseer series. The bastard of an abdicating prince becomes a royal assassin after being raised as a stable boy. He inherits the skill for magic from his royal sire and also has a mysterious ability to communicate with animals.

Assassins • Politics.

 Assassin's Apprentice. 1996 Compton Crook Award Winner.

Royal Assassin.

Assassin's Quest.

The Liveship Traders series.

Pirates • Adventure.

NEW **Ship of Magic.** Althea Vestrit is forced to fight both pirates and her in-laws to regain her family's most treasured possession, an intelligent sentient Liveship made of wizard wood.

Jones, Diana Wynne

Dalemark Quartet.

Assassins • Magic • Music • Talismans • Quest • Younger Readers.

Cart and Cwidder.

Drowned Ammet.

The Spellcoats.

 The Crown of Dalemark. 1996 Mythopoeic Award Winner.

Jordan, Robert

Four of these titles have made it to the top ten positions on *Publishers Weekly* Bestseller List. Jordan's fans also have a newsgroup devoted to his work at alt.fan.jordan.

YA The Wheel of Time series. Seven youths are assembled on a world where only a precarious balance is maintained due to the necessity of magic being practiced only by women and the fact that males performing it go insane. Entwined with religious motifs, some sections hearken back to the Bene Geserit of *Dune*, Frank Herbert's classic SF novel.

Quest • Magic.

The Eye of the World.

The Great Hunt.

The Dragon Reborn.

The Shadow Rising.

The Fires of Heaven.

Lord of Chaos.

Crown of Swords. Spent eight weeks on the *Publishers Weekly* Bestseller List, making it to the number two spot.

 The Path of Daggers.

The World of Robert Jordan's The Wheel of Time, by Robert Jordan and Teresa Patterson, is a guide to the series. It serves as an atlas with maps of the world, the Seanchan Empire, the nations of the Covenant of the Ten Nations, and historical maps of the nations as they were when Artur Paendrag Tanreall began his rise to fame. It also includes illustrations of landscapes, objects of power, and portraits of central characters.

Kerr, Katharine

Deverry series. Four-hundred years of political intrigue, religion, magic, and fighting in a Celtic-like land.

Celtic Fantasy • Magic • Reincarnation.

Daggerspell. "Jill was a favorite of the magical, mysterious Wildfolk, who appeared to her from their invisible realm. Little did she know her extraordinary friends represented but a glimpse of a forgotten past and a fateful future. Four hundred years—and many lifetimes—ago, one selfish young lord caused the death of two innocent lovers. Then and there he vowed never to rest until he'd righted that wrong–and laid the foundation for the lives of Jill and all those who he would hold dear: Her father, the mercenary soldier Cullyn; the exiled berserker Rhodry Maelwaedd; and the ancient and powerful herbman Nevyn, all bound in a struggle against darkness . . . and a quest to fulfill the destinies determined centuries ago."—Jacket copy.

Darkspell.

The Bristling Wood.

The Dragon Revenant.

A Time of Exile.

A Time of Omens.

Days of Blood and Fire.

Days of Air and Darkness.

Lee, Adam

The Dominions of Irth series. A hero rose up to save the land from an evil lord, but now his very presence has poisoned the unborn child of a goddess.

Assassins • Witches • Swordsmen.

The Dark Shore.

 The Shadow Eater.

McKiernan, Dennis L.

Hèl's Crucible duology. Two ordinary people, Tipperton Thistledown and Beau Darby, are swept into the conflict of the Great War of the Ban, which sweeps over much of Mithgar.

War • Magic • Alternate Worlds.

Into the Forge.

Into the Fire.

Tales of Mithgar. Short stories told against the backdrop of an inn in a blizzard give a broader view of Mithgar.

Other Mithgar books are listed in the Quest section earlier in this chapter (p. 27).

Stackpole, Michael A.

Once a Hero. Neal Elfward is a legendary human hero who, 500 years ago, had fought against the tyranny of the sorcerous Reithrese's empire, thus starting a genocidal war. Can he now bring stability to the land?

Elves • Swords.

Tarr, Judith

Avaryan Rising series. Mages and politics in a richly detailed culture and setting.

The Hall of the Mountain King.

The Lady of Han-Gilen.

A Fall of Princes.

Arrows of the Sun.

Spear of Heaven.

Politics • Magic • Parallel Worlds.

Williams, Tad

Memory, Sorrow, and Thorn series. The world is much like an alternate tenth-century Britain. A kitchen boy assumes the responsibility of learning magic to try to stop a new king and his advisor from totally destroying the land.

Romance • Religion • Magic.

🆈 The Dragonbone Chair. Simon, a castle scullion, finds himself spearheading a quest for the solution of a riddle that offers the only hope of salvation for the peaceful world of Osten Ard. Prester John, the High King, lies dying, and with his death the ancient evil of the Storm King will be unleashed. "Memory, Sorrow and Thorn, [are] the names of three legendary swords, one of which unfortunately is already in the new king's possession, which does not bode well for his realm. Simon had advanced from scullery boy to magician's apprentice in the old king's court, but with the death of the monarch, he throws in his lot with young Prince Joshua and sets out to find the other two legendary swords, before it is too late."—Bonnie Kunzel.

Stone of Farewell. Simon now wields the sword Thorn. The evil forces and wild magic of the undead Sithi ruler, Ineluki the Storm King, are spreading across Osten Ard as the last remnants of the human army seek refuge at the mysterious Stone of Farewell.

To Green Angel Tower. Both humans and Sithi are turned against their own blood as the call goes out to all who would stand against the Storm King and try to stop the unstoppable evil. "Young Prince Joshua and Simon, now a knight, lead their forces in a final confrontation between good and evil."—Bonnie Kunzel.

Heroic

In heroic fantasy, magic is used only sparingly. The emphasis is on adventure in exotic locales and the brave deeds of a muscular hero. Swashbuckling fights and physical agility play a big role. A barbaric or feudal society is usually the setting. Another popular theme in heroic fantasy is for the protagonist, through some terrible miscalculation, to unleash evil that he or she must then combat to be redeemed.

Brackett, Leigh

Stark series. Originally set on Mars and later moved to Skaith. Eric John Stark bears similarities to John Carter of Mars. Leigh Brackett, one of the female pioneers of fantasy, also wrote westerns, science fiction, and mystery.
Eric John Stark of Mars series.

Adventure • Science Fantasy.

Eric John Stark: Outlaw of Mars.

The Secret of Sinharat.

People of the Talisman.

The Ginger Star.

The Hounds of Skaith.

The Reavers of Skaith.

The last three volumes were also published together as *The Book of Skaith.*

Brust, Steven

Taltos series. Vlad Taltos, assassin and more, is actually more of an anti-hero, but as in heroic fantasy, the action revolves around his exploits in the Taltos series (annotated in Chapter 10).

Burroughs, Edgar Rice

Barsoom series. This series has a Martian setting.

Adventure • Science Fantasy.

A Princess of Mars.

The Gods of Mars.

The Warlord of Mars.

Thuvia, Maid of Mars.

The Chessmen of Mars.

The Master Mind of Mars.

A Fighting Man of Mars.

Llana of Fathol.

John Carter of Mars.

Carter, Lin

The Thongor of Lemuria series and the Green Star Rises series are both long out of print and extremely difficult to find, but they are important to know about because Carter was a seminal figure in the creation and popularity of heroic fantasy in the barbarian mode. If it were not for Lin Carter and other pioneers of the heroic barbarian, we might not be enjoying *Xena: Warrior Princess* today.

Thongor of Lemuria series.

The Wizard of Lemuria (Thongor and the Wizard of Lemuria).

Thongor Against the Gods.

Thongor in the City of Magicians.

Thongor at the End of Time.

Thongor Fights the Pirates of Tarakus.

Green Star Rises series.

Under the Green Star.

When the Green Star Calls.

By the Light of the Green Star.

As the Green Star Rises.

In the Green Star's Glow.

Cooper, Louise

Indigo series. Indigo is condemned to roam the earth with wolf companion Grimya until she can slay the demons that have wreaked havoc on her life and the world since she released them from the box that bound them.

Wolves • Immortality • Demons.

Nemesis.

Inferno.

Infanta.

Nocturne.

Troika.

Avatar.

Revenant.

Aisling.

Delany, Samuel R.

Nevèrÿon series. Gorgik, a barbarian, evolves, as does his world.

Barbarians.

Tales of Nevèrÿon.

Nevèrÿon.

Flight from Nevèrÿon.

Gemmell, David

Drenai series.

Swordsmen • Adventure.

Legend (also published as *Against the Horde*).

Waylander.

The King Beyond the Gate.

Quest for Lost Heroes.

Waylander II: In the Realm of the Wolf.

The First Chronicles of Druss the Legend. Druss and his legendary ax in the service of good.

Sipstrassi series.

Gods • Science Fantasy.

Wolf in Shadow.

The Jerusalem Man (also published as *The Last Guardian*).

Bloodstone. John Shannow tries to save the world from legions of unleashed demons.

Stones of Power series. Set in the same world as the Sipstrassi series, but at a different time, this features Merlin and Uther Pendragon.

Arthurian Legend.

Ghost King.

Last Sword of Power.

Heinlein, Robert A.

Glory Road. In the great master of science fiction's only sword and sorcery tale, a Vietnam War veteran faced with dim prospects takes a chance on a job advertisement for a "hero," finding himself traveling through many alternate worlds while accompanying a beautiful and talented woman.

Vietnam War • Parallel Worlds.

Howard, Robert E.

The prolific Howard, who died at age thirty, is best known for the barbarian world of sword and sorcery he created for his Conan series. It was continued by L. Sprague de Camp, Lin Carter, Poul Anderson, Robert Jordan, and others. Conan is a brawny, brawling, sword-swinging adventurer in a mythical land. Two Conan movies were made by Raffaella De Laurentiis with Arnold Schwarzenegger in the sword-wielding role, *Conan the Barbarian* and *Conan the Destroyer*. Howard's Conan works were originally published in *Weird Tales* magazine.

Film • Barbarians.

Conan the Conqueror.

The Sword of Conan.

King Conan.

The Coming of Conan.

Conan the Barbarian.

Tales of Conan.

The Return of Conan.

The People of the Black Circle.

A Witch Shall Be Born.

Red Nails.

The Tower of the Elephant.

The Devil in Iron.

Rogues in the House.

The Hour of the Dragon.

The Pool of the Black One.

Some books have been published under the following alternate titles.

Conan the Defender.

Conan the Destroyer.

Conan the Invincible.

Conan the Magnificent.

Conan the Triumphant.

Conan the Unconquered.

Conan the Victorious.

Several Conan books that were not written by Howard and are not directly linked to Howard's stories were popular in the 1980s.

Conan.

Conan of Cimmeria.

Conan the Freebooter.

Conan the Wanderer.

Conan the Adventurer.

Conan the Buccaneer.

Conan the Warrior.

Conan the Usurper.

Conan the Conqueror.

Conan the Avenger.

Conan of the Isles.

Conan of Aquilonia.

Conan the Swordsman.

Conan the Liberator.

The Blade of Conan.

The Spell for Conan.

Conan and the Spider God.

Treasure of Tranicas.

Conan the Barbarian. By Roland Green.

Conan and the Mists of Doom. By John C. Hocking.

Conan and the Emerald Lotus.

La Plante, Richard

Tegne: Soul Warrior. Tegne was marked from birth for a great destiny as a key player in the epic struggle between good and evil. Prophecies foretold that he would overthrow a tyrant, attain a throne, and free his people from slavery. Raised by Zen monks, Tegne becomes a master of meditation and martial arts.

Martial Arts • Religion • Demons.

McKinley, Robin

The Hero and the Crown. Aerin, a young princess, is recuperating from a poisoning. She takes solace in the palace library, where she learns how to make a salve that resists dragon flame. When the kingdom is threatened, she is the only one who may be able to save her people. Newbery Medal Winner.

Women Warriors • Dragons • Younger Readers.

The Blue Sword. Hundreds of years after the events in *The Hero and the Crown*, Harry finds herself following in the footsteps of her heroic ancestor, Aerin. She is swept into an adventure involving horses, a magical sword, and epic battles to save the people of Damar.

Women Warriors • Magic • Younger Readers.

Moon, Elizabeth

The Deed of Paksenarrion series. "Better a soldier's life than a pig farmer's wife."—Jacket copy.

Women Warriors.

Sheepfarmer's Daughter. Paks is not under any circumstances going to follow her father's orders to marry the pig farmer down the road. Instead, she leaves to join the army and become a legendary hero.

Divided Alliance. Now a seasoned veteran, Paks is accepted as a paladin-candidate by the Fellowship of Gird where she will learn diplomacy and magic as well as increasing her fighting skills. She is called to her first mission before completing her training.

Oath of Gold. Paks proves she is a hero fit to be chosen by gods.

Niles, Douglas

Watershed trilogy. One world but three lands—one mundane, one of good magic, and one of evil—each with its own river, can only be saved by Rudy Appenfell, a hero who has drunk the water of all three rivers simultaneously.

Elves • Dwarves.

A Breach in the Watershed.

Darkenheight.

War of Three Waters.

Pierce, Tamora

The Song of the Lioness quartet.

Women Warriors.

"The making of a hero. The most stubborn girl in the world, Alanna of Trebond, wants to be a knight of the realm of Tortall, in a time when girls are forbidden to be warriors. Rather than give up her dream, she and her brother—who wants to be a mage, not a knight—switch places. She becomes Alan; Thom becomes a student wizard in the school where she would have learned to be a lady. The quartet is about her struggle to achieve her goals and to master weapons, combat, polite behavior, her magic, her temper, and even her own heart. It is about the power of friendships—with the heir to the throne, the King of Thieves, a wise and kindly knight—and her long struggle against a powerful enemy mage. She sees battle as a squire and as a knight, lives among desert people and tries to rescue an independent princess. Singled out by a goddess, accompanied by a semi-divine cat with firm opinions, somehow she survives her many adventures to become a most unlikely legend."—found on the Internet at www.sff.net/people/Tamora.Pierce/about.htm alanna.

> **Alanna: The First Adventure.**
>
> **In the Hand of the Goddess.**
>
> **The Woman Who Rides Like a Man.**
>
> **Lioness Rampant.**

Wizards, Sorcerers, and Enchantresses

Magic wielded for good is often the focus of this subdivision of sword and sorcery. While heroes, battles, and even quests can play into the mix, the use of powers beyond our ken serves as the impetus for the action.

Bujold, Lois McMaster

> **YA** **The Spirit Ring.** After her sorcerer father is murdered and his spirit enslaved, Fiametta, with the assistance of an earnest young metalworker, sets out to rescue him and free the dukedom.
>
> *Talismans • Quest.*

Clayton, Jo

Duel of Sorcery trilogy.

> **Moongather.**
>
> **Moonscatter.**
>
> **Changer's Moon.**

Dancer trilogy. These books are set in the same world as Duel of Sorcery. Awaking after a long ensorcellment, woman warrior Serroi uses her Earth magic to battle an evil enemy who can bend minds and souls.

> *Women Warriors • Healers.*
>
> **Dancer's Rise.**
>
> **Serpent Waltz.**
>
> **Dance down the Stars.**

YA Wild Magic series. In a world filled with many magics, young Faan seeks her mother, who is under a spell.

> **Wild Magic.**
>
> **Wildfire.**
>
> **Magic Wars.**

Drums series.

Drum Warning. See the annotation in Chapter 10. One of the most fascinating aspects of this series is the way in which magical powers are invoked by the three mages trying to manipulate events so they come out on top. One mage has magic devices tattooed all over his body, while another paints magical designs on when he needs them, and the third gowns herself in silvery wire twisted into magical meaning.

Tattoos.

Drum Calls.

Drums of Chaos.

Coe, David B.

LonTobyn Chronicle.

Children of Amarid. Something is seriously awry in LonTobyn, and the mages known as the Children of Amarid must find out what—as the populace loses confidence in them and their bird familiars.

Familiars • Talismans • Quest.

Cole, Allan

Wizard of the Winds. In a land where humans and demons are deadly enemies only one ruler has ever held the title King of Kings, lord over men and demons alike. Now, Iraj Protarus, an orphaned prince, wants to be the next great conqueror and will use his friend Safar Timura, who has an awesome gift for sorcery, to reach his goal.

Demons • Psionic Powers.

de Camp, L. Sprague, and Fletcher Pratt

Harold Shea series. Shea visits worlds created by literature and legend as he slides through parallel worlds.

Humor • Parallel Worlds

The Incompleat Enchanter.

The Castle of Iron.

Wall of Serpents (sometimes titled *The Enchanter Compleated*). An omnibus edition of the three de Camp-Pratt titles was released as *The Intrepid Enchanter: The Complete Magical Misadventures of Harold Shea* in some editions and *The Complete Compleat Enchanter* in others.

The series continued in the 1990s with Christopher Stasheff as co-author, replacing the late Pratt.

Sir Harold and the Gnome King.

The Enchanter Reborn.

The Exotic Enchanter.

Drake, David

Lord of the Isles series.

Time Travel • Dreams • Woman Sorcerer.

Lord of the Isles. When the Kingdom of the Isles is destroyed, Tenoctris, a female wizard, is cast 1,000 years into the future.

NEW **Queen of Demons.** The saga of Garric, Sharina, Cashel, and Tenoctris continues as they travel across the world toward their confrontation with contending forces of evil.

Franklin, Cheryl J.

Sable, Shadow, and Ice. In a decaying society, Avalon mage Morita, member of a politically powerful family but in a declining mage guild, becomes embroiled in a battle between powerful mages and a prince who embraces outlawed education and Empire technology. The stately pace of this intricately wrought epic is appropriate for the multiple viewpoints and philosophies espoused.

Religion • Alternate Worlds • Politics.

Fire Lord series. Features conflict between magic users and anti-magic forces. Interestingly enough the third volume is marketed as science fiction and the first as fantasy.

Parallel Worlds • Science Fantasy.

Fire Get. The wizards of Serii only have a remnant of the power that once had been used to enslave entire lands. Because magic is hated and feared, Lady Rhianna has been taught to deny the power she possesses. Now she discovers that the man she is in love with, Lord Venkaral, is the first master sorcerer to have been born in a millennium, and he is bent on finding the Taormin, a power focus that must be kept safe at all costs.

Fire Lord.

Fire Crossing. The Taormin Matrix is the ultimate tool of sorcery and it is used by three wizards to reopen a time/space portal that the people of the Network—the science-ruled universe that completely surrounds the wizards' world—had thought was closed forever.

Goodkind, Terry

YA Sword of Truth series (annotated by Bonnie Kunzel).

Parallel Worlds • Swords.

Wizard's First Rule. The Wizard's First Rule is that people are stupid and will believe almost anything. But if Richard Cypher refuses to believe Kahlen, the young woman in white he rescues from assassins, when she tells him that he is the Seeker of Truth and must battle the powerful wizard Darken Rahl for the three boxes of Orden, life as he knows it could be destroyed.

Stone of Tears. The adventures of Richard Cypher and Kahlen, now his betrothed, continue; he must study wizardry so that he can stop the Keeper of the Underworld, leaving Kahlen in charge of the bloody battle to save the Midlands.

Blood of the Fold. Blood flows freely as reluctant wizard Richard Cypher wields his Sword of Truth to save his beloved Kahlen and close the gate that is threatening his world.

Temple of the Winds. Richard and Kahlen battle on, this time against a magic-induced plague that can only be defeated by the discovery of the long-lost Temple of the Winds.

Greenberg, Martin H., ed.

Wizard Fantastic. DAW, 1997. Includes twenty-one stories of those who would deal with magic, by Jane Yolen, Andre Norton, Kristine Kathryn Rusch, Diana L. Paxson, Mickey Zucker Reichert, John De Chancie, Michelle West, Jane Lindskold, Dennis L. McKiernan, Josepha Sherman, Jody Lynn Nye, Tanya Huff, and others.

Short Stories.

Huff, Tanya

YA **Child of the Grove.**

YA **Last Wizard.** Crystal must slay the only other wizard in the world, who is evil, if she and the world are to survive.

Keyes, J. Gregory

Chosen of the Changeling series. This series features intricate world building with a solid anthropological basis. Two young people from vastly different cultures, one animistic and the other monotheistic, find their lives linked.

Gods • Barbarians • Ghosts • Assassins.

The Waterborn.

The Black God.

Lackey, Mercedes, and Larry Dixon

The Mage Wars series is a prequel to the World of Valdemar. It deals with magical wars. It is included in Chapter 12 to keep it with the other Valdemar books.

Lee, Adam

Dominions of Irth series. "Griffins, ogres, dragons and trolls inhabit the wilderness of Irth, and sorcerers and witches compete with guilds of assassins and swordmasters for control of the realm's outlandish cities. Evil thrives, heroes strive."—Adam Lee.

Dragons • Assassins • Swordsmen • Animals.

The Dark Shore.

The Shadow Eater.

Massie-Ferch, Kathleen M., ed.

Ancient Enchantresses. DAW, 1995. These tales of women and magic include "The Lady's Gift," by Melanie Rawn; "The Last Spell," by Andre Norton; "The Offering Place," by Diana L. Paxson; "Suffer a Sorceress," by Harry Turtledove; "Saxon Flaxen," by Tanith Lee; "Beyond the Wide World's End," by Susan Shwartz; "The Seven Flowers of Autumn," by Claudia O'Keefe; "Ancient Enchantresses of War," by Kathleen M. Massie-Ferch; "Her City of Ladies," by Steven Rogers; "Unmasking the Ancient Light," by Deborah Wheeler; "A Dying at Blackwater," by Hugh B. Cave; "The Shiksa," by Mike Resnick and Lawrence Schimel; "Mehitabel Goodwin," by Lawrence Watt-Evans; "A Craving for Oysters," by Mary Frances Zambreno; "On the Sun and Moon Mountain," by William F. Wu; "But One Son Living," by Lois Tilton; "A Wind from Heaven," by Laura Resnick; "In His Name," by Jennifer Roberson; and "Erdeni's Tiger," by Pamela Sargent.

Short Stories.

McKillip, Patricia A.

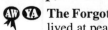 **The Forgotten Beasts of Eld.** World Fantasy Award Winner. "The wizard Sybel lived at peace on Eld Mountain with her legendary beasts until agreeing to raise the infant heir of Eldwold brings her to the attention of King Drede and embroils her in a struggle which only her beasts can help her resolve."—Bonnie Kunzel.

Animals • Romance • Literary Fantasy.

Pierce, Tamora

YA Circle of Magic Quartet.

Younger Readers • Pirates • Weaving • Gardening.

Sandry's Book. Four young people who are all outcasts among their own people are taken by Niklaren Goldeye to Winding Circle, a monastery-like isolated community. All four, not fitting in well in the dorms, are sent to live in a cottage called Discipline. Each of the four has an unusual talent, a magical talent uncommon enough to be unrecognized until Nik finds them. As the four housemates learn to tolerate each other they also begin to learn to deal with their magic. Even though this is Sandry's story, everyone in the quartet is evenly featured until they are trapped in the bowels of the earth and Sandry must bind their unique abilities together to survive. Like Pierce's previous quartets, The Song of the Lioness and The Immortals, Circle of Magic will be popular with fantasy readers of all ages.

Tris's Book. A pirate invasion could spell disaster for Winding Circle.

Daja's Book.

Briar's Book.

Rawn, Melanie

Exiles series. Three sisters of the exiled mageborn find themselves opposing each other in a conflict long after the war between dissenting factions has ended.

Women • Politics • Alternate Worlds.

The Ruins of Ambrai. After years of peace and recovery from the devastating Wild Magic used in the war, the people are no longer threatened by genetic damage and Mageborns practice their craft under strict constraints. But someone has been planning for a new war in the conflict between the Mage Guardians and the Lords of Malerris.

The Mageborn Traitor. Using her own son, Glenin prepares to strike at the heart of her sisters' power by betraying the Ambrai's most closely guarded family secret.

Reimann, Katya

Tielmaran Chronicles.

Gods • Swordsmen.

Wind from a Foreign Sky. In a hideous plot to overthrow the peaceful government of Tielmark, the chancellor plans a forbidden arcane ritual to forge a bride of Glamour from the blood and magic of twin sisters, Gaultry and Mervion.

A Tremor in the Bitter Earth. Gaultry captures an assassin but must thwart his imperial masters in order to save her prince.

NEW Assassins.

Russell, Sean

Moontide and Magic Rise series.

Scientists • Familiars.

World Without End. Tristam Flattery, a young naturalist, is summoned to the royal court at Farrland to tend a failing species of plant that seems to possess magical healing properties on a world where magic is thought to have been lost forever.

 Sea Without a Shore. Led by a mysterious white bird, Tristam travels to a remote island where he comes to realize that he has inherited more than he thought from his uncle Erasmus. In a decision that will determine the fate of the world, he has to decide whether to open a dangerous door or to keep a magical gateway locked forever. 1997 Locus Poll winner.

River into Darkness series.

Beneath the Vaulted Hills. Most mages have already disappeared from Earth, but Lord Eldritch, living in seclusion, has dedicated his life to eliminating all remaining vestiges of magic from the world. He summons Erasmus Flattery, who must lead an expedition into the labyrinthine caves where a secret has remained hidden since the time of the first mages.

Science.

Salvatore, R. A.

Demon Awakens series.

Demons • Elves • Goblins • Dwarves.

The Demon Awakens. Gemstones that rain from the heavens have the potential for magic, both good and evil. Salvatore is particularly known for his excellent fight scenes.

The Demon Spirit.

Shinn, Sharon

 The Shape-Changer's Wife. Aubrey discovers that even the wizard's wife has been shape-changed from an animal as he tries to learn to shapeshift himself. 1996 Crawford Award Winner.

Shapeshifting • Dark Fantasy • Romance.

Wurts, Janny

The Wars of Light and Shadows series. Half-brothers control the powers of light and shadow. Lysaer, the prince of light, is sworn to uphold justice and free humanity from the sorcerer's rule. Arithon, the master of shadow, is a Masterbard and a trained mage who wishes for nothing but an end to war and strife.

Curses • Music • Politics.

The Curse of the Mistwraith.

The Ships of Merior.

Warhost of Vastmark.

Alliance of Light series.

Fugitive Prince. With the Vastmark Warhost destroyed, the balance of power in the Five Kingdoms is reshaped as Koriani enchantresses join forces with Lysaer.

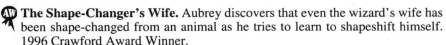

D's Picks

Chapter 4

Saga, Myth, and Legend

Many readers come to fantasy through a love of the types of tales that some consider a precursor of fantasy and others a subset. Here the reader will find tales based on familiar myths and legends. Many of the following are sword and sorcery adventures set against a backdrop made familiar because of its basis in a myth, legend, or saga.

Arthurian Legend

The most enchanting of the legendary backgrounds is the Arthurian, with Merlin often the dominating figure. Since Marion Zimmer Bradley's groundbreaking *The Mists of Avalon* was published, women have been playing a larger role in these stories.

Ashley, Michael, ed.

The Camelot Chronicles. Carroll & Graf, 1992.

The Chronicles of the Round Table. Carrol & Graf, 1997.

Anthologies of Arthurian short stories.

Short Stories.

Bradley, Marion Zimmer

The Mists of Avalon. 1984 Locus Poll Winner. "The story of King Arthur is told from a different point of view, that of the women in his life: his sister Morgaine, his aunt Viviane and his wife, the lovely Guinevere."—Bonnie Kunzel.

Women.

Bradshaw, Gillian

Gawain trilogy (annotated by Bonnie Kunzel).

Hawk of May. "Another version of the Arthurian legends, this time featuring Gawain, who tells the story from his own point of view. After fleeing from the magical black arts practiced by Morgause, his mother, he winds up in Arthur's court."

Kingdom of Summer. "A body servant of Gawain tells the story of his master's search for a woman he had wronged by slaying her brother."

In Winter's Shadow. "Arthur versus his nephew Medraut, a battle between the light and the dark for the fate of his kingdom, narrated by Guinevere (Gwynhwyfar), who is aware of the damage Medraut is causing but is in danger herself when she tries to stand up to him."

Cary, James

King & Raven. Raven goes to the thirteenth-century court of King Arthur to try to avenge a grave wrong done his family.

Charrette, Robert N.

A Prince Among Men. Arthur in a dystopian twentieth-first century. "In a heavily-computerized future, a young college student gets involved with King Arthur, recently awakened after slumbering through the centuries. In their quest to find Arthur's sword Caliburn, the two encounter elves, goblins, demons, fairies, etc., in a world where Faery has crossed over into the realm of mankind."—Bonnie Kunzel.

Futuristic Fantasy • Faerie.

Cochran, Molly, and Warren Murphy

The Forever King. Arthur Blessing, an orphaned ten-year-old Chicagoan, ends up on the run with his aunt after he finds a mysterious cup-like object that possesses the power to heal. Hooking up with ex-FBI agent Hal Woczniak, the reincarnated Galahad, Arthur strives to survive and bring Merlin back from the limbo in which he has been languishing. When he pulls Excalibur from a stone, Arthur discovers that he is the reincarnated King Arthur. It may sound hokey, but it is a satisfying read, blending the magic of Camelot with the twentieth century. Saladin is a unique and reprehensible villain.

Contemporary Fantasy • Reincarnation.

The Broken Sword. This rare blend of action, adventure, and history is the sequel to *The Forever King*. In a Middle Eastern marketplace, a former American president is shot but then is miraculously healed by a humble cup that rolls into the hands of Beatrice, who has been blind from birth but suddenly can see. After further attempts on their lives, Arthur and Beatrice stow away with Taliesin on a ship bound for America. Hal Woczniak swept away in a strong ocean current, eventually finds himself shepherding the rowdy knights of the roundtable, who have been released into this reality in New York to try to save Arthur from once again losing his life to evil forces.

Contemporary Fantasy • Reincarnation.

Crompton, Anne Eliot

Merlin's Harp. A feminist version of the Arthur story, told from the viewpoint of Niviene, who is Merlin's apprentice and the daughter of the Lady of the Lake.

Women.

Gemmell, David

The Stones of Power sequence is part of Gemmell's Sipstrassi series in that Maedhlyn or Merlin owes his power to the Sipstrassi meteor.

Science Fantasy.

Ghost King.

Last Sword of Power. Young Thuro grows up to be Uther Pendragon.

Godwin, Parke

Includes a very human portrayal of Arthur, followed by an account of Guenevere's subsequent attempts to hold the kingdom together and her life as a Saxon lord's servant.

Historical Fantasy.

Beloved Exile.

Firelord.

Hollick, Helen

Pendragon series.

Kingmaking: Book One of Pendragon. As the Roman legions are driven from Britain, a young Arthur must assume a leadership role.

Pendragon's Banner.

Shadow of the King. A fifth-century version of the great romance between the King and his Queen Gwenhwyfar.

Jones, Courtway

Dragon's Heirs trilogy. This is a fresh view of the tale, set in the fifth century, with different perspectives on King Pellas, Morgan, and Mordred.

In the Shadow of the Oak King.

Witch of the North.

A Prince in Camelot.

Kane, Gil, and John Jakes

Excalibur! Explores the whys and hows of the legend more than some of the other versions.

Kennealy-Morrison, Patricia

The Keltiad series. The widow of rocker Jim Morrison sets her Arthurian tales on a distant planet.

Science Fantasy.

The Copper Crown.

The Throne of Stone.

The Silver Branch.

The Hawk's Gray Feather.

The Oak Above the Kings.

The Hedge of Mist.

Lawhead, Steve

🅐Pendragon series. This is a Christian take on the legend, full of spirituality.

Christianity.

Taliesin.

Merlin.

Arthur.

Monaco, Richard

Parsival sequence.

Parsival; or, A Knight's Tale. "First of a trilogy that is a dark, brooding treatment of the legend of Parsifal, the young knight of the Round Table who is judged so pure and innocent by his companions that he is the logical one to search for the Holy Grail."—Bonnie Kunzel.

The Grail War.

The Final Quest.

Munn, H. Warner

King of the World's Edge. "An entirely new twist to the Arthurian canon, in which Merlin, accompanied by Sir Gawain, travels to America and is recognized by the Aztecs as Quetzalcoatl, one of their gods." —Bonnie Kunzel

Gods • Mexico • Quetzalcoatl.

The Ship from Atlantis. Sir Gawain leaves Merlin to return to Rome, is trapped in the Sargasso Sea, and encounters a survivor from Atlantis.

Atlantis.

Merlin's Godson. This is an omnibus edition of *King of the World's Edge* and *The Ship from Atlantis.*

Merlin's Ring. The love story of Sir Gawain and the Atlantean sorceress Corenice across the centuries, from the fall of Atlantis to the time of Joan of Arc.

Immortality.

Newman, Sharan

Told from Guinevere's viewpoint, this gently humorous series contains more fantasy elements, including a unicorn, than many Arthurian tales.

Humor • Women • Unicorns.

Guinevere.

The Chessboard Queen.

Guinevere Evermore. Guinevere's affair with Lancelot is discovered, leading to the end of an era.

Norton, Andre

Merlin's Mirror. Merlin and Arthur are aliens in possession of advanced scientific knowledge.

Science Fantasy.

Nye, Robert

Merlin. Is Merlin writing the story of his life, or is the author the devil, his father?

Paterson, Katherine

🅐 **Parzival: The Quest of the Grail Knight.** This is a short, beautifully presented telling of the Percival/Galahad part of the legend.

Younger Readers.

Paxson, Diana L.

The White Raven.

Rice, Robert

🅐 **The Last Pendragon.** "In this variation of the Arthurian legends, a dying Arthur asks Sir Bedwyr to throw his sword Caliburn in the lake. Bedwyr can't make himself do it, hides the sword in a tree and flees to Rome. Eleven years later he returns to England to complete Arthur's last request and in his search for the missing sword meets the most viable candidate for Arthur's replacement. Irion is Arthur's grandson as well as the son of the man who killed the king, which is why Bedwyr is not willing to trust him, until it is almost too late."—Bonnie Kunzel.

Swords.

Roberson, Jennifer, ed.

Return to Avalon. DAW, 1996. Includes twenty original stories set in Marion Zimmer Bradley's version of the Arthurian legend. Contributors include Judith Tarr, C. J. Cherryh, Katharine Kerr, Diana L. Paxson, Charles de Lint, and Melanie Rawn.

Short Stories.

Saberhagen, Fred

Merlin's Bones. Many are interested in the bones of the great wizard found on a mysterious spit of land near a strangely unfinished castle: Morgan le Fay, beautiful and catlike; Mordred, power-hungry; a skeptical twenty-first-century physicist; the ambitious Viking leader Hakon; and Merlin himself.

Time Travel • Parallel Worlds • Futuristic Fantasy.

Springer, Nancy

🆕 🅐 **I Am Mordred.** Mordred's only wish, when he discovers his own history, is to escape his fate.

Stewart, Mary

The Merlin trilogy. This is the story told from Merlin's viewpoint. The first book takes place before Arthur's birth and follows Merlin's life from childhood to his last enchantment (annotated by Bonnie Kunzel).

Romance • Historical Fantasy.

🅐🅥 **The Crystal Cave.** Merlin narrates the story of his early life as the son of a Welsh princess and a Roman commander, who realizes that he must make a place for himself at his father's side if he is to survive. His special talents develop under the tutelage of Galapas, his first teacher in the Crystal Cave. 1971 Mythopoeic Award Winner.

Weaving.

The Hollow Hills. Merlin has foreseen the need of a champion to unite Britain and personally takes on the challenge of seeing that Arthur is born and later recognized as the High King. This he accomplishes, but what he cannot do is keep Arthur from sleeping with his half-sister Morgause, a union that produces Mordred, Arthur's personal nemesis. 1974 Mythopoeic Award Winner.

The Last Enchantment. In his old age Merlin falls in love with Nimue, his young apprentice, who takes over as Arthur's advisor when the magician becomes ill and infirm. He sees the love triangle forming among Arthur, Guinevere, and in this version, Bedwyr, but he can do nothing to prevent the final tragedy because it is too late—he has been imprisoned in the Crystal Cave.

The Wicked Day. Describes Mordred's rebellion against Arthur.

Tolstoy, Nikolai

The Coming of the King: The First Book of Merlin. Covers Merlin's Celtic past, the story of his birth, and all that befell him during the period before he met Arthur.

Celtic Fantasy.

White, T. H.

The Once and Future King. For those who read this classic first it represents the definitive version. *Camelot* the movie also bears a strong resemblance to White's version of events. *The Once and Future King* is the collective title for:

The Sword in the Stone (the basis of the Disney movie of the same title).

The Witch in the Wood (The Queen of Air and Darkness).

The Ill-Made Knight.

The Candle in the Wind.

The Book of Merlyn (concludes the series).

Film.

Wolfe, Gene

Castleview. The fabric of time and space is very thin between Arthur's England and contemporary Castleview, Illinois. A phantom castle sometimes appears there. Shortly after Will E. Shields decides to buy a house there, a giant horseman comes thundering out of the rain and a brutal murder is discovered. Centuries of pent-up fury are loosed on the small midwestern town when Morgan le Fay sends her minions through the breach.

Woolley, Persia

Includes the trials and tribulations as well as the joys of Guinevere and Camelot.

Child of the Northern Spring.

Queen of the Summer Stars.

Guinevere: The Legend in Autumn.

Yolen, Jane

⚠️ Young Merlin trilogy.

Passager.

Hobby.

Merlin.

Younger Readers.

Robin Hood and Sherwood Forest

Cadnum, Michael

⚠️ The Wild Wood. This take on the Robin Hood tale portrays a sympathetic sheriff who likes and respects Robin. There is no Maid Marion in this very adult version, published as a young adult title.

Godwin, Parke

Sherwood. This is the Robin Hood legend set in the time of the Norman Conquest, with Robin upholding the Saxon traditions.

Robin and the King. A middle-aged Robin continues to fight for what he thinks is right.

McKinley, Robin

⚠️ Outlaws of Sherwood. This is a feminist version of Robin Hood.

Morpurgo, Michael

⚠️ Robin.

Roberson, Jennifer

⚠️ Lady of the Forest. A prequel, this story tells of the assemblage of the well-known characters of the Robin Hood legend.

Ancient Civilizations

The setting could be ancient Greece or Rome or even the lost worlds of Atlantis or Mu.

Bradley, Marion Zimmer

Fall of Atlantis.

Atlantis.

The Firebrand. Kassandra, a princess of Troy, is at the center of cataclysmic events.

Greece • Troy.

Lindskold, Jane

The Pipes of Orpheus. The Pied Piper's true identity is discovered in a book from his library by his child prisoners.

Greece • Music • Libraries • Fairy Tales.

Norton, Andre, and Susan Shwartz

Empire of the Eagle. Quintus is a member of a defeated legion who is sent east with the Roman golden Eagle into the mists of legend to see wonders previously unknown to any Roman.

Romans.

Saberhagen, Fred

Book of the Gods series.

NEW **The Face of Apollo.** Young Jeremy Redthorn and the world he inhabits will never be the same since the ancient gods are back: Apollo, the sun god; Hades, lord of the Underworld; Thanatos, a Trickster; and Hephaestus the Smith.

Gods • The Paranormal.

Silverberg, Robert

Letters from Atlantis. Correspondence between two time travelers, one of whom is in Atlantis.

Time Travel • Atlantis.

Wolfe, Gene

AW **Soldier of the Mist.** After a soldier, possibly a Roman legionnaire, suffers a grievous head wound he wakes each day to amnesia and his journal. 1987 Locus Poll Winner.

Celtic Fantasy

Alexander, Lloyd

YA The Prydain Chronicles. Although written for the young, these are also read by adults. Based on the Mabinogion of Welsh legend. The adventures of Taran, an assistant pig-keeper; Hen-Wen, a pig who is also an oracle; Gwydion; and the dark lord Arawan have also appeared in a computer game.

Younger Readers • Gaming.

The Book of Three.

The Black Cauldron.

The Castle of Llyr.

Taran Wanderer.

AW **The High King.** Newbery Award Winner.

Berry, Liz

🅨 The China Garden. Clare Meredith, ready to go to university, insists on accompanying her mother to Ravensmere instead, where she discovers that the legends of the Guardians go deep into the past. Each generation of the Kenwards from the farm and the Aylwards from the castle were to marry, but something went wrong in the past, threatening the survival of Ravensmere and all connected to it. Clare meets a handsome, leather-clad biker and together they must find the mysterious treasure of legend, the Benison, and restore the tradition of the Guardians to ensure the well-being of the community. A labyrinth motif plays a pivotal role.

Labyrinths • Romance.

Bradley, Marion Zimmer

The Forest House. Before the time of Avalon, a secret circle of Druidic priestesses guards the ancient rites of learning, healing, and prophecy against the inexorable approach of the Roman Empire.

Chant, Joy

🅨 Vandarei series. These are Celtic and pre-Arthurian. Three children oppose the Dark Lord.

🅰🅦 Red Moon and Black Mountain. 1972 Mythopoeic Award Winner.

The Grey Mane of Morning.

🅰🅦 When Voiha Wakes. 1984 Mythopoeic Award Winner.

The High Kings.

Cooper, Susan

🅨 The Dark Is Rising sequence. This is a beloved children's series. Will Stanton is the seventh son of a seventh son (as is Alvin in Orson Scott Card's Alvin Maker series, Chapter 10) who is the last of the Old Ones, a race of guardians involved in the battle between Light and Dark.

Over Sea, Under Stone.

The Dark Is Rising.

Greenwitch.

The Grey King.

Silver on the Tree.

Immortality • Younger Readers.

de Lint, Charles

Into the Green. Angharad travels "the Kingdoms of the Green Isles with a witch staff in her hand, a harp on her back, a puzzle to solve and a quest to fulfill."—Jacket copy.

Music.

Edgerton, Teresa

Green Lion series. A young woman is the heroic figure who learns to use her magic to fight an evil princess.

Women • Shapeshifting • Wolves.

Child of Saturn.

The Moon in Hiding.

The Work of the Sun.

Celeydonn series. Gwenlliant must use her Wild Magic to keep herself and the children of Celeydonn safe.

The Castle of the Silver Wheel.

The Grail and the Ring.

The Moon and the Thorn.

Flint, Kenneth C.

Flint and Morgan Llywelyn both use the same heroes in their works, with quite different effects.

Finn MacCool • Ireland • Heroes.

Finn MacCumhal series. The heroic Finn MacCool rallies forces to defend Ireland. (Note that there are many different ways to spell the name of this legendary character.)

Challenge of the Clans.

Storm Shield.

The Dark Druid.

Isle of Destiny. Depicts the early life of the hero Cuchulain. Readers looking for a different version of the legendary hero may want to try Morgan Llywelyn's *Red Branch*.

Sidhe series. Features the legend of Tuath De Danann.

Riders of the Sidhe.

Champions of the Sidhe.

Master of the Sidhe.

Cromm. A twentieth-century man's dreams lead to a bloody confrontation with the fourth century.

Darkening Flood.

Godwin, Parke

The Tower of Beowulf. Beowulf and Grendel.

Jones, Diana Wynne

Fire and Hemlock. Elements from Tam Lin appear in this story.

Younger Readers • Fairy Tales.

Lawhead, Stephen R.

Song of Albion series.

The Paradise War. A college student, seduced by the lure of the Otherworld, crosses a hidden border that takes him into a Celtic past as a warrior for Nudd, the lord of the eternal damned.

The Silver Hand.

The Endless Knot.

Christianity.

Llywelyn, Morgan

Red Branch. The hero Cuchulain in a version quite different from that of Kenneth C. Flint in *Isle of Destiny*.

Finn MacCool. This details Finn's rise to leadership told in one volume. Diana L. Paxson and Adrienne Martine-Barnes wrote about MacCool in *Master of Earth and Water*, as did Kenneth C. Flint in his Finn MacCumhal series.

Finn MacCool • Ireland • Heroes.

McAvoy, R. A.

Grey Horse. A magnificent stallion brings magic to an Irish town.

Book of Kells.

Ireland.

Morris, Kenneth

Morris, who died in 1937, is credited with creating the modern genre of Celtic fantasy.

The Fates of the Princes of Dyfed.

Book of the Three Dragons.

Paxson, Diana L.

The Serpent's Tooth. This is a Celtic take on King Lear set five centuries before the Roman conquest of England. King Lear, a Celtic chieftain who conquered three kingdoms, married the three ruling queens and fathered one daughter with each of them.

Shakespeare.

Paxson, Diana L., and Adrienne Martine-Barnes

Master of Earth and Water. This is about third-century Irish outlaw/poet Fionn MacCumhal.

Shield Between the Worlds.

Sword of Fire and Shadow.

Finn MacCool.

Tarr, Judith

AW **YA** Hound and the Falcon trilogy: Medieval Wales. 1987 Crawford Award Winner.

The Isle of Glass.

The Golden Horn.

The Hounds of God.

Vance, Jack

Lyonesse series. Set two generations before Arthur on a series of now sunken islands, these stories feature political intrigue and magic.

Suldrun's Garden.

The Green Pearl.

AW **Madouc.** 1990 World Fantasy Award Winner.

Walton, Evangeline

The Mabinogion series.

> **The Prince of Annwn.**
>
> **The Children of Llyr.**
>
> **The Song of Rhiannon.** 1973 Mythopoeic Award Winner.
>
> **The Virgin and the Swine.**

The Americas

Bell, Clare

> **The Jaguar Princess.**

Bruchac, Joseph

> **Dawn Land.** Sensing impending doom, Young Hunter and his three dog companions set out on a quest to save his people.
>
> *Native Americans • Dogs.*

de Lint, Charles

> **Someplace to Be Flying.** The Crow Girls, Jack Daw, and other shapeshifting animal people interact with ordinary humans and people with animal blood as they try to stop the cuckoos from obtaining the pot that holds the power of creation itself.
>
> *Contemporary Fantasy • Animal People.*

Morris, Kenneth

> **The Chalchiuhite Dragon.** Based on Toltec history and mythology, this story recounts the rise of Quetzalcoatl, the great philosopher king.
>
> *Mexico • Quetzalcoatl.*

Asia

Anthony, Piers

> **Willing Spirit.** A young man is the object and victim of a wager between two Hindu gods.
>
> *Gods • India.*

Dalkey, Kara

Blood of the Goddess series (annotated in Chapter 10).

Hughart, Barry

Master Li series. Fans of this may also enjoy Robert van Gulick's Judge Dee mystery series.

> **Bridge of Birds: A Novel of Ancient China That Never Was.** 1985 World Fantasy Award winner. 1986 Mythopoeic Award Winner.
>
> **The Story of the Stone.**

Eight Skilled Gentlemen.

China • Detection.

Norton, Andre, and Susan Shwartz

Imperial Lady. (Han China).

China • Women.

Russell, Sean

The Asian Duology.

Initiate Brother.

Gathering of Clouds.

Martial Arts • Poets • Magic.

Europe

Cherryh, C. J.

Rusalka sequence. In a medieval Ukrainian setting with its roots in the folklore of the area, these stories follow the fortunes of a family talented with magic.

Rusalka. A father's sacrifice brings life to Eveshka, a formerly destructive ghost with whom Peytr had unwillingly fallen in love.

Chernevog. Eveshka's nights are plagued by fears and a summoning that takes her away from her husband, Peytr, and the half-taught young wizard Sasha. She goes to the north, to a stone where Kavi Chernevog, the dark wizard who had killed her, sleeps bespelled by the forest guardians. But dark magic is loose in the world in human form.

Yvgenie.

Folktales.

Grundy, Stephan

Rhinegold. Follows the story of two warrior lines––the Saxon Walsings and the Burgundian Gevicungs––through seven generations. They are bound together by Wodan and a treasure under the Rhine.

German Stories.

King, Bernard

Lambisson series. Hather Lambisson has been blessed by Odin with three lives and cursed by Thor with death and dishonor.

Scandinavian Stories.

Starkadder.

Vagr-Moon.

Death-Blinder.

Milan, Victor, and Melinda Snodgrass

Runespear. Features Nordic gods versus Nazis.

Scandinavian Stories.

Paxson, Diana L.

The Wolf and the Raven.

The Dragons on the Rhine. Based on the Nibelungen, the Nordic myth that inspired Wagner's Ring Cycle of operas.

Scandinavian Stories.

Reichert, Mickey Zucker

The Renshai trilogy. These stories are very loosely based on Norse legend. Just before the battle of Ragnarok, both humankind and the gods hover on the brink of destruction. "And what hope was there for mere humans when Odin, the leader of the gods, was himself doomed to die in the upcoming battle? Yet Odin had long planned to cheat his fate. His chosen weapon to slay his nemesis, Fenris Wolf, was the demigod Colbey Calistinsson, the son of Thor and the last true survivor of the warrior race known as the Renshai. But Colbey had loyalties far older and stronger than those he owed to the gods. He, too, was determined to change the foreordained path of the future—though Colbey's success would seal Odin's doom."—Jacket copy.

Scandinavian Stories.

The Last of the Renshai.

The Western Wizard.

Child of Thunder.

The Renshai Chronicle is a sequel series.

Beyond Ragnarok. A new ruler must be found for Bearn to maintain the balance between Law and Chaos, but an unidentified enemy seems bent on destroying all who stand in line for the throne. When no likely heir is apparent after the Test of the Staves a party consisting of the king's granddaughter, a knight in training, an apprentice bard, a young and untested Renshai warrior, and a thief set out on a quest to find the true heir to the throne.

Prince of Demons. The Staffs of Law and Chaos have been brought back, and Colbey Calistinsson must select a champion to fight the elves who are preparing to claim vengeance on humankind.

Schaefer, Frank

Whose Song Is Sung. Musculus, a bastard dwarf, embarks on a remarkable odyssey that leads him to the land of the Northmen, where he becomes the companion of Einarr, Slayer of Monsters, also known as Beowulf.

Africa and the Middle East

When we think of myths and legends of the Middle East, genies, djinn, flying carpets, and other denizens of 1,001 Arabian Nights come to mind. We think of Aladdin and his magical lamp and even Sidney Sheldon's television series *I Dream of Jeannie.*

Friesner, Esther

YA **Wishing Season.** A trainee genie, with his thoughts on love rather than magic rules, messes up his first assignment.

Myers, Walter Dean

YA **The Legend of Tarik.** Features a heroic young African man on a quest to become someone who can stop the annihilation of his people. Even though this has been out of print for several years it is still available in many libraries.

Younger Readers.

Resnick, Mike, ed.

Aladdin: Master of the Lamp. DAW, 1992. This contains forty-three stories inspired by the tale of Aladdin and his magical lamp.

Tarr, Judith

Lord of Two Lands. Features Alexander the Great's conquest of Egypt.

Throne of Isis. Tells of Cleopatra's romance with Marc Antony.

Byzantium

Shwartz, Susan

Shards of Empire. Leo Dorcas leaves a failing tenth-century Constantinople. On the borders of the empire he finds wonders, magic, and a woman who may hold the key to unite the peoples of Asia Minor.

D's Picks

Chapter 5

Fairy Tales

The publication of retellings of fairy tales and old folktales is a growing trend. Some of the stories told in the following novels will be familiar; others will seem to be new, but with an underlying feeling that they have been told before. Tor's Fairy Tale series, created by Terri Windling, was written for adults. About the books in this series, Lisa Goldstein wrote, "difficult truths can sometimes only be told through the medium of fantasy." The familiar fairy tale is sometimes taken into other subgenres and books that fit into them are noted here and annotated in the other sections.

Readers who enjoy fantasy with the flavor of fairy tales and folktales may also want to check out collections and compilations of the original stories. They are often shelved in the nonfiction sections in the children's and adult areas of libraries, places that fantasy readers may not think to visit without the suggestion of a reader's advisor.

An overview of the last 150 years of the short form of fairy tale can be found in Alison Lurie, ed., *The Oxford Book of Modern Fairy Tales* (Oxford University Press, 1993). The vast variety and evolution of the fairy tale over the years is demonstrated in the diverse stories included: "Uncle David's Nonsensical Story About Giants and Fairies" (1839), by Catherine Sinclair; "Feathertop" (1846), by Nathaniel Hawthorne; "The King of the Golden River" (1850), by John Ruskin; "The Story of Fairyfoot" (1856), by Frances Browne; "The Light Princess" (1864), by George MacDonald; "The Magic Fishbone" (1868), by Charles Dickens; "A Toy Princess" (1877), by Mary De Morgan; "The New Mother" (1882), by Lucy Lane Clifford; "Good Luck Is Better Than Gold" (1882), by Juliana Horatia Ewing; "The Apple of Contentment" (1886), by Howard Pyle; "The Griffin and the Minor Canon" (1887), by Frank Stockton; "The Selfish Giant" (1888), by Oscar Wilde; "The Rooted Lover" (1894), by Laurence Housman; "The Song of the Morrow" (1894), by Robert Louis Stevenson; "The Reluctant Dragon" (1898), by Kenneth Grahame; "The Book of Beasts" (1900), by E. Nesbit; "The Queen of Quok" (1901), by L. Frank Baum; "The Magic Shop" (1903), by H. G. Wells; "The Kith of the Elf-Folk" (1910), by Lord Dunsany; "The Story of Blixie Bimber and the Power of the Gold Buckskin Whincher" (1922), by Carl Sandburg; "The Lovely Myfanwy" (1925), by Walter De la Mare; "The Troll" (1935), by T. H. White; "Gertrude's Child" (1940), by Richard Hughes; "The Unicorn in the Garden" (1940), by James Thurber; "Bluebeard's Daughter" (1940), by Sylvia Townsend Warner; "The Chaser" (1941), by John Collier; "The King of the Elves" (1953), by Philip K. Dick; "In the Family" (1957), by Naomi Mitchison; "The Jewbird" (1963), by Bernard Malamud; "Menaseh's Dream" (1968), by I. B. Singer; "The Glass Mountain" (1970), by Donald Barthelme; "Prince Amilec" (1972), by Tanith Lee; "Petronella" (1973), by Jay Williams; "The Man Who Had Seen the Rope Trick" (1976), by Joan Aiken; "The Courtship of Mr. Lyon" (1979), by Angela Carter; "The Princess Who Stood on Her Own Two Feet" (1982), by Jeanne Desy; "The Wife's Story" (1982), by Ursula K. Le Guin; "The River Maid" (1982), by Jane Yolen; "The Porcelain Man" (1987), by Richard Kennedy; and "Old Man Potchikoo" (1989), by Louise Erdrich.

Short Stories.

The Familiar

Sometimes the classic fairy tale is elaborated upon by developing the characters beyond stereotypes and giving them backgrounds and motivation. Other familiar fairy tales are used as jumping-off points, with the original premise there, but used as a springboard into something entirely different, such as taking the heroine into another century or situation. One of the defining moments in modern fantasy fairy tales was when Terri Windling signed with Tor books to gather some of the best of contemporary fantasy writers to tell their versions of the classic tales.

Bemmann, Hans

The Broken Goddess. After delivering a skeptical lecture on the importance of fairy tales, a young college professor steps into a world of living fairy tales.

de Lint, Charles

Jack of Kinrowan. This is a contemporary feminist Jack the Giant Killer (see annotation in "Urban Fantasy," Chapter 9).

Dean, Pamela

NEW **Juniper, Gentian, and Rosemary.** Three sisters become fascinated by Dominic, but their father fears that he may be the Devil himself. Inspired by the traditional ballad.

Contemporary Fantasy • Literary Fantasy.

Lackey, Mercedes

Fire Rose. "Lackey's story of a young turn of the century female who is brought to the wilds of San Francisco to read books for a reclusive alchemist recreates the fable of the monster who wins the heart of a young woman yet forbids her to view him. For the monster here is a magician caught in a werewolf spell, and the young girl is a destitute young woman with no other choices."—*Midwest Book Review*.

Werewolves • Beauty and the Beast.

Firebird. Based on the Russian tale, in this story a young man guarding his father's orchards manages to stay awake to meet the fantastical Firebird, who gives him one of her feathers, which allows him to understand the speech of animals. Bound and sent into the wilds by his jealous brothers, he encounters many adventures before freeing the Firebird from the spell that binds her.

Russian Stories.

5

Levine, Gail Carson

YA **Ella Enchanted.** Although published for children or young adults, this down-to-earth, yet magic-filled take on the Cinderella story delights adult readers. Poor Ella is given the "gift" of obedience, which causes her to do whatever she is told. When her mother dies and she is sent off to boarding school with the odious daughters of her father's girlfriend, she must find a way to rebel.

Younger Readers • Cinderella • The Paranormal.

McKinley, Robin

Beauty. This is a retelling of *Beauty and the Beast*.

Beauty and the Beast.

Deerskin. This tale unveils the horrors of incest in a tale of a beautiful princess and her dog, based on the fairy tale "Donkeyskin."

Incest • Dogs • Donkeyskin.

The Rose Daughter. This is a most unusual story in that McKinley had previously, and in a very different manner, retold the same story years before in *Beauty*. This lovely, lyrical retelling of the "Beauty and the Beast" story is a wonderful addition to the canon of retold fairy tales. McKinley has created complex, fully realized characters in the three sisters and their failed merchant father. Unlike the traditionally told versions, Beauty's sisters are pretty likable. Roses and their cultivation play a large role in this tale, as does the magical castle of the Beast.

Beauty and the Beast • Gardening.

Napoli, Donna Jo

(YA) The Magic Circle. This retelling of the "Hansel and Gretel" story from a different view-point is an example of a dark fairy tale told in a way that changes one's views of villain and hero. In an attempt to become better and help more children, a midwife starts to use little spells that result in her being condemned to burn at the stake. A demon is willing to save her in exchange for transforming her into a witch. Unwilling to eat children, she flees deep into the forest, where she lives a lonely existence of housekeeping until two unsuspecting children come knocking at her door.

Hansel and Gretel • Witches • Dark Fantasy.

(YA) Zel. The motivations of the characters from the traditional "Rapunzel" story are brought to life in this tale of an adopted daughter living in a remote cottage who meets a boy in the village, setting off a horrifying train of events. On the eve of Zel's birthday, Zel and Mother go to town, a rare event that happens only twice a year. When Zel catches the eye of a young nobleman, Konrad, while helping the smith with a horse, her life changes forever. After returning to the cottage on the mountain where they live, Mother takes Zel to a tower, where she tells her she will be safe from bad people who are trying to find and kill her. Told from the perspectives of Zel, Mother, and Konrad, the story provides us with a sense of the emotional turmoil experienced by all as Zel, isolated and suffering from the horrendous headaches caused by her magically long hair, descends into madness. Mother struggles with her decisions and the issues of eternal damnation, and Konrad relentlessly searches for the young woman who is inextricably linked to him on a level no one else can understand.

Rapunzel • Romance • Psychology.

Osborne, Mary Pope

(YA) Haunted Waters. Inspired by the German fairy tale "Undine," in this story a lord falls in love with a child of the sea who can only be with him in death, a death caused by drowning in tears, leading to a life in the sea.

Younger Readers • Undine • Demons.

Scarborough, Elizabeth Ann

Godmother. In a fractured fairy tale manner, Scarborough sets her tales of a fairy god-mother in contemporary Seattle.

Godmother's Apprentice.

Fairy Godmothers • Contemporary Fantasy.

Tepper, Sheri S.

(AW) (YA) Beauty. Beauty pricks her finger on her sixteenth birthday and instead of sleeping for 100 years, she travels to the twenty-first century. 1992 Locus Poll Winner.

Futuristic Fantasy • Time Travel.

Wrede, Patricia C.

Snow White and Rose Red (annotated in Chapter 8).

(YA) The Enchanted Forest Chronicles. Written for teens, this series is always sneaking in little tidbits of fairy tales, such as magic carpets, giants, and beanstalks.

Dealing with Dragons. Cimorene doesn't like what life has laid out for her, so she sets out on her own, becoming librarian to a dragon.

Searching for Dragons. Holes have started appearing in the magic of the Enchanted Forest and the young king, Mendabar, must find out why, so he ventures forth to seek advice from Kazul, the king of the dragons. Unfortunately Kazul has been captured by horrible wizards, so Mendabar hooks up with Cimorene, who is unlike any princess he has ever met.

Calling on Dragons.

Talking to Dragons. Shortly after his sixteenth birthday, Daystar is sent on a quest into the Enchanted Forest, but doesn't know why.

> *Dragons • Humor • Magic • Romance.*

Yolen, Jane

 Briar Rose. When her dying grandmother says "I am Briar Rose, find the castle," a young journalist sets off on a journey of discovery that combines the tale of Sleeping Beauty with the horrors of the Holocaust's death camps. 1993 Mythopoeic Award Winner.

> *Holocaust • Contemporary Fantasy • Sleeping Beauty.*

Originals

Barnes, John

One for the Morning Glory. In this parody of a traditional fairy tale, a prince is literally turned into half a person when he drinks the Wine of the Gods. The four people present at the time and responsible for his safety are graphically beheaded. A year and a day later, four people apply for the four vacant positions—witch, alchemist, fighter, and nursemaid—starting the adventures that will lead to the restoration of Prince Amatus's left side. Barnes delightfully manipulates language with hilarious results. People hunt and eat gazebos, shoot omnibuses, and keep their screes in their swashes. Predictable because of its fairy tale format, this story still surprises because of the frequent and excessive violence.

> *Parody • Humor • Quest.*

Furlong, Monica

Wise Child. Juniper, a witch who practices white magic, adopts a girl child. ALA Notable Children's Book.

> *Magic • Witches • Younger Readers.*

Juniper. A princess spends a year and a day being raised by a wise woman—or is she a witch? A prequel to *Wise Child*.

> *Younger Readers • Magic • Witches.*

Goldman, William

The Princess Bride: S. Morgenstern's Classic Tale of True Love and High Adventure, The "Good Parts" Version, Abridged by William Goldman. This is the basis of the movie *The Princess Bride*.

> *Film • Adventure.*

Jones, Diana Wynne

🆅🅐 Howl's Moving Castle.

🆅🅐 Castle in the Air (annotated in Chapter 6).

McKillip, Patricia A.

The Book of Atrix Wolfe. Atrix, a powerful mage, unleashed a savage uncontrollable force that not only defeated the invading army but also killed his own beloved king. After twenty years among the wolves he has finally been summoned to find a princess, the daughter of the Queen of the Wood, who disappeared into the human realm during the battle.

Animals • Wolves.

Meynard, Yves

The Book of Knights. The pages of a marvelous book show a young boy the world outside his village, inspiring him to go on a quest, become a knight, and discover the secret of his heritage.

Medieval Times • Quest • France • Women Warriors • Books.

Weis, Margaret, and Tracy Hickman

Rose of the Prophet series. This is based on Middle Eastern tales, complete with djinns.

The Will of the Wanderer.

The Paladin of the Night.

The Prophet of Akhran.

Legends • Middle East • Djinns.

Wolfe, Gene

The Devil in a Forest. "A young man finds himself torn between his hero-worship for a charming highway man named Wat and his growing suspicion of Wat's cold savagery; and Mother Cloot, a sorcerer whose suspicious friendliness may serve good, or perhaps evil, purposes. He must decide which of these powers to stand by in the coming battle between Good and Evil, a battle that even his isolated village will be unable to avoid."—Jacket copy.

Medieval Times.

Yolen, Jane

The Books of Great Alta is a two-in-one volume that contains *Sister Light, Sister Dark,* and *White Jenna.* "White Jenna, born in sorrow, raised among warrior women, and taught to call forth her shadow sister under the light of the moon. And we learn what posterity makes of the lives of the white-haired girl, her princely lover, and her shadow-self: what legends are told of the White Queen, what songs are sung of King Longbow, what tales are whispered of Dark Skada; what tragic myths and glorious histories time makes out of their lives—and their deaths."—Publisher's catalog copy.

Women Warriors • Myths.

Fairy Tale Short Stories

Fairy tales and folktales seem to be particularly well suited to the short story form. Many outstanding writers have turned their hands to this genre of short story, giving readers a chance to sample a great variety of talents. Fans of the following should be reminded of the pleasures to be found in the Dewey decimal system's 398s.

Brooke, William J.

🆈🅰 Teller of Tales. HarperCollins, 1994. Told in a tale within a tale format as a young girl tells an old writer nursery tales and he adds his own twist to them when writing them down.

> *Younger Readers • Humor.*

Datlow, Ellen, and Terri Windling, eds.

Black Swan, White Raven. Avon, 1997. Contains "The Flounder's Kiss," by Michael Cadnum; "The Black Fairy's Curse," by Karen Joy Fowler; "Snow in Dirt," by Michael Blumlein; "Riding the Red," by Nalo Hopkinson; "No Bigger Than My Thumb," by Esther M. Friesner; "In the Insomniac Night," by Joyce Carol Oates; "The Little Match Girl," by Steve Rasnic Tem; "The Trial of Hansel and Gretel," by Garry Kilworth; "Rapunzel," by Anne Bishop; "Sparks," by Gregory Frost; "The Dog Rose," by Sten Westgard; "The Reverend's Wife," by Midori Snyder; "The Orphan the Moth and the Magic," by Harvey Jacobs; "Three Dwarves and 2000 Maniacs," by Don Webb; "True Thomas," by Bruce Glassco; "The True Story," by Pat Murphy; "Lost and Abandoned," by John Crowley; "The Breadcrumb Trail," by Nina Kiriki Hoffman; "On Lickerish Hill," by Susanna Clarke; "Steadfast," by Nancy Kress; and "Godmother Death," by Jane Yolen.

Black Thorn, White Rose. Avon, 1994. Contains "Words Like Pale Stones," by Nancy Kress; "Stronger Than Time," by Patricia C. Wrede; "Somnus's Fair Maid," by Ann Downer; "The Frog King, or Iron Henry," by Daniel Quinn; "Near-Beauty," by M. E. Beckett; "Ogre," by Michael Kandel; "Can't Catch Me," by Michael Cadnum; "Journeybread Recipe," by Lawrence Schimel; "The Brown Bear of Norway," by Isabel Cole; "The Goose Girl," by Tim Wynne-Jones; "Tattercoats," by Midori Snyder; "Granny Rumple," by Jane Yolen; "The Sawing Boys," by Howard Waldrop; "Godson," by Roger Zelazny; "Ashputtle," by Peter Straub; "Silver and Gold," by Ellen Steiber; "Sweet Bruising Skin," by Storm Constantine; and "The Black Swan," by Susan Wade.

Ruby Slippers, Golden Tears. Avon, 1995. Contains the stories "Ruby Slippers," by Susan Wade; "The Beast," by Tanith Lee; "Masterpiece," by Garry Kilworth; "Summer Wind," by Nancy Kress; "This Century of Sleep or, Briar Rose Beneath the Sea," by Farida S. T. Shapiro; "The Crossing," by Joyce Carol Oates; "Roach in Loafers," by Roberta Lannes; "Naked Little Men," by Michael Cadnum; "Brother Bear," by Lisa Goldstein; "The Emperor Who Had Never Seen a Dragon," by John Brunner; "Billy Fearless," by Nancy A. Collins; "The Death of Koshchei the Deathless (a Tale of Old Russia)," by Gene Wolfe; "The Real Princess," by Susan Palwick; "The Huntsman's Story," by Milbre Burch; "After Push Comes to Shove," by Milbre Burch; "Hansel and Gretel," by Gahan Wilson; "Match Girl," by Anne Bishop; "Waking the Prince," by Kathe Koja; "The Fox Wife," by Ellen Steiber; "The White Road," by Neil Gaiman; "The Traveler and the Tale," by Jane Yolen; and "The Printer's Daughter," by Delia Sherman.

Snow White, Blood Red. Avon, 1993. Contains "Like a Red, Red Rose," by Susan Wade; "The Moon Is Drowning While I Sleep," by Charles de Lint; "The Frog Prince," by Gahan Wilson; "Stalking Beans," by Nancy Kress; "Snow-Drop," by Tanith Lee; "Little Red," by Wendy Wheeler; "I Shall Do Thee Mischief in the Wood," by Kathe Koja; "The Root of the Matter," by Gregory Frost; "The Princess in the Tower," by Elizabeth A. Lynn; "Persimmon," by Harvey Jacobs; "Little Poucet," by Steve Rasnic Tem; "The Changelings," by Melanie Tem; "The Springfield Swans," by Caroline Stevermer and Ryan Edmonds; "Troll Bridge," by Neil Gaiman; "A Sound, Like Angels Singing," by Leonard Rysdyk; "Puss," by Esther M. Friesner; "The Glass Casket," by Jack Dann; "Knives," by Jane Yolen; "The Snow Queen," by Patricia A. McKillip; and "Breadcrumbs and Stones," by Lisa Goldstein.

Kerr, Katharine, ed.

Enchanted Forests. DAW, 1995. Contains "The Forest's Not for Burning," by Katherine Lawrence; "I'll Give You Three Wishes," by Kevin Andrew Murphy; "The Triple Death," by Ken St. Andre; "Out of the Woods," by Lawrence Watt-Evans; "Viridescence," by Connie Hirsch; "Fiat Silva," by Jack Oakley; "Weeds," by Julia and Brook West; "Benbow," by Nancy Etchemendy; "The Prism of Memory," by Jo Clayton; "The Force That Through the Green Fuse," by Mark Kreighbaum; "My Soul into the Boughs," by Teresa Edgerton; "These Shoes Strangers Have Died Of," by Bruce Holland Rogers; "The Clearing," by Lois Tilton; "How the Ant Made a Bargain," by Karawynn Long; "In Fear of Little Nell," by Gregory Feeley; "Wood Song," by Kate Daniel; "Virginia Woods," by Janni Lee Simner; "Ties of Love," by Lawrence Schimel; "The Heart of the Forest," by Dave Smeds; "Holy Ground," by Thomas S. Roche; "Ghostwood," by Michelle Sagara; "The Monsters of Mill Creek Park," by Susan Shwartz; "The Memory of Peace," by Kate Elliott; "Everything Has a Place," by Barbara A. Denz; and "Trees Perpetual of Sleep," by Nina Kiriki Hoffman.

McKinley, Robin

The Door in the Hedge. Greenwillow, 1981. Includes imaginative retellings of classic fairy tales, featuring magical new versions of "The Twelve Dancing Princesses," "The Princess and the Frog," "The Hunting of the Hind," and "The Stolen Princess."

Vande Velde, Vivian

YA Tales from the Brothers Grimm and the Sisters Weird. Harcourt Brace, 1995. These twisted retellings include "Jack and the Beanstalk," "Hansel and Gretel," "Little Red Riding Hood," "Three Billy Goats Gruff," and others.

Younger Readers • Humor • Parody.

D's Picks

Chapter 6

Humor

Humor plays a major role in fantasy. It appears in all the subgenres but is especially prominent in fantasy based on fairy tales and folktales. In fact, many of the following titles have a foundation in the old stories. Often full of topical jokes, such books provide more humor to the well read.

Anthony, Piers

Xanth series. Books in this series are full of puns and plays on words. Xanth is surrounded by Mundania where magic doesn't work. The first three books are vastly entertaining, but only devoted fans will want to continue through the series, which also seems to become more racy as it develops.

Puns • Parallel Worlds.

A Spell for Chameleon. 1978 British Fantasy Award (August Derleth Award) Winner.

The Source of Magic.

Castle Roogna.

Centaur Isle.

Ogre, Ogre.

Night Mare.

Dragon on a Pedestal.

Crewel Lye: A Caustic Yarn.

Golem in the Gears.

Vale of the Vole.

Heaven Cent.

Man from Mundania.

Isle of View.

Question Quest. This book recaps many of the events found in earlier books, making it a good choice for those who have skipped earlier volumes in the series but want to dip into it again.

> **The Color of Her Panties.**
>
> **Demons Don't Dream.**
>
> **Harpy Thyme.**
>
> **Geis of the Gargoyle.**
>
> **Roc and a Hard Place.**

Asprin, Robert Lynn

🔞 The M. Y. T. H. series. These are humorous tales with humorous titles: slapstick adventures of a magician and demon duo reminiscent of the Bob Hope and Dean Martin *Road to . . .* movies.

> *Demons • Magic.*

> **Another Fine Myth.**
>
> **Myth Conceptions.**
>
> **Myth Directions.**
>
> **Hit or Myth.**
>
> **Myth-ing Persons.**
>
> **Little Myth Marker.**
>
> **M. Y. T. H. Inc Link.**
>
> **Myth-Nomers and Im-pervections.**
>
> **M. Y. T. H. Inc in Action.**
>
> **Sweet Myth-tery of Life.**

Brooks, Terry

🔞 **Magic Kingdom of Landover series** (annotated in Chapter 10).

Cook, Rick

> **Mall Purchase Night.** A mall has been built on the actual gateway between Elfland and Earth and security guard Andy Westin may be the only thing between a major elfin battle and thousands of innocent shoppers.

> *Parallel Worlds • Elves.*

Wiz Zumwalt series. Wiz Zumwalt finds himself in an alternate world where magic works like a computer program.

> *Science Fantasy• Computers• Magic.*

> **Wizard Compiled.**
>
> **Wizard's Bane.**
>
> **Wizardry Consulted.** "You would think that a 20-foot dragon walking down the street of an American city would attract at least some attention. You would be wrong. Anyone who has been in Las Vegas more that 48 hours has seen stranger things than that on the breakfast buffet."––Jacket copy.
>
> **Wizardry Cursed.** Wiz and his fellow Silicon Valley hackers are up against the forces of primal chaos, who are in cahoots with a couple of computer criminals.
>
> **Wizardry Quested.**

DeChancie, John

Castle Perilous series. The castle, ruled by Lord Incarnadine, is a portal to 144,000 worlds where anything can happen. Readers may also enjoy Zelazny's Amber series.

Parallel Worlds • Science Fantasy • Computers.

Castle Perilous.

Castle for Rent.

Castle Kidnapped.

Castle War!

Castle Murders.

Castle Dream.

Castle Spellbound.

Bride of the Castle.

Friesner, Esther

🆈🅰 Majyk series.

Parallel Worlds • Cats.

Majyk by Accident. A student magician's future is changed with the arrival of a dimension-traveling cat.

Majyk by Hook or Crook.

Majyk by Design.

Gaiman, Neil, and Terry Pratchett

Good Omens: The Nice and Accurate Prophecies of Agnes Nutter, Witch. A demon and an angel try to stop the apocalypse because they are having too good a time in this world to see it all end.

Witches • Demons • Angels.

Gardner, Craig Shaw

🆈🅰 The Cineverse Cycle. With his Captain Crusader Decoder ring, Roger cruises the various alternate worlds of a universe based on movie genres.

Film • Parallel Worlds.

Slaves of the Volcano God.

Bride of the Slime Monster.

Revenge of the Fluffy Bunnies.

Gentle, Mary

Grunts. Some editions have the subtitle *A Fantasy with Attitude,* which says it all. Orc marines obtain modern weapons in a hilarious but earthy, and to some obscene, tale of fantasy warfare told from the "bad guy's" point of view.

Orcs • Technology.

Jones, Diana Wynne

(YA) Howl's Moving Castle. When seventeen-year-old Sophie is transformed into a seventy-year-old crone by the wicked witch of the waste, she seeks relief by decamping in a mobile castle, where she has accepted employment from a mysterious wizard.

Parody • Magic.

(YA) Castle in the Air. A sequel to *Howl's Moving Castle*, it brings Arabian tales into the mix.

Djinns • Magic Carpets.

Moore, Christopher

Island of the Sequined Love Nun. This is a wacky romp featuring a fired pilot now working for a missionary on a Micronesian island.

Ghosts • Gods • Cannibals • Sexuality.

Pratchett, Terry

Discworld series. "Geography is only physics slowed down, with a few trees stuck on it. . . ." Discworld, a world that really is flat, floats through space on the backs of four giant elephants standing on a gigantic turtle. As of 1998 there were twenty-one Discworld novels.

Alternate Worlds • Wizards • Gods • Witches.

Eric: A Discworld Novel.

Lords and Ladies. An infestation of Faerie Trash has invaded the Kingdom of Lancre, wreaking havoc with the Royal Wedding plans. Fortunately, Granny Weatherwax thinks it is fun to kill the cute, vicious little monsters.

The Light Fantastic.

Guards! Guards!

Small Gods.

Men at Arms.

Wyrd Sisters.

Moving Pictures.

Pyramids: The Book of Going Forth.

Witches Abroad.

Strata.

Interesting Times. The directions delivered to the "Great Wizard" Rincewind by a carrier albatross were unclear as to whether his mission is to defend or destroy the Forbidden City of Hunghung, to which he has traveled with Cohen the Barbarian, an ant farm-powered computer named Hex, the Silver Horde (an army of six old men), and a fractal weather-making butterfly.

Feet of Clay. An unauthorized killer is loose in Ankh-Morpork. Commander Vimes of the City Guard hires a Dwarf to help him stop this unprincipled assassin, who has gone so far as to kill one of his victims with a loaf of her own Battle Bread.

Maskerade. A mask-wearing ghost is terrorizing the Opera House of Ankh Morpork, wreaking havoc among the company. Fortunately Granny Weatherwax and Nanny Ogg are in the capital city trying to recruit a third witch so they can have a real coven, so it could be quite convenient to take care of the ghost at the same time.

Jingo. A long-lost sunken island erupts in the sea causing a war to erupt, too!

Book of Nomes series (also sometimes called The Book of the Bromeliad series). A band of tiny beings exists on the edge of our world. These are somewhat reminiscent of Mary Norton's *The Borrowers,* but not nearly so nice in a pleasantly wicked kind of way.

> *Tiny People • Science Fantasy.*

Truckers. A specific band finds that they must move on when the department store they inhabit is closed for demolition.

Diggers. The nomes continue their quest for a new home.

Wings. The nomes summon a spaceship that has been waiting for them on the moon.

Rogers, Mark E.

Samurai Cat series. Questing through time and space, sixteenth-century samurai cat Miaowara Tomokato and his faithful sidekick Shiro seek to revenge his murdered warlord.

> *Cats • Japan • Martial Arts.*

The Adventures of Samurai Cat.

More Adventures of Samurai Cat.

Samurai Cat in the Real World.

The Sword of the Samurai Cat.

Samurai Cat Goes to the Movies. "Tomokato and Shiro deflate major Hollywood 'sacred cows' in a hilarious laugh fest."--Nathan Sundance Herald.

> *Film.*

Samurai Cat Goes to Hell. After they die at the end of a long and illustrious career, Miaowara abandons his cushy spot in heaven to rescue Shiro from eternal damnation.

Turtledove, Harry

The Case of the Toxic Spell Dump. Even on magic carpets, accidents can happen, and a wild series of events turns an inspector for the Environmental Perfection Agency into a detective.

> *Magic Carpets • Contemporary Fantasy • Detection.*

Rowling, J. K.

Harry Potter and the Sorcerer's Stone (Harry Potter and the Philosopher's Stone). At age eleven, Harry Potter goes off to Hogwarts School of Witchcraft and Wizardry. British Book Award winner.

> *Magic • Witches • Orphans • Younger Readers.*

Watt-Evans, Lawrence, and Esther Friesner

Split Heirs. Triplets are split up at birth, the girl to be raised as a prince (yes, prince) and the two princes to be raised as a magician's apprentice and a shepherd.

> *Magic • Politics.*

Wrede, Patricia C.

Ⓨ Book of Enchantments. Ten enchanting stories and a recipe by a master of humorous fantasy showcase a variety of settings and types. "Utensil Strength," a tale that is laugh-out-loud funny, takes place in the same world as Wrede's popular novel series, the Enchanted Forest Chronicles, set in a familiar but slightly twisted fairy tale realm. A stranger turns up with a mysterious magical weapon called the Frying Pan of Doom. "Roses by Moonlight" is a sensitive story with a contemporary setting and a powerful, though not in the least bit preachy, message. The other stories range between, but all have a delicious dollop of humor.

Ⓨ Enchanted Forest Chronicles. A series featuring tongue-in-cheek humor and an assortment of characters that lurk just on the edge of familiarity. Also included in Chapter 5.

Short Stories • Younger Readers.

Dealing with Dragons. Princess Cimorene searches for happiness and fulfillment by moving in with a dragon.

Librarians.

Searching for Dragons. The king of the enchanted forest meets a most unusual princess and together they are able to save the kingdom.

Flying Carpets • Romance.

Calling on Dragons.

Talking to Dragons.

Zelazny, Roger, and Robert Sheckly

Bring Me the Head of Prince Charming. The world as we know it *really* does end every millennium, but only the Forces of Good and Evil know it. In the battle for control of the universe for the next 1,000 years, until the year 2000, demon Azzie Elbub contrives a plan for the Dark Forces to win, using a Prince Charming and a Sleeping Beauty.

Demons • Millennium.

If At Faust You Don't Succeed. "Azzie has been deposed in favor of a newer demon. A wry twist on the original Faustian legend."—Nathan Sundance Herald.

Demons • Faust.

D's Picks

Jones, Diana Wynne. *Howl's Moving Castle.* (p. 76)

Rowling, J. K. *Harry Potter and the Sorcerer's Stone.* (p. 77)

Turtledove, Harry. *The Case of the Toxic Spell Dump.* (p. 77)

Watt-Evans, Lawrence, and Esther Friesner. *Split Heirs.* (p. 77)

Wrede, Patricia C. Enchanted Forest Chronicles. (p. 78)

Chapter 7

A Bestiary

Animals play a large role in fantasy. It seems that every fantasy has some kind of non-human creature in it whether it is a major character with a speaking role or mere window dressing in the form of a cat soaking up some sunshine. Fantasy with the emphasis on animals ranges from animal fables in which humans play no role (the characters are sentient beasts), to books in which the emphasis is on the relationship between humans and animals. The preponderance of magic workers in fantasy brings with it animal familiars who may facilitate the magic of humans or even work magic of their own.

The urge to know what animals are thinking is so great that many tales use it as a major theme. Some books dealing with animal communication feature telepathic animals who are linked to specific humans through magical amulets that allow the wearer to speak with the animals. Hugh Lofting's *Adventures of Dr. Dolittle* is an example of an early work dealing with animal communication.

Anthologies

Animals are a popular topic for fantasy in its short form. Both fantastical beasts and everyday animals are popular subjects. Cats seem to appear often as major characters.

Beagle, Peter S., and Janet Beliner

Immortal Unicorn. Harper Prism, 1995. Includes twenty-seven new tales of unicorns by the two editors as well as contributions from Judith Tarr, Edward Bryant, Charles de Lint, Ellen Kushner, Eric Lustbader, Lisa Mason, Elizabeth Ann Scarborough, Will Shetterly, Susan Shwartz, Nancy Willard, Tad Williams, and others. This is the first volume of a two-volume anthology with the second volume due to be published in 1999.

Greenberg, Rosalind M., and Martin H. Greenberg, eds.

Christmas Bestiary. DAW, 1992.

Dinosaur Fantastic. DAW, 1992.

Dinosaurs.

Horse Fantastic. DAW, 1991.

Horses.

Norton, Andre, and Martin H. Greenberg, eds.

Catfantastic. v. 1, DAW, 1989; v. 2, DAW, 1991; v.3, DAW, 1994; v. 4, DAW, 1996. This anthology has been so popular that it was turned into a series.

Cats.

Resnick, Mike, and Martin H. Greenberg, eds.

Dragon Fantastic. DAW, 1993.

Dragons.

Unicorns

Often portrayed as one-horned horses, unicorns in the following books are viewed in different ways. They are generally good creatures that possess magic.

Beagle, Peter S.

(YA) The Last Unicorn. Fearing she is the last of her kind, a unicorn embarks on a quest to see if others survive. Basis of the animated film.

Film • Quest.

Bishop, Michael

(AW) Unicorn Mountain. The problems of dying unicorns in another dimension and the AIDS epidemic in our world intersect. 1989 Mythopoeic Award Winner.

Parallel Worlds • AIDS.

Coville, Bruce

(YA) Unicorn Chronicles.

Parallel Worlds • Dragons • Younger Readers.

Into the Land of Unicorns.

(NEW) A Glory of Unicorns.

Lee, John

Unicorn Quest series. When an epic war is waged against the Outlanders, the people of Strand are able to win because of Jarrod Courtak, Mage of Paladine's ability to communicate with a powerful race of unicorns. Filled with political intrigue.

Politics • Magic • Quest • Technology.

The Unicorn Quest.

The Unicorn Dilemma.

The Unicorn Solution.

The Unicorn Peace.

The Unicorn War

Lee, Tanith

 Unicorn series. Tanaquil's mother is a sorceress and her sister is an empress, which makes her own life as a mender difficult in this series written for teens but enjoyed by adults, too.

> *Technology • Magic • Parallel Worlds.*

The Black Unicorn.

The Gold Unicorn.

The Red Unicorn.

Pierce, Meredith Ann

 Firebringer series. A young unicorn saves his clan by bringing them fire.

> *Younger Readers.*

Birth of the Firebringer.

Dark Moon.

The Son of Summer Stars. "Jan, the prince of the unicorns, uses his knowledge of fire to form a historic alliance between his people and their former enemies and to return the unicorns to their ancestral homeland."—Publisher's catalog copy.

Salitz, Rhondi Vilott

 The Twilight Gate. A unicorn, along with forces of evil, crosses through a gate that fifteen-year-old George creates with his art.

> *Younger Readers • Art • Parallel Worlds.*

Dragons

Dragons are often portrayed as telepathic creatures. They have been portrayed in many different ways throughout history (for example, Western and Eastern art portray dragons differently).

Bertin, Joanne

 The Last Dragonlord. Linden, the last weredragon, gives up his centuries-old quest for love to try to stop the outbreak of civil war.

> *Shapeshifting.*

Bradshaw, Gillian

 Dragon and the Thief. Prahotep, failing at many of the occupations he has tried in ancient Egypt, decides to take a stab at tomb robbing. He finds Hathor, the last remaining dragon in Thebes.

> *Africa • Egypt • Younger Readers.*

🔞 **The Land of Gold.** Prahotep and Hathor save princess Kandaki from being sacrificed to a water dragon and journey across Nubia to reclaim the throne that was stolen by her parents' murderer.

Africa • Nubia • Quest • Younger Readers.

Brown, Mary

🔞 **Master of Many Treasures.** Summer is traveling with dog Growch to try to find the Dragon/Man she had lost her heart to in *Pigs Don't Fly*. The odious Dickon finds her again as she travels, disguised as a boy, in trading caravans through bogs, deserts, and mountains. The companions she meets on her journey include a slave boy, a dancing bear, and a figurine that comes to life as a spectacularly multi-colored, hoofed, antennaed, omni-lingual magical creature. This story stands well alone, succinctly imparting necessary information from the previous book, *Pigs Don't Fly*, but not spoiling the plot.

Quest • Dogs • Romance • Magic.

Callander, Don

Dragon Companion. "A dragon appears to a quiet employee of the Library of Congress and whisks him away to a magical kingdom where librarians are among the most powerful of humans, especially if they are a dragon's best friend."—Amazon. com.

Librarians • Parallel Worlds.

Dragon Rescue. Fearing that his friend, young dragon Arbitrance Constable, is not still out hunting treasure, Murdan of Overhall organizes a search.

Parallel Worlds • Quest.

Dickson, Gordon R.

The Dragon and the George series. Jim Eckert and Angie, his fiancée, are transported back to medieval Europe where she is herself and he is a dragon. After he discovers how to get his body back, Jim is known as the Dragon Knight, because he can shift into his dragon body as needed.

Shapeshifting • Time Travel.

 The Dragon and the George. 1977 August Derleth Award Winner.

The Dragon Knight.

The Dragon on the Border.

The Dragon at War.

The Dragon, The Earl, and the Troll.

Dragon and the Gnarly King.

Shapeshifting • Parallel Worlds.

Fletcher, Susan

🔞 Dragonsayer series.

Younger Readers • Psionic Powers.

Dragon's Milk. When she tries to make a deal with a dragon for the dragon's milk needed for her own ailing first sister, Lyf, outcast Kaeldra becomes foster mother to a trio of draclings.

Flight of the Dragon Kyn. A young woman who was twice spared by dragons is commanded to call them to the waiting archers of the king. A prequel to *Dragon's Milk.*

Sign of the Dove. In this sequel to *Dragon's Milk,* Lyf tries to save the dragon mothers and their hatchlings from their enemies.

Hambly, Barbara

🅨 Dragonsbane. Jenny, a witch, has conflicting feelings about slaying dragons.

Witches.

Kellogg, Marjorie B.

The Dragon Quartet. As of 1998, only two of the books in the series have been published.

Shapeshifting • Ecology • Time Travel • Medieval Times • Futuristic Fantasy.

The Book of Earth. Feisty young Erde finds that her future involves a dragon called Earth.

The Book of Water.

Kerner, Elizabeth

Song in the Silence. This dragon romance features Lanen Kaelar, a young horse farmer who has dreamed of dragons and sets out on a perilous journey to find them.

Romance • Quest • Dreams.

McCaffrey, Anne

Even though McCaffrey contends, and even presents evidence to prove, that her works are science fiction, dragon-loving fantasy fans claim the books set on the planet Pern as their own. Pern is a planet on which deadly Thread falls from the sky when it passes too closely to another planet in the solar system. When this happens, the only way to preserve life is to burn the Thread out of the air, using genetically engineered fire-breathing dragons, ridden by skilled and telepathic bond-mates. The titles are listed in Chapter 12.

Murphy, Shirley Rousseau

🅨 Dragonbards series.

Younger Readers • Otters • Shapeshifting • Music • Alternate World • Animals.

7

Nightpool. Sixteen-year-old Tebriel recovers from her wounds, incurred while fighting the Dark, in the care of a band of talking otters.

The Ivory Lyre. Dragonbards, Tebriel and Kiri are helped in their search for a magical ivory lyre by four shape-changing dragons.

Dragonbards.

Norton, Andre, and Mercedes Lackey

🅨 Halfblood Chronicles.

Multiracial Beings (Elfin and Human).

The Elvenbane. On a world where elves rule and humans are their slaves, a concubine flees to the desert to give birth to her half-breed child. A prophecy had foretold that a child with human and elfin blood would lead to the fall of the elves. Orphaned at birth, Shana is raised by dragons not realizing until she comes of age that she isn't one herself.

Elvenblood. Shana, a halfblood known as the Elvenbane, challenges the power of the elfin lords with her band of outcasts, slaves, and dragons.

Elves • Libraries • Women • Fostering.

Radford, Irene
Dragon Nimbus.

Magic • Alternate Worlds.

Glass Dragon. Magic is fading from the land of Coronnan as dragons become an endangered species. Jaylor is a journeyman wizard whose unconventional magic may be the only hope of stopping the extinction of dragons and magic in the land.

The Perfect Princess. Prince Darville, recently freed from an enchantment that imprisoned him in the form of a wolf, is to marry Princess Rossemikka, who has also been the helpless victim of magic.

The Loneliest Magician. Magic is gone from Coronnan, the dragons and their magic vanished, the Commune magic forbidden. King Darville is having trouble maintaining order and Senior Magician Jaylor is in hiding. The dragons must be found. It is not Jaylor who will find them, but rather Yaakke, an untested orphan.

The Dragon Nimbus History.

The Dragon's Touchstone. Three hundred years before the time of *The Glass Dragon*, wild magic and uncontrolled magicians are tearing Coronnan apart. Nimbulan, a Battlemage, founds a University of Magicians to train a generation to fight the rogue spellworkers who are getting rich on the endless war. He is joined by the witchwoman and healer, Myrilandel, who can offer the gift of dragon magic to the spellcasters of the University.

Rowley, Christopher
Bazil Broketail series. Features battledragons and their dragoneers.

Bazil Broketail.

A Sword for a Dragon.

Dragons of War.

Battledragon.

A Dragon at World's End.

NEW **Dragons of Argonath.** Redkin must draw on his own untested magic to try to destroy the Dominator, the crusher of worlds who has invaded the Empire of the Rose.

Stasheff, Christopher, ed.

Dragon's Eye. Pocket, 1994. Includes short stories by Mike Resnick, Jody Lynn Nye, Diane Duane, William R. Forstchen, S. M. Stirling, and others. Provides various takes on the world of the fabulous dragons of folklore and legend.

Short Stories.

Vande Velde, Vivian

YA **Dragon's Bait.** After she is staked out as dragon bait, a young woman teams up with a dragon to get revenge upon the villagers who caused her father's death.

Younger Readers.

Yolen, Jane
YA Pit Dragons series. Like McCaffrey's dragon series, this is actually science fiction but is read as fantasy.

Younger Readers • Science Fantasy.

Dragon's Blood. "Jakkin, a bond boy who works as a Keeper in a dragon nursery on the planet Austar IV, secretly trains a fighting dragon of his own in hopes of winning his freedom."—Library catalog copy.

Heart's Blood. Now free, Jakkin is asked to infiltrate rebel forces, changing his dragon-training plans.

A Sending of Dragons. Jakkin has been sent into the wilderness after being unjustly accused of sabotage. His dragon makes a heroic sacrifice to save him.

Uncommon Common Animals

Animals from our world, ordinary creatures such as rabbits, ants, dogs, cats, skunks, and horses don't seem to fit the fabric of fantasy—in the following books they do. The animals can range from the mundane and ordinary to sentient members of complex societies.

Adams, Richard

Watership Down. A modern classic of rabbits heroically seeking a new home.

Rabbits • Quest.

Bell, Clare

Ⓨ The Named, a clan of intelligent catlike creatures living in prehistoric times is featured in this un-named series.

Cats • Politics.

Ratha's Creature.

Clan Ground.

Ratha and Thistle-Chaser. Thistle-Chaser is Ratha's abused and outcast daughter.

Ratha's Challenge. The Named meet another clan of cats, but something is very wrong with them. They are controlled by a ruler called True-of-Voice, who uses "the song" to govern their thoughts. Ratha, now leader of the Named, and Thistle-Chaser must make some hard decisions.

7

Brown, Mary

Ⓨ **Pigs Don't Fly.** Typically, in quests a band of stalwart companions is assembled. Sometimes the quest starts out with an individual who picks up companions along the way. In *Pigs Don't Fly,* instead of picking up human companions, the protagonist picks up animal companions. Somerdai starts out with a dog but quickly adds a horse, a bird, a turtle, and a flying pig to her entourage. Her magical ring, which allows her to communicate with animals, helps.

Dogs • Horses • Dragons • Turtles • Birds.

Greeno, Gayle

Ghatti's Tale series. Features telepathic catlike creatures. See Chapter 12.

Finder's Keepers.

Mind-Speaker's Call.

Exile's Return.

Cats • Psionic Powers • Science Fantasy.

Hawdon, Robin

A Rustle in the Grass. Their world in peril, a colony of ants takes on a devastating army of killer red ants.

Younger Readers • Ants.

Horwood, William

Duncton Chronicles. This is a series about romance and adventure in a neighborhood of moles.

Moles • Adventure • Romance.

Duncton Wood.

Duncton Quest.

Duncton Found.

Duncton Tales.

Duncton Rising.

Duncton Stone.

Jacques, Brian

The Redwall series. Woodland creatures battle evil in this fantasy adventure popular with all ages.

Adventure • Romance.

Redwall. In 1998 a tenth-anniversary edition with new illustrations was published.

Mossflower.

Mattimeo.

Mariel of Redwall.

Salamandastron.

Martin the Warrior.

The Bellmaker.

Pearls of Lutra.

The Long Patrol.

King, Gabriel

The Wild Road. Tag, a pampered kitten, is sent dreams that send him out into a world far more dangerous and harsh than he had ever imagined on a quest to find the King and Queen of cats.

Cats • Quest.

Lackey, Mercedes

Valdemar series. Features telepathic horselike companions. See Chapter 12.

Murphy, Shirley Rousseau

Catswold Portal.

Parallel Worlds • Shapeshifting • Cats.

Joe Grey, cat detective series (annotated in chapter 17).

Cat on the Edge.

Cat Under Fire.

Cat Raise the Dead.

> *Cats • Detection.*

Tolkien, J. R. R.

NEW **Roverandom.** A dog, transformed into a toy, searches for the wizard who cursed him.

> *Dogs • Magic.*

Wangerin, Walter

AW **The Book of the Dun Cow.** Chaunticleer the Rooster, ruler of the barnyard, takes on evil when it threatens his domain. American Book Award Winner.

> *Christianity • Religion • Allegory • Roosters.*

The Book of Sorrows. The barnyard animals are unaware that evil has not been vanquished as they try to rebuild their lives.

> *Christianity • Religion • Allegory • Roosters.*

Williams, Tad

Tailchaser's Song. Ginger tomcat Fritti Tailchaser is on a magical quest that will take him to cat hell and beyond as he searches for his catfriend Hushpad.

> *Cats • Quest.*

D's Picks

7

Chapter 8

World of Faerie

The world of faerie is not the same as the world of fairy tales. It is a place inhabited by elven-type people with powers that, to humans, seem magical. Often, the interaction of humans and residents of faerie sets up the conflict. Time moves at a different pace in this world that coexists side by side with ours. Sometimes, a rift between the worlds allows someone of faerie to descend into our world, or vice versa. There also seems to be a great proclivity for humans and those of faerie blood to fall in love with each other. Changelings, a faerie child and a human child switched at birth, often appear. Lord Dunsany and George MacDonald have influenced modern writers of fantasy.

While this is not a large subgenre it is an important one. The legends of faerie magic crop up often in all types of literature. They often play an important role in urban fantasy (Chapter 9) and have subtly influenced the entire fantasy genre. The idea of a place existing side by side with our world with different rules of nature and passage of time has surely played a role in the development of fantasy dealing with parallel worlds.

Baudino, Gael

Spires of Spirit. Six novellas of elfin magic, three set in the medieval village of St. Brigid and three in contemporary Colorado.

Medieval Times • Contemporary Fantasy • Short Stories.

Charrette, Robert N.

Artos series (annotated in Chapter 4).

A Prince Among Men.

King Beneath the Mountain.

Knight Among Knaves.

Arthurian Legend.

Cherryh, C. J.

The Dreaming Tree. As magic is driven out of the world by men, a small forest remains where elven magic survives. The title of the duology is also the title of an omnibus edition issued in 1997.

Magic • Immortality.

Dreamstone.

Tree of Swords and Jewels.

de Lint, Charles

Greenmantle. An ancient wood lies not far from the city, forgotten by most but not abandoned by the horned man who wears a cloak of leaves and is summoned by the music of the pipes. A classic reissued in 1998.

Horned God • Contemporary Fantasy.

The Wild Wood. Part of Brian Froud's Faerielands shared world series.

Ecology • Canada • Contemporary Fantasy.

Jack of Kinrowan. An omnibus edition containing *Jack the Giant Killer* and *Drink down the Moon.*

Fairy Tales • Urban Fantasy • Women • Contemporary Fantasy.

The Ivory and the Horn. A collection of stories about the interface of Faerie and de Lint's city of Newford Canada.

Short Stories.

Dean, Pamela

Tam Lin. Set in a Vietnam-era Midwest college town, a young woman rescues her love from the Queen of Faerie.

Contemporary Fantasy • Vietnam War • Romance.

Dietz, Tom

David Sullivan has a kind of second sight that allows him to see into the Faerie realm.

Parallel Worlds • Psionic Powers • Contemporary Fantasy • Celtic Fantasy • Native Americans.

Windmaster's Bane.

Fireshaper's Doom.

Darkthunder's Way.

Sunshaker's War.

Stoneskin's Revenge.

Ghostcountry's Wrath.

Dreamseeker's Road.

NEW **Landslayer's Law.**

Dunsany, Lord

The King of Elfland's Daughter (1924). A classic that has influenced much of the later works set in Faerie.

Edghill, Rosemary

Sword of Maiden's Tears.

Cup of Morning Shadows. An elfin prince goes to New York seeking a sword and combating evil.

Librarians • Contemporary Fantasy • Swords.

Goldstein, Lisa

Strange Devices of the Sun and Moon. An Elizabethan stationer believes that her son may be the changeling prince of Faerie.

Changelings • Women • Literary Fantasy.

Holdstock, Robert

Mythago Cycle. Ryhope Wood is an enchanted world where mythic images come to life.

Myths • Legends • Celtic Fantasy.

Mythago Wood. 1985 World Fantasy Award Winner.

Gate of Ivory, Gate of Horn. Christian Huxley goes into Ryhope Wood, where he and Guiwenneth (a Celtic warrior) and a band of crusaders discover the meaning of the two gates.

Kushner, Ellen

Thomas the Rhymer. Thomas's disappearance into the faerie realm is told from varying points of view. 1991 Mythopoeic Award Winner. World Fantasy Award Winner.

Romance • Literary Fantasy.

MacDonald, George

Phantastes: A Faerie Romance for Men and Women (1858). This was written by a nineteenth-century author of children's books.

McKillip, Patricia A.

Something Rich and Strange. This is a part of Brian Froud's Faerielands illustrated series. 1995 Mythopoeic Award Winner.

Art • Music • Contemporary Fantasy.

Sherman, Josepha

A Strange and Ancient Name. Trying to defeat a curse, a prince of Faerie must sojourn in our world and seek out his family history.

Quest • Multiracial Beings (Elfin and Human).

Windleaf. A human count goes on a quest to win the hand of a princess of Faerie.

Younger Readers • Romance.

Prince of the Sidhe. The exploits of elfin prince Ardagh Oathbreaker.

Runes Magic • Celtic Fantasy.

The Shattered Oath.

Forging the Runes.

Snyder, Midori

The Flight of Michael McBride. This unique blend of Faerie and the Old West could almost be considered a historical urban fantasy. When his mother dies, Michael McBride finds that there was more to her tales of the Fair Folk than he had thought. He flees the evil magical folk in New York and goes to Texas, where a different kind of magic exists.

The sense of magic co-existing but invisible to us is also found in Charles de Lint's books, set in Newford, and in Terri Windling's *The Wood Wife*.

Shapeshifting • Animal People • Literary Fantasy.

Warner, Sylvia Townsend

Kingdom of Elfin (1977). Sophisticated series of stories, first published in *The New Yorker*.

Short Stories.

Windling, Terri

 The Wood Wife (annotated in Chapter 9).

Animal People • Poets • Art • Literary Fantasy.

Wrede, Patricia C.

Snow White and Rose Red. Blanche and Rosamund come to the rescue of the changeling son of the Queen of Faerie.

Fairy Tales • Changelings.

D's Picks

de Lint, Charles. *Jack of Kinrowan.* (p. 90)

Goldstein, Lisa. *Strange Devices of the Sun and Moon.* (p. 91)

Kushner, Ellen. *Thomas the Rhymer.* (p. 91)

Snyder, Midori. *The Flight of Michael McBride.* (p. 92)

Windling, Terri. *The Wood Wife.* (p. 92)

Chapter 9

Contemporary Fantasy

The cornerstone of contemporary fantasy is a setting that is readily recognizable to us. While some stories exhibit the extreme facets of fantasy, there are always parts that are identifiable in our world. Sometimes stories set in our mundane world are called low fantasy or realistic fantasy (an oxymoron much like jumbo shrimp). For some the recognizable settings make this fantasy more accessible, while for others the settings detract from the escapism of a completely made-up world.

Urban Fantasy

In this cyberpunk version of the fantasy world, magic and technology share a place in gritty, dangerous cities. Drugs, racism, gangs, and other scourges of modern life are evident. This is the world in which our contemporary cities, or maybe even the cyberpunk cities of the future, are the sites of a rift between our world and the world of Faerie. Such works are not pastoral, as most fantasy tends to be.

Brust, Steven, and Megan Lindholm

The Gypsy. "Neither Stepovich, a seasoned cop, nor Cigany, a gypsy who stalks the city streets in a cloud of magic, seem to be able to find the killer who is leaving a trail of dead bodies all over the city."—Publisher's catalog copy.

Detection • Demons • Ohio.

Bull, Emma

War for the Oaks. A mortal woman is drawn into the war between the Seelie and Unseelie Faerie forces.

Minneapolis • Music • Shapeshifting.

Finder. Orient is dragged into a drug-dealing scheme that threatens to destroy Bordertown.

Bordertown • Faerie • Psionic Powers.

Charnas, Suzy McKee

(YA) The Sorcery Hill trilogy. Valentine Marsh fights evil from another universe.

New York.

The Bronze King. Valentine notices odd things disappearing from the city.

The Silver Glove. Valentine and her grandmother, a sorceress, team up to protect her mother from her new evil wizard boyfriend.

The Golden Thread.

Younger Readers.

Dalkey, Kara

Steel Rose. In a secret corner of Pittsburgh's Schenley Park, performance artist T. J. Kaminski conjures up something with steel-gray eyes, razor-sharp teeth, and the power to grant T. J. her every wish. The elves are furious at her use of magic and draw her into a battle between immortal foes.

Art • Pittsburgh • Magic.

de Lint, Charles

Dreams Underfoot. A collection of stories set in Newford, an imagined Canadian city where magic and our reality frequently collide.

Short Stories.

Memory and Dream. Isabelle Copley has the ability to craft images so real they come alive, setting free ancient spirits and unleashing awesome power.

Native Americans • Newford • Art.

(AW) Moonheart. 1985 Crawford Award Winner.

Native Americans • Music • Celtic Fantasy.

(AW) Jack the Giant-Killer. Contemporary woman Jackie Rowan becomes a heroine without trying. This was part of Terri Windling's Fairy Tale series. 1988 Prix Aurora Award Winner.

Fairy Tales.

Drink down the Moon. This sequel to *Jack the Giant-Killer* was published with it in one volume as *Jack of Kinrowan.*

Gaiman, Neil

Neverwhere. Richard Mayhew is drawn into the mysterious subterranean world under London when he goes to the aid of a girl called Door.

London • Dark Fantasy.

Huff, Tanya

Gate of Darkness, Circle of Light. Unicorns are turning up in Toronto.

Unicorns • Toronto.

Lackey, Mercedes

YA The Serrated Edge series. A shared world urban fantasy, involving the elves who have formed SERRA, the South Eastern Road Racing Association.

Born to Run. Mercedes Lackey and Larry Dixon. Mixes hot cars, rock and roll, abused youth, and elves.

Music • Car Racing • Child Abuse • Shared Worlds.

Wheels of Fire. Mercedes Lackey and Mark Shepherd. Involves a parental kidnapping, a racing car, and an elf to the rescue.

Shared Worlds.

When the Bough Breaks. Mercedes Lackey and Holly Lisle. A girl with psionic powers could wreak havoc on Faerie if her pain is not relieved.

Shared Worlds.

Chrome Circle. Mercedes Lackey and Larry Dixon. Mixes Celtic rock, elves and dragons, and romance.

Music • Shared Worlds.

Spiritride. Mark Shepherd. Set in Albuquerque, it features motorcycles and skateboards.

Skateboarding • Shared Worlds.

Elvendude. Mark Shepherd. Features a prince of Faerie who is raised in our world so he can grow to adulthood and take on the dark elves.

Changelings • Shared Worlds.

Lackey, Mercedes, and Ellen Guon

A Knight of Ghosts and Shadows. Music frees an elfin noble and changes the life of flautist Eric Banyon, who now must fight against an evil elf lord who wants to conquer California.

Summoned to Tourney.

Bedlam's Bard. This title combines *A Knight of Ghosts and Shadows* and *Summoned to Tourney* in one volume.

Music • California.

Lindskold, Jane

Brother to Dragons, Companion to Owls. Sarah, who hears inanimate objects and can only speak in literary quotations, is forced out of the asylum and rescued from the streets by Abalone, who uses his computer skills to delve into her past.

Psionic Powers.

9

Shetterly, Will

Elsewhere. "Ron, a teenage runaway, comes of age among the punk elves and humans of Bordertown, a run-down city on the border between the real world and the magic world of Faerie."—Library catalog copy.

Bordertown • Music • Shared Worlds.

NeverNever. Ron, now transformed into a wolf-boy, discovers what life is really about.

Bordertown • Werewolves • Shared Worlds.

Spencer, William Browning

Zod Wallop. A writer fears that his creation is coming to life.

Fairy Tales.

Springer, Nancy

Fair Peril. (1996). A dowdy storytelling mother refuses to kiss a frog, but takes him home anyway. He runs off to Fair Peril (the Faerie Realm) with her teenage daughter.

Librarians • Fairy Tales.

Windling, Terri, and Delia Sherman, eds.

NEW The Essential Borderland. Tor, 1998. Contains original stories by Charles de Lint, Steven Brust, Patricia A. McKillip, Ellen Kushner, Delia Sherman, Caroline Stevermer, and seven others, set in a once-normal American city where Faerie and the human world meet. It is a place "where young human runaways mix with errant High Elves, to fight, trade, make music, and build a new and strange world."—Jacket copy.

Short Stories • Bordertown • Shared Worlds.

The Human Condition

The triumphs and trials and tribulations of being human are examined in the following books where fantasy helps highlight the problems and sometimes the solutions.

Anthony, Piers

The Incarnations of Immortality series.

Parallel Worlds • Fate • Time • Death • War • Earth.

On a Pale Horse. A potential suicide changes his mind at the last minute, slaying Thanatos instead, and as a result must himself become the incarnation of Death.

Bearing an Hourglass. Living backwards in time is not any fun when everyone else is moving in the opposite direction, even though Chronos does have the ability to sometimes stop time altogether.

With a Tangled Skein. The incarnation of fate is made up of three different aspects. Niobe in turn becomes Clotho, Atropos, and Lachesis.

Wielding a Red Sword. Mars is the incarnation of war.

Being a Green Mother. Gaia is the incarnation of Earth itself.

For Love of Evil. Satan has appeared throughout the series but is he actually all that evil or is he constrained by being an incarnation himself?

And Eternity. The story of the incarnation of Good wraps up the series.

Bishop, Michael

Brittle Innings. The setting is rural Georgia in 1943 (not exactly contemporary, but this century). This is a story of redemption in which a brutalized young baseball player discovers friendship with Hank Clervall, Frankenstein's gentle monster. 1995 Locus Poll Winner.

Baseball • Georgia • Legends.

Bisson, Terry

Talking Man. The silent talking man operates a junkyard in Kentucky and leads his relatives to an alternate America.

Kentucky • Parallel Worlds.

Blaylock, James P.

All the Bells on Earth. Humans try to beat the forces of evil after the devil tries to claim three souls brokered by a bogus minister.

Dealings with the Devil • Dark Fantasy.

de Lint, Charles

Trader. Max Trader, a luthier, awakes one morning to find that he has been dreamed into the body and life of deadbeat scumbag Johnny Devlin. When he tries to reclaim his apartment and shop, he winds up losing even Devlin's cruddy apartment. Homeless and on the streets, he is befriended by an Indian and one of the most likable canine characters ever, the stalwart Buddy. Peopled by characters so real you expect to run across them when walking through the park, *Trader* is a compelling look at identity and a good story well told.

Dogs • Animal People.

Gaiman, Neil

Neverwhere. A girl named Door leads Richard Mayhew into the weird subterranean world that exists under London.

London • Urban Fantasy.

Heinlein, Robert A.

Job: A Comedy of Justice. 1985 Locus Poll Award Winner.

Religion • Gods.

Nylund, Eric S.

Dry Water. An author with some precognitive abilities flees his life in the city for a New Mexico filled with magical battles.

Psionic Powers• New Mexico • Magic.

9

Reed, Robert

Exaltation of Larks. This tale of strange goings on at a 1970s college, long out of print, was reissued in 1998.

Time Travel • Shapeshifting • Immortality.

Resnick, Mike

A Miracle of Rare Design.

Springer, Nancy

Larque on the Wing. Larque can make doppelgangers, sometimes even without doing it consciously. When she creates Sky, who has a surprising solidity and is who she was as a child, her life begins to change. When Sky disappears, her talent for decorative painting, which keeps the family financially afloat, disappears too. In the course of Larque's search for Sky, she finds the bizarre Popular St., with its odd collection of shops and a gay nightclub. She also meets Shadow, who gives her a makeover that turns her into the studly young Lark, with all the accoutrements normally found on a healthy young man. However, she does not change her woman's heart or soul, which leaves Lark attracted to men in the same way that Larque was. When she discovers that her mother has the ability to blink someone into her own reality, she realizes that she is in terrible danger of losing herself. This complex novel, winner of the James Tiptree, Jr. Award, is a stunning tour de force, giving the reader much to ponder while being wildly entertaining. It is a great choice for open-minded book groups.

Doppelgangers • Homosexuality.

Tepper, Sheri S.

A Plague of Angels.

Archetypes.

Willard, Nancy

Things Invisible to See. Ben throws a baseball into the air; it comes down and cripples Clare. After time adrift at sea during World War II, Ben enters into a "deal with the devil" and must play a baseball game against death. 1986 Crawford Award Winner.

World War II • Baseball • Dealings with the Devil.

Magic Realism

Magic realism features an ordinary work-a-day setting in which magic and mythology are an integral part of the spiritual makeup. The contemporary settings are similar to those in Urban Fantasy, but with more spirituality and less emphasis on urban problems such as gangs and drugs. For years the name was applied only to Latin American literary works, but readers like the term for the following works as well.

Blaylock, James P.

The Paper Grail. Many are in on the hunt in California for a nineteenth-century woodcut sketch that is imbued with magical powers.

California • Talismans • Ghosts.

Block, Francesca Lia

Dangerous Angels: The Weetzie Bat Books. This is an omnibus title for the five rollicking, surrealist punk fairy tales about a teen family made of love, not blood, in modern-day Venice Beach. While published as young adult books, they have a huge following of twenty-something readers and older teens.

Weetzie Bat.

Witch Baby.

Cherokee Bat and the Goat Guys.

Missing Angel Juan.

Baby Be-Bop.

de Lint, Charles

Someplace to Be Flying. The huge cast of well-developed characters in this book may be confusing to readers who are not already accustomed to the mythos of Newford, a town on the cusp between our mundane world and a New World version of Faerie. A cab driver going to the assistance of a woman photographer under attack finds himself being rescued by two seemingly identical and strange young women, who slay the attacker. Released from a nearly lifelong stay in a mental institution, a young woman tries to take up a new life in Newford, moving into an apartment where her neighbors are close friends of the photographer and two young girls, called the Crow girls, who claim to live in a tree. All these and more come together to fight an evil family that is seeking something that will destroy the world. A brief sojourn in Tucson as well as a certain brand of magic exhibit similarities to Terri Windling's *The Wood Wife*.

Native Americans • Animal People • Newford • Tucson.

Goldstein, Lisa

Walking the Labyrinth. Goldstein, who won the American Book Award for *The Red Magician,* creates a world so real and inviting that the reader is compelled to keep going nonstop until the book is finished. A reviewer in *The New Yorker* wrote of this author: "She has given us the kind of magic and adventure that once upon a time made us look for secret panels in the walls of wardrobes, or brush our teeth with a book held in front of our eyes, because we couldn't bear to put it down." While that was written about *Tourists*, it is also true for *Walking the Labyrinth*. Goldstein has a rare and powerful gift for conveying truth through fantasy.

The world is our own, and Molly Travers is an ordinary contemporary woman. That is, until a private detective turns up with questions about her family. Molly, orphaned at age two, was raised by her now-elderly aunt Fentrice, believing that she is her only family. Discovering that she is descended from a family of Vaudeville magicians who may have come from England, Molly goes to investigate and finds a mystical labyrinth in the basement of the estate of a friend of her great-great grandmother's. Faced with murder, betrayal, new friendships, and discovery of long-lost secret diaries and family members, Molly finds real magic and herself. Readers of *Walking the Labyrinth* may also enjoy *The China Garden,* by Liz Berry, which also deals with magic, mazes, and unknown lost relatives.

Labyrinths • Detection • Magicians.

Kindl, Patrice

YA The Woman in the Wall. Anna, "small and thin, with a face like water," fades into the walls of her family's dilapidated Victorian home, her shyness making her invisible to her family.

Romance.

Scarborough, Elizabeth Ann

The Healer's War. A military nurse serving in Vietnam during the war is given a powerful talisman. 1989 Nebula Award Winner.

Talismans • Vietnam War • Healers.

Shetterly, Will

Dogland. Florida of the 1950s is the setting for this tale of a family-run theme park featuring a variety of dog breeds.

Dogs • Florida.

Windling, Terri

The Wood Wife. Poet Maggie Black has inherited a desert home near Tucson from her mentor, the prizewinning poet Davis Cooper, whom she has never met. Leaving her sophisticated life, she goes to Tucson to try to assemble a biography of this mysterious man, former lover of dead Mexican artist Anna Naverra, and a notorious recluse. In the desert Maggie begins to see things that don't jibe with her sense of reality. She comes to love the desert and see it in Davis's work, where before she had seen only the England where he had grown up. A complex and magical work, this story is rich and moving, conjuring up visions of that which is just beyond our view. The prose is beautiful, and it has a fully fleshed-out, coherent plot. The reader is rewarded by knowing Maggie, Fox, and Dora and finding mystery, romance, and magic in its pages. While *The Wood Wife* is definitely fantasy, readers who like it may also enjoy Barbara Kingsolver's *Animal Dreams*. 1997 Mythopoeic Award Winner.

Animal People • Tucson • Poets.

D's Picks

Bull, Emma. *Finder.* (p. 93)

de Lint, Charles. *Someplace to Be Flying.* (p. 99)

Shetterly, Will. *NeverNever.* (p. 96)

Springer, Nancy. *Larque on the Wing.* (p. 98)

Windling, Terri. *The Wood Wife.* (p. 100)

Chapter 10

Alternate and Parallel Worlds

Alternate and parallel worlds are fully developed. They are either our own world transformed by a difference in history or one that can be traveled to from our world. Sometimes the alternate world is a fully fleshed-out one that has no relation to our own, but has its own fully developed history and rules.

Alternate History

Due to a divergence somewhere in time, the worlds presented in these books are very different from the world we know. Sometimes the divergence was far in the past, as in the Lord Darcy books (annotated in Chapter 17), in which the alternate world and ours diverged during the reign of Richard I. As a result, magic in that world achieved the status held by science in ours.

Alternate history is an element that is most often employed in science fiction, but because most of it does not scientifically explain the divergence, it can arguably be placed in fantasy. Harry Turtledove, the reigning dean of alternate history, is discussed in John Clute and Peter Nicholls's *The Encyclopedia of Science Fiction* (St. Martin's Press, 1995) but not in John Clute and John Grant's *The Encyclopedia of Fantasy* (St. Martin's Press, 1997).

Prehistoric epics such as Jean Auel's Earth's Children series could also fit into the alternate history category, especially when the gods are present or magic is manifest.

Anthony, Piers

Geodyssey series.

Prehistoric.

Isle of Woman. "The story of humanity itself, from its savage origins to its troubled future, told through the lives of one family reborn throughout history."—Jacket copy.

Shame of Man.

Hope of Earth.

Ball, Margaret

Tamai series. In an alternate nineteenth century, Tamai uses her magic to protect her people, keeping Chin an isolated country by refusing contact with the British.

Flameweaver.

Changeweaver.

China • Magic • Weaving.

Blaylock, James P.

The Paper Grail. Many are in on the hunt in northern California for a nineteenth-century woodcut sketch that is imbued with magical powers.

California • Talismans • Ghosts • Magic Realism.

Bova, Ben

Triumph. Their history diverged from ours when Roosevelt started taking better care of himself, thus surviving World War II and a ceremonial sword awarded to Stalin had a deadly secret hidden in its hilt.

World War II • Espionage.

Brust, Steven, and Emma Bull

Freedom and Necessity. This is a magical, mysterious romp through mid-nineteenth-century England.

England • Politics • Romance • Detection.

Card, Orson Scott

YA Chronicles of Alvin Maker. In this alternate nineteenth-century North America, hexes and spells work and the states never became a union. It is American history, but it has many parallels to the life of Joseph Smith, founder of the Church of Latter Day Saints (Mormons).

Hexes • Magic • America • Politics • Religion.

Seventh Son. Alvin is born the seventh son of a seventh son on his family's westward journey. 1988 Locus Poll Winner. Mythopoeic Award Winner.

Red Prophet. 1989 Locus Poll Winner.

Prentice Alvin. 1990 Locus Poll Winner.

Alvin Journeyman. 1996 Locus Poll Winner.

Heartfire. Alvin travels to Salem, New England, to confront the legacy that has branded all knacks as witchcraft. His wife Peggy, who can read the heartfires and futures of people, journeys south to Charleston to meet with the exiled king and try to stop a war between the free and slave nations of North America.

Ciencin, Scott

Elven Ways series. When elves desert a dying faerie in the fifteenth century, they pass themselves off as angels in our world, taking control and changing the destiny of humankind.

Elves • Angels.

The Ways of Magic.

Ancient Games.

Conner, Mike

Archangel. An alternate 1920s Minneapolis is the sight of a viral epidemic that is draining its victims of blood.

Disease • Detection • Minneapolis.

Dalkey, Kara

Blood of the Goddess series.

Science • India • Gods • Quest.

Goa. At the end of the sixteenth century, Thomas Chinnery, an apothecary's apprentice, is voyaging toward China on a quest for rare herbs and curatives when his ship captures a small galleon being pursued by the Portuguese near the colony of Goa in western India. On board are a woman accused of heresy and an alchemist, who are fleeing the Inquisition. They are in possession of a vial of dried blood called the Blood of the Goddess, which kills the living and restores the dead to life.

Bijapur. Now the captive of the Inquisition's Black Friars, Thomas is guiding an expedition across India, pretending he knows the source of the Blood of the Goddess.

Bhagavati. Thomas Chinnery's quest continues.

Dreyfuss, Richard, and Harry Turtledove

The Two Georges. Our world would be very different if George Washington had reconciled the rebellious colonies with King George. Americans, as loyal subjects of the Crown, may not have been so innovative or inventive, or perhaps in that reality there would have been no Revolution because the colonists were not as independent as in ours. This thought-provoking tale takes Colonel Thomas Bushell of the Royal American Mounted Police on a trek from sea to shining sea as he tries to recover the famous Gainsborough painting, the *Two Georges,* which is emblematic of America as a loyal subject nation. At a gala reception in New Liverpool (Los Angeles), Tricky Dicky (Richard Nixon), the used steamer magnate, is killed by gunfire, a most unusual occurrence. At the same time the *Two Georges* is stolen by the Sons of Liberty, a radical group that wants American autonomy. On the trail of the painting, along with his friend and co-worker Sam Stanley, Tom once again runs into the curator of the traveling exhibit, the lovely Kathleen Flannery, who claims to be conducting her own investigation into the abduction of the painting.

Detection • Romance • Politics.

Edgerton, Teresa

Goblin sequence. The harmony of an alternate Europe is shattered when an inept alchemist awakens a malign force.

Romance • Magic.

Goblin Moon.

Gnome's Engine.

Gemmell, David

Dark Prince. King Philip of Macedon from the evil parallel universe kidnaps four-year-old Alexander into his reality. Sequel to *Lion of Macedon.*

Alexander the Great • Parallel Worlds.

Gentle, Mary

Rats and Gargoyles. Humans led by the White Crow plot to overthrow the ruling giant rats in the "city called the heart of the world."

Rats • Politics • Magic.

The Architecture of Desire. The White Crow and her husband, the Lord-Architect Casaubon, both powerful magicians, become embroiled in a deadly game of politics and magic in an alternate seventeenth-century London.

Politics • Magic.

Goldstein, Lisa

The Red Magician. "Turns the hidden world of Eastern European Jews during the 1940s into a world of wonders, then transcends the Holocaust with magical optimism." —*The New York Times.*

Holocaust.

Harrison, Harry

Hammer and the Cross trilogy.

Scandinavian Stories • Heroes.

The Hammer and the Cross. Shef, a Norseman, leads the Viking army to victory over England

One King's Way. After defeating his enemies among the Norsemen, Shef becomes the King of the North.

King and Emperor. Shef faces the power of a reborn Holy Roman Empire.

MacAvoy, R. A.

Trio for Lute series. Renaissance Italy. Damiano Delstrego, a witch boy, and his dog familiar meet the Archangel Raphael.

Renaissance • Italy • Angels • Music.

Damiano. A musician at heart, gifted witch Damiano is thrilled when the Archangel Raphael teaches him to play the lute. When his city is invaded, the men of the city are too afraid to fight, and Raphael refuses to help him, so he makes a bargain with Satan.

Damiano's Lute. Magic has become an obstacle to his music, so Damiano gives his powers to Saara and sets out to be a full-time lutenist. But life is harsh without the protection of magic. Damiano may be able to alleviate a great grief if he can get his magic back.

Raphael. When Saara falls into the devil's clutches, Raphael offers himself in exchange for her life. Guilt-stricken Saara teams up with a dragon, Gaspare, and Damiano to find him.

McIntyre, Vonda N.

The Moon and the Sun. "The discovery of a sea-woman by a Jesuit explorer sends the court of Louis XIV into a tizzy, revealing the range of human response to a confrontation with the unknown."—*Publishers Weekly* "Best Science Fiction '97."

France • Paranormal Beings • Religion.

Roessner, Michaela

The Stars Dispose. Red-haired Tommaso is the son of the head carver and Piera, a cook in the kitchens of the Ruggieros, occultists with close ties to the de Medici family. He is tied to Caterina, the de Medici heir, by love, magic, and kinship on the wrong side of the blankets. As Florence faces peril first from the Black Plague and then under siege by the Pope, Tommaso becomes apprentice to an artist and also becomes the lover of Michelangelo. This richly textured, intimate look at sixteenth-century Florence is a rewarding read. It does seem like the first of a series, though sequels are not mentioned. The exact instructions for summoning beings from alternate worlds are not included, but there are recipes for some of the delicacies from the Ruggiero and de Medici kitchens.

Italy • Cookery.

Rohan, Michael Scott

The Lord of Middle Air.

Magic • Sir Walter Scott.

Rohan, Michael Scott, and Allan Scott

The Spell of Empire: The Horns of Tartarus. A conflict arises between Scandinavian and Mediterranean cultures in Europe.

Humor • Europe.

Snyder, Midori

The Innamorati. Set in an alternate Renaissance Venice, in this story four companions journey across Italy to meet at the great labyrinth, where curses may be lost.

Labyrinths • Italy.

Turtledove, Harry

Between the Rivers. At the dawn of history, Sharur lives in the thriving city-state of Gibil, which is in danger from the gods of other cities, who do not like the burgeoning creativity of the townspeople.

Prehistoric • Gods.

10

Parallel Worlds

The following works all present characters who travel from one world to another. Frequently the traveler goes from our world to one on an alternate plane or place. Some go from one fantasy world to another. The conflict in the story often arises from the main character being a stranger in a strange land. Usually there is no scientific explanation given for the journey or transformation to the other world. These fantasies are grounded in the soil of our earth, by virtue of having characters that have experienced the world as we have. They find wonder in magic and in mythical creatures come to life. Some of the worlds in the books in this section do not have concrete relationships to our world either in time or in place, but take place in lands seemingly familiar—our world but not the world we know.

Anderson, Poul

Three Hearts and Three Lions. Twentieth-century engineer Holger Carlsen is transported into a world of knights, dragons, witches, and fairy folk to battle evil and fight dragons, giants, elfin warriors, and the beautiful sorceress Morgan le Fay. If he can live long enough, he may even be able to discover his true identity.

Engineers • Dragons • Witches • Elves • Magic.

Anthony, Piers

YA The Apprentice Adept series. The ecological balance between science and magic and two worlds is constantly threatened.

Technology • Magic • Humor.

Split Infinity.

Blue Adept.

Juxtaposition.

Out of Phaze.

Robot Adept.

Unicorn Point.

Phaze Doubt.

Anthony, Piers, and Robert Kornwise

YA **Through the Ice.** When he falls through the ice, a boy from our world is transported to one filled with magic and peril. The most remarkable thing about this book is that it was started by a teenaged fan of Anthony who was killed in an accident, and then finished by the prolific author.

Adventure.

Ball, Margaret

Lost in Translation. Allie is thrilled to learn magic under Dean Aigar instead of going to the university, but she is unaware that he is really a ruthless traveler from another world.

Magic.

Bear, Greg

Songs of Earth and Power. "The Song of Power opened the gateway to the Realm of the Dishe, allowing young Michael Perrin to slip through. Now Michael faces years of captivity and deadly struggles for the future of the Realm and of Earth–leading finally to a terrible confrontation on the streets of Los Angeles, with the soul of humanity at stake."–-Jacket copy.

    Los Angeles • Contemporary Fantasy.

Bradley, Marion Zimmer

House Between Worlds. A parapsychology experimental drug takes a young man out of his body and into many different realms to stop a war between a world of elven magic and one of technology.

    Drugs • Technology • Magic • Elves.

Bradley, Marion Zimmer, and Holly Lisle

Glenraven series.

    Humor • Heroes • Women.

Glenraven. The people of Glenraven were looking for a couple of heroes from outside to free them from the depredations of life under an evil dictator. Instead they got two women from our world who thought they were going on a vacation in an Alpine principality. Sophie had lost a child, and Jay was a three-time loser in the marriage market. Can they actually be of any assistance to a magic kingdom in trouble?

In the Rift. After embracing a pagan religion, Kate Beacham has been disowned by her parents and assaulted by bigots. She returns home to find her beloved stallion dead in her driveway, with a note nailed to his head saying that she is next. In her house she gets out her shotgun, then notices a book titled *Glenraven* on her nightstand. Opening it, she sees the words "get out of the house, quick" appear. Still holding the shotgun, she goes outside and sees a hole opening up in midair; a group on horseback rides out, pursued by a nightmarish horror that looks like a cross between a dragon and a shark. Her shotgun and quick reactions may mean the survival of her world and another.

Brooks, Terry

 Magic Kingdom of Landover series.

    Humor • Magic.

Magic Kingdom for Sale—Sold! Lawyer Ben Holiday, disenchanted with his life, sees an ad and cashes in everything to come up with the required million dollars, only to discover that owning one's own magic kingdom isn't everything it's cracked up to be.

The Black Unicorn. A fictional unicorn finds himself brought to life outside his magical book; Ben Holiday finds himself and his kingdom in deep trouble.

    Unicorns.

Wizard at Large. The tale continues, with Landover at peace as Meeks, the evil wizard, has been dealt with. But peace never lasts for long.

The Tangle Box. Ben, the witch Nightshade, and the dragon Strabo are trapped in the Tangle Box with no memories. They must wait for Queen Willow, who is lost in an endless dance herself. Dreams may be their only salvation.

    Dragons.

YA **Witches' Brew.** Ben's daughter Mistaya is kidnapped and the court wizard, Questor Thews, is magically detained on Earth.

Carroll, Jerry Jay

Top Dog. A vicious Wall Street executive suddenly finds himself in a medieval fantasy world in the form of a dog. For a kinder, gentler take on life as a dog, readers may enjoy *Dogsbody*, by Dianna Wynne Jones, which is also great for younger readers.

Chalker, Jack L.

Changewinds. Originally published as *When the Changewinds Blow, Riders of the Winds,* and *War of the Maelstrom.* Two young women have been caught up in the Changewinds, the winds that blow through worlds, changing realities.

Magic • Physics • Demons • Women.

Donaldson, Stephen R.

AW **Mordant's Need duology.** A repressed young woman is drawn into another, more primitive, world through one of the mirrors she surrounds herself with in an attempt to believe in herself.

Magic • Mirrors.

The Mirror of Her Dreams.

A Man Rides Through.

AW **The Chronicles of Thomas Covenant, the Unbeliever.** A modern leper is transported in what he thinks are dreams to a land that is paralleling his own diseased decline. The series won the 1979 August Derleth Award.

Contemporary Fantasy • Leprosy • Quest.

First Chronicle:

Lord Foul's Bane.

The Illearth War.

The Power That Preserves.

Second Chronicle:

AW **The Wounded Land.**

AW **The One Tree.** 1983 Balrog Award Winner.

White Gold Wielder.

Douglas, Carole Nelson

The Taliswoman series.

Women • Quest • Talismans.

Cup of Clay. Allison Carver is transported to Veil, where she finds that women have a peculiar place in society and, while some children are cherished, others are discarded. She embarks on a quest for a magical cup.

Seed upon the Wind. Allison was glad to return to her world, leaving Veil behind, but she finds she must return to free the innocent from the devastation that is plaguing Veil. The key to Veil's salvation or its destruction may be our world.

Duncan, Dave

Great Game series. During World War I, Edward Exeter flees our world and enters Nextdoor, an alternate world where he is imbued with magical qualities needed to liberate the populace from a pantheon of evil gods.

Magic • Gods.

Past Imperative: Round One of the Great Game.

Present Tense: Round Two of the Great Game.

Future Indefinite: Round Three of the Great Game.

Foster, Alan Dean

 The Spellsinger series. Features a land of intelligent, talking animals and wizards.

Music • Otters • Animals.

Spellsinger. Jonathan Meriweather is plucked from university life in our world and catapulted into a world in which he is the spellsinger and animals talk and carry blades.

The Hour of the Gate. Jon and his companions must make a perilous journey across Helldrink, through a tunnel of cold flame, and into the center of the Earth.

The Day of the Dissonance. With Mudge the otter as his guide, the Spellsinger sets out across the Glittergeist Ocean in search of healing for Clothahump the Wizard, who seems to be dying.

The Moment of the Magician. A powerful magician is holding a beleaguered city in thrall. Clothahump asks Jon and Mudge to help free it. Could the evil come from Jon's own world?

The Paths of the Perambulator. Do Jon, Mudge, and Clothahump have any chance to defeat the mysterious Perambulator, a threat to the very fabric of the universe?

Son of the Spellsinger. Buncan, not wanting to be a spellsinger, forms a band with Mudge's kids; the rap-based music they play creates a wild, unpredictable magic.

Gardner, Craig Shaw

Dragon Circle series. An entire suburban street is transported by a dragon to a world of magic, wizards, and warriors.

Dragons • Magic • Warriors.

Dragon Sleeping.

Dragon Waking.

Dragon Burning.

Hambly, Barbara

Darwath series. Gil, a historian, and bad-boy biker Rudy are drawn from our world into Darwath, where they join forces with a wizard and a barbarian warrior in an effort to save the people from a hideous evil.

Gods • Quest • Weather • Barbarians • Magic.

The Time of the Dark.

The Walls of Air.

The Armies of Daylight.

Mother of Winter. Two individuals from our world live in a society that is very different from our world. Gil is the warrior guard of her lover, the Archmage Ingold, who is on a search for lost knowledge to help sustain life in his world, which is suffering from a chilling of the climate and the growth of a strange substance called slunch. Slunch is almost impossible to destroy and is quickly overrunning the fields, destroying the food crops and invading everywhere. Strange creatures are also appearing. One of them bites Gil, causing her to suffer dreams that compel her to want to murder Ingold. Rudy is the lover of the young king's mother and is trying to preserve the life of all in the keep. Statues of a mysterious new saint have appeared and a strange smell is permeating the distant reaches of the keep. A bizarre ice storm, previously unknown in the area, destroys all the livestock and crops as well as the beloved young herd children, making the quest for a new food source of utmost importance.

Ice Falcon's Quest. The barbarian Ice Falcon is the only one from the Keep of Dare who has any chance of rescuing the queen's abducted son.

Heinlein, Robert A.

Glory Road (annotated in Chapter 3).

Jones, Diana Wynne

A Sudden Wild Magic. The witches of England discover that the sorcerers on a parallel Earth called Arth have been visiting disasters (such as global warming) upon us to analyze how we face such crises and steal the solutions we develop.

Science Fantasy • Witches • Technology.

🆈🅰 Hexwood. This is a bizarre tale in which events seem to keep repeating themselves, but with different results. Hume encounters a robot and a dragon in the wood and Ann meets a tormented wizard named Mordion.

Arthurian Legend • Technology.

Jones, J. V.

The Barbed Coil. When she is transported from Southern California to another land, Tessa's art skills give her magical powers. She just may be what is needed to depose an evil king.

Art • Magic.

King, Stephen

The Dark Tower series. Roland is involved in an epic battle against the Men in Black, combating evil.

Futuristic Fantasy • Dark Fantasy • Quest.

The Gunslinger.

The Drawing of the Three.

The Waste Lands.

Wizard and Glass.

L'Engle, Madeleine

🆈🅰 The Time Fantasy quartet also called the Murray Family saga.

Younger Readers • Science Fantasy • Time Travel.

🅰🆆 A Wrinkle in Time. Meg and her brother Charles Wallace are off on a journey through the dimensions to rescue their scientist father. Newbery Award Winner.

A Wind in the Door.

A Swiftly Tilting Planet.

Many Waters. The twins, Sandy and Dennys time travel to Noah's era. For the young, but read by all ages.

Le Guin, Ursula K.

The Lathe of Heaven. George Orr's dreams become reality.

Dreams • Film.

Modesitt, L. E., Jr.

The Spellsong Cycle.

Music.

The Soprano Sorceress. A college music teacher makes a wish to get out of Iowa and ends up in a world where music is magic but women are second-class citizens.

The Spellsong War. Now regent of the kingdom of Defalk, Anna Marshal must defend it against the greedy rulers of neighboring kingdoms.

Moorcock, Michael

Blood: A Southern Fantasy. New technology has caused a rift to open into chaos. Denizens of the Terminal Cafe find there is more than meets the eye when they start manipulating reality in the parallel worlds exposed by the rift.

Technology.

O'Donohue, Nick

🔼 Crossroads series. A team of veterinary students go into Crossroads, where a war is being fought between good and evil, featuring unicorns, griffins, and even Morgan le Fay.

Animals • Veterinarians • Unicorns.

The Magic and the Healing. A veterinary student travels to a parallel world to doctor unicorns and other mystical creatures injured in a deadly war.

Under the Healing Sign.

The Healing of Crossroads.

Pullman, Philip

🔼 His Dark Materials.

Magic • Quest • Bears • Familiars • Younger Readers.

The Golden Compass. Lyra Belacqua has been pretty much raising herself in one of the colleges of Oxford. Like all humans in her world, she has a daemon. Hers is named Pantalaimon. It will continue to change shape until she reaches adulthood. Children start disappearing, reputedly stolen away by Gobblers, and Lyra is given an alethiometer, a fortune-telling device, and sent to London to live with the elegant and sinister Mrs. Coulter. She escapes with the help of the Gyptians. With a cohort of stalwart companions, including Iorek Byrnison, an armored bear whom she rescues from a life of slavery and degradation, Lyra heads for the North, where strange occurrences have been happening and where the mystery of the missing children may be solved.

 10

The Subtle Knife. This is definitely the middle book of a trilogy, but it does offer thrills and chills of its own. Lyra hooks up with Will, a boy from our world, and they escape to a recently deserted city in a parallel world to try to recover from past events, he from killing an invader in his home and she from the cataclysmic events in *The Golden Compass*.

Rawn, Melanie, Jennifer Roberson, and Kate Elliott

The Golden Key. In a world where paintings are a binding legal record, the Grijalva family of artists are master painters. Certain males of the line are born with a talent to manipulate time and reality with their paintings. Sario Grijalva has learned a whole new way to use his talent, and because of his obsession for his beautiful cousin Saavedra, he uses it in a way that will cost his family a terrible price.

Art • Magic.

Reichert, Mickey Zucker

The Bifrost Guardians. An American soldier is shanghaied from the Vietnam War to fight in a war between gods of Norse myth.

Vietnam War • Scandinavian Stories • Myths.

Godslayer. Al Larson is snatched from a fire fight in Vietnam and transported into an elfish body in another place, where sword and spell are the weapons of choice, not grenades and guns.

Shadow Climber. Taziar Medakan had turned to stealing for survival after his father was wrongly executed. Now he is the Shadow Climber, stealing for the challenge and, like Robin Hood, giving to those in need. Through a cunning politician's treachery he finds himself in the baron's dreaded dungeons, where he meets Moonbear, swordsman and prince among barbarians.

Dragonrank Master. Al Larson, having earned the name Godslayer, teams up with master swordsman Gaelinar and the Shadow Climber on a quest that will take them from the citadel of Dragonrank powers to war-torn Vietnam, and even to Hel's dark realm and beyond.

Shadow's Realm. Chaos was unleashed when the Chaos Dragon was slain, driving the most powerful Dragonmage into madness. Now insanely bent on revenge, he is after Al Larson, Shadow, and the two Dragonmages, Silme and Astryd.

By Chaos Cursed. Chaos has pursued Al, Shadow, Silme, and Astryd into the heart of twentieth-century New York City.

Rohan, Michael Scott

Winter of the World trilogy. The evils of ice and darkness are advancing and threatening the land. 1991 Crawford Award Winner.

Magic • Weather.

The Anvil of Ice.

The Forge in the Forest.

The Hammer of the Sun.

Rosenberg, Joel

Keepers of the Hidden Ways series.

Myths • Norse Tales • Swordsmen.

The Fire Duke. Attacked by werewolves, three vacationing college fencers go down a tunnel to Tir Na Nog.

The Silver Stone.

Sarti, Ron

Chronicles of Scar series. Arn knows the gutters, having lived in them for seven years, until it is discovered that he is the long-lost illegitimate heir to the throne. Set in a post-apocalyptic North America.

Ohio • Quest.

Chronicles of Scar.

Legacy of the Ancients.

Savage, Felicity

Ever series.

Sexuality • Demons.

The War in the Waste. "Our world is like water to them. The daemons swim invisibly through rock and trees, men and beasts—until they are summoned by a handler, collared, and imprisoned in oak and silver to power entire cities with their rage."—Jacket copy.

The Daemon in the Machine. "Crispin became a daemon handler as a boy, taught by an exiled courtier who had become a circus bum. The gift gave him wings, carrying him all the way to far Kirekune, the home of his long-lost love. And on to contact with the most exotic civilization of all. America."—Jacket copy.

NEW **A Trickster in the Ashes.**

Stasheff, Christopher

Rod Gallowglass series. Science fiction trappings of space travel and robots are abundant in the first series about Rod Gallowglass, who discovers he can work magic on the planet Gramarye.

Technology • Magic • Science Fantasy.

The Warlock in Spite of Himself.

King Kobold Revived.

The Warlock Unlocked.

Escape Velocity.

The Warlock Enraged.

The Warlock Wandering.

The Warlock Is Missing.

The Warlock Heretical.

The Warlock's Companion.

The Warlock Insane.

The Warlock Rock.

Warlock and Son.

Rogue Wizard series. Magnus, the headstrong son of Rod Gallowglass, sets out to sow anarchy across the stars.

A Wizard in Mind.

A Wizard in Bedlam.

> **A Wizard in War.**
>
> **A Wizard in Peace.**

The Warlock's Heirs series.

> **A Wizard in Absentia.**
>
> **M'Lady Witch.**
>
> **Quicksilver's Knight.**
>
> **A Wizard in Midgard.** Gar Pike finds himself on a Norse version of Earth, where he ends up in the middle of a conflict between three warring races when he rescues a young girl.

Wizard in Rhyme series.

> **Her Majesty's Wizard.**
>
> **The Oathbound Wizard.**
>
> **The Witch Doctor.**
>
> **The Secular Wizard.**

Turtledove, Harry

Videssos cycle. A Roman legion and a Celtic chieftain find themselves in a world similar to Byzantium, where magic works.

> **Misplaced Legion.**
>
> **An Emperor for the Legion.**
>
> **Legion of Videssos.**
>
> **Swords of the Legion.**
>
> *Roman Legions • Byzantium • Celtic Fantasy.*

Alternate Worlds

Fully realized worlds with their own histories of politics and culture are found in much of fantasy. While many of the books in this section would fit just as well in sword and sorcery, some of them are of a more unique nature. All the following emphasize building worlds of complexity.

Aiken, Joan

🆈🅰 The Stolen Lake.

> *South America • Celtic Fantasy • Arthurian Legend • Adventure.*

Anderson, Poul

🅰🆆 A Midsummer Tempest. The worlds of Shakespeare come to life in the era of Roundheads and Cavaliers. 1975 Mythopoeic Award Winner.

> *Magic • Adventure • Alternate History • England.*

Bradley, Marion Zimmer

Darkover series. Later books in the series demonstrate that they are actually SF, but to many readers they have a definite feel of parallel world fantasy. Psionic powers are used for communications. Titles are listed in Chapter 12.

Brust, Steven

Vlad Taltos series.

Assassins • Familiars.

Taltos. Vlad journeys to the land of the dead.

Jhereg.

Teckla. Vlad is drawn into a rebellion against the Dragaeran Empire.

Phoenix. At the bidding of his patron goddess, Vlad is called upon to use his skills as an assassin.

Clayton, Jo

Drums of Chaos series.

Magic • Politics.

Drum Warning. Master fantasist Clayton introduces the reader to a huge cast of characters, living in a variety of lands on different worlds. The one thing they have in common is that a huge disruption in the pneuma has started. Sometimes the sky writhes and boils, assuming a cottage cheesy-type texture. It portends a time of chaos and change, when the worlds of Glandair and Iomard will meet. The huge cast of characters is sometimes hard to follow. The most memorable are Cymel, a young daughter of both worlds who seems to have powerful magic of unknown dimensions, and Lyanz, a wealthy merchant's son who may be the hero needed for the time of Chaos. Jo Clayton is always enjoyable to read, but be forewarned that this work is merely the first part of a series and one must wait for subsequent books to be published to find out what happens. One of the most fascinating aspects is the way in which magical powers are invoked by the three mages to manipulate events to come out on top. One mage has magic devices tattooed all over his body, while another paints magical designs on when he needs them, and the third gowns herself in silvery wire twisted into magical meaning.

Drum Calls. This book was finished while Clayton was hospitalized with multiple myeloma.

Drums of Chaos. Clayton completed half of this book before her death in 1998. Katherine Kerr, her literary executor, is planning to have it finished for publication in 1999.

Coney, Michael Greatrex

Fang, the Gnome.

King of the Scepter'd Isle.

Cross, Ronald Anthony

The Eternal Guardians series. "The walls of space and time dissolve as we rollercoaster between lewd, pagan Los Angeles and haunted, mystic Rome, in a nightmare where only the blood is real."—Robert Anton Wilson.

Los Angeles • Roman • Humor.

The Fourth Guardian.

The Lost Guardian.

10

The White Guardian. History has become frozen because a Guardian has become lost in time. The White Guardian must find him to save the world as we need it to be.

Delany, Samuel R.

They Fly at Ciron (1993). This early work defies description.

Dorsey, Candas Jane

Black Wine. Dorsey's elegant, poetic writing makes the reader take time to savor the prose while reading this tale of sex, depravity, and lost memories. This complex, convoluted tale tells of several different women—or is it really only one or two?—in different lands and places in their lives. A waiflike slave sneaks food to an old crazy woman kept in a cage in the town square. A queen flees her sadistic husband. A mother in a mannerly, well-run mountain village deserts her young daughter. A new slave in the royal palace learns the sign language of her mute lover. A trader finds love in a multiple handfasted relationship. A young princess and her half sister watch as their perverted grandmother sexually abuses a slave. Complex, sometimes confusing, the diverse elements of this tale come together eventually to form an intricate whole from what seem to be disconnected fragments.

Literary Fantasy • Abuse • Fairy Tales.

Eddison, E. R.

The Worm Ouroboros (1922). Strong elements of myth and legend are found in this challenging read from early in the century.

Myths • Hedonism.

The Zimiamvian trilogy.

Mezentian Gate.

A Fish Dinner in Memison.

Mistress of Mistresses.

Elliott, Kate

Crown of Stars series. The war-torn kingdoms of Wendar and Varre are the setting for these tales.

Politics • Magic • Epic • Ghosts.

Kings Dragon. Wendar is torn by internal strife: Sabella contests her brother, King Henry's, right to the crown and deadly raids by the inhuman Eika threaten the land. Thrust into this conflict, where sorcery, not swords, will win, are Liath and Alain, each trapped in a personal struggle for survival.

NEW Prince of Dogs. Sanglant, captain of the Dragons and King Henry's illegitimate son, is believed dead, but he is actually being held captive by Bloodheart, the Eika warlord. While grieving over Sanglant, Liath is trying to discover the secrets of her own past and evade traps set for her.

Haggard, H. Rider

She series. Some of the titles are still in print over a century after they were first published. They take place in a lost alternate world African setting.

Adventure • Reincarnation • Immortality.

She (1887).

Ayesha (1905).

She and Allen (1921).

Wisdom's Daughter (1923).

Hodgell, P. C.
Kencyrath series.

God Stalk.

Magic • Cats.

Dark of the Moon
"Jame and her friend Mark journey over the mountains to find Jame's twin brother Tori, but they must face great dangers, including planet-threatening enemies."—Publisher's catalog copy.

Seeker's Mask.

Huff, Tanya

No Quarter (annotated in Chapter 12).

Sing the Four Quarters.

Fifth Quarter.

Kay, Guy Gavriel

Tigana. In a land similar to Italy, two tyrants using powerful magic battle to divide up the provinces. 1991 Prix Aurora Award Winner.

Italy.

King, Stephen, and Peter Straub

The Talisman.

Quest • Sword and Sorcery.

Kurtz, Katherine
Deryni saga.

Magic • Politics • Religion.

Chronicles of the Deryni.

Deryni Rising.

Deryni Checkmate.

High Deryni.

Legends of Camber of Culdi series.

Camber of Culdi.

Saint Camber.

Camber the Heretic. 1982 Balrog Award Winner.

Heirs of Saint Camber series.

The Harrowing of Gwynedd.

King Javan's Year.

The Bastard Prince.

Histories of King Kelson series.

The Bishop's Heir.

The King's Justice.

The Quest for Saint Camber.

Kushner, Ellen

Swordspoint. Accustomed to performing duels to the death for the entertainment of nobles, swordsman Richard St. Vier is drawn into the intrigue of multiple conspiracies as nobles plot against each other using him as a pawn in their deadly political games. An elegant and sophisticated first book by the author who went on to write the beautifully told *Thomas the Rhymer*.

Fairy Tales • Politics.

Moorcock, Michael

(AW) (🏵) Gloriana; or, The Unfulfill'd Queen. Elizabeth in Albion, a Faerie world. 1979 World Fantasy Award Winner.

Sexuality • Elizabethan England.

Nix, Garth

(AW) (YA) Sabriel. When she receives her father's necromancy tools, Sabriel is off on a quest to find him (if he is still alive) to free him from the dead. Won both the Best Fantasy Novel and Best Young Adult Novel in the 1995 Australian Aurealis Awards.

Necromancy • Quest.

Nye, Jody Lynn

Waking in Dreamland. In a world where people's appearances constantly shift, Roan was odd because he always looked the same.

Dreams • Shapeshifting.

O'Leary, Patrick

The Gift. In intricately wrought tales within tales within tales, O'Leary vividly depicts the lives of two great wizards. While trying to have his deafness cured, Simon, the prince, is struck by the curse of hearing everyone's thoughts. As he spirals into madness in the horrendous cacophony, he seeks magical knowledge to cure himself and be avenged upon the Usher of the Night, who caused his affliction. When his parents are killed by a horrible, sweeping fire started by Tomen, the ominous bird who accompanies the Usher, Tim, a twelve-year-old woodcarver's son, starts his quest for magical knowledge and the ability to ride the winds.

Magic • Quest • Dark Fantasy.

Peake, Mervyn

Gormenghast trilogy. The world of the Gothic imagination follows Titus through life and the immense edifice Gormenghast.

Dark Fantasy • Labyrinths.

Titus Groan (1946).

Gormenghast (1950).

Titus Alone (1959).

Scott, Melissa, and Lisa Barnett

(YA) Point of Hopes (annotated in Chapter 17).

Detection • Astrology.

Volsky, Paula

The Wolf of Winter. In a Russia-like alternate world, a young prince takes up necromancy and uses his power over ghosts to try to secure rule for himself.

Russia • Necromancy • Ghosts.

Wells, Angus

Lords of the Sky. Daviot, a Dhar storyteller, wants peace between his people and the Ahn, who send magical airboats to wage war on them. On his quest to the lost lands of the North with an amnesiac Ahn warrior and a beautiful blind mage, Daviot finds that a weapon of peace can wreak more destruction than generations of war.

Quest • Technology • Storytelling • Magic.

Willey, Elizabeth

Prospero series. Rich in language and characterization, this series may be too slow moving for aficionados of swashbuckling adventure fantasy.

Literary Fantasy • Politics • Dragons.

The Well-Favored Man. After his father and uncle have disappeared, Prince Gwydion is forced into ruling the Dominion of Argylle. While he just wants to enjoy a life of intrigue, gossip, and viniculture, he is instead forced to deal with a plague of monsters, a dragon, and a mysterious long-lost sister.

A Sorcerer and a Gentleman.

The Price of Blood and Honor.

Williamson, Jack

Demon Moon. Zorn struggles to learn the secrets of his homeworld before it falls prey to malign creatures from another world.

Science Fantasy • Technology.

Wolfe, Gene

Book of the New Sun tetralogy. This is a science fantasy tetralogy featuring some of the best world building ever seen. Wolfe's Book of the Long Sun series, while set in the same world, is more science fiction than fantasy.

Science Fantasy.

 The Shadow of the Torturer. 1981 World Fantasy Award Winner.

 The Claw of the Conciliator (combined in *Shadow and Claw*). 1981 Nebula Award Winner. 1982 Locus Poll Winner.

 The Sword of the Lictor. 1983 Locus Poll Winner. 1983 August Derleth Award Winner.

The Citadel of the Autarch (combined in *Sword and Citadel*).

D's Picks

Brooks, Terry. Magic Kingdom of Landover series. (p. 107)

Card, Orson Scott. Chronicles of Alvin Maker. (p. 102)

Dreyfuss, Richard, and Harry Turtledove. *The Two Georges.* (p. 103)

Foster, Alan Dean. The Spellsinger series. (p. 109)

Jones, Diana Wynne. *A Sudden Wild Magic.* (p. 110)

L'Engle, Madeleine. *A Wrinkle in Time.* (p. 110)

Le Guin, Ursula K. *The Lathe of Heaven.* (p. 111)

Pullman, Philip. His Dark Materials series. (p. 111)

Chapter 11

Time Travel

Time travel is common in both science fiction and fantasy. The distinction I make between the two types of time travel is the mode used. Time travel involving a machine, a computer, or some kind of scientific explanation is not included here. Time travel involving magic or other inexplicable methods of travel is included. Time travel is a huge genre in and of itself, when science fiction and romance are added. Bontly and Sheridan annotate 219 time travel romances in volumes 1 and 2 of *Enchanted Journeys Beyond the Imagination* (Blue Diamond Publications, 1996). Readers who like time travel should check the science fiction and romance sections of libraries and bookstores for more books they will enjoy.

Curiously enough, time travel is one of the subgenres in fantasy in which adult and teen reader's interests do not have much overlap.

Bond, Nancy

YA **Another Shore.** Working at a historical site in costume precipitates a journey into the past.

Younger Readers.

Cherryh, C. J.

Morgaine series. Morgaine travels through time and space to destroy gates that have been used by an alien race to manipulate time.

Science Fantasy.

Gate of Ivrel.

Well of Shiuan.

Fires of Azeroth.

Cooney, Caroline B.

🟡 Time Travel Trilogy.

> **Both Sides of Time.** Annie falls in love and through time to 1895.
>
> **Other Side of Time.** Strat's life in the Victorian era becomes unbearable and he travels forward to Annie's time.
>
> *Romance.*
>
> **Prisoner of Time.** Devonny wishes she could follow her older brother Strat through time to escape being forced by her father to marry a stuffy English lord. Drawn into the 1990s by Annie's brother Tod, Devonny discovers she can't escape all of her problems.
>
> *Younger Readers.*

Gabaldon, Diana

Outlander series. These extremely lengthy and spicy novels are discussed in Chapter 18. This series is popular with older teens even though it is most definitely for adult readers.

> *Romance • Scotland.*
>
> **Outlander.**
>
> **Dragonfly in Amber.**
>
> **Voyager.**
>
> **Drums of Autumn.**

Griffin, Peni R.

> 🟡 **Switching Well.** Involves two girls, two eras, and one well that switches them in time.
>
> *Younger Readers.*

L'Engle, Madeleine

> 🟡 **An Acceptable Time.** Polly travels 3,000 years into the past to the time of the druids.
>
> *Younger Readers.*

Lindbergh, Anne

> 🟡 **Nick of Time.** Nick, a boy from 2094, shows up at the Mending Wall school in 1994.
>
> *Younger Readers.*

Matheson, Richard

> 🔴 **Bid Time Return** (also published as *Somewhere in Time*, which was also the title of the movie based on it starring Christopher Reeve). A man falls in love with a woman he saw in a picture, and through willing himself to be with her, travels back in time. 1976 World Fantasy Award Winner.
>
> *Romance • Film.*

Millhiser, Marlys

> **The Mirror.** On the eve of her wedding, a young woman looks into an antique mirror and is transported back in time, switching places with her grandmother on the eve of her wedding.
>
> *Romance • Mirrors • Colorado.*

Park, Ruth

 Playing Beatie Bow. When she follows a raggedy girl from the playground, Abigail finds that she was meant to go back in time.

Younger Readers • Australia.

Tepper, Sheri S.

 Beauty. Beauty travels through time to a future without magic. Locus Poll Winner.

Fairy Tales.

Vande Velde, Vivian

 A Well-Timed Enchantment. When she accidentally drops her watch down a well, a young teen goes back in time. Her only friend, a cat, is turned into a boy and carried back to medieval times with her.

Younger Readers • Cats • France.

Yolen, Jane

 The Devil's Arithmetic. Hannah is thrust back in time to a Polish village and ends up in a Nazi concentration camp.

Younger Readers • Holocaust.

D's Picks

Chapter 12

Paranormal Powers

Paranormal powers, not necessarily created by magic, allow the talented ones to do more than ordinary humans. In many cases telepathic abilities link a human with an animal, much as a wizard is linked to a familiar. Other paranormal powers include telepathy between humans or even one-sided telepathy, where the telepath can hear what is in others' minds; telekinesis; precognition, or the ability to see the future; immortality; and shapeshifting, changing from a human to an animal.

Psionic Powers

Psionic powers include the abilities to communicate telepathically with other beings, to see into another's thoughts, to see the future, and to move objects or oneself through space.

Bradley, Marion Zimmer

Darkover series. Telepathy called *laran* is used as the form of long-distance communication in this series. Although the series was begun as science fiction, Bradley's fans, like fans of McCaffrey's Pern series, consider it fantasy. There are several series or groupings of titles set in this world.

Science Fantasy • Telepathy • Women Warriors • Romance • Technology.

Ages of Chaos series. The Towers are conducting a tyrannical breeding program to create people with unnaturally powerful *laran*.

Stormqueen! A thousand years after landfall, Darkover has returned to a feudal level, depending on psi powers and psi weapons.

Hawkmistress! Rejecting humanity, Romilly is happy with the rare *laran* called the MacAran Gift, which gave her mastery over horse and hawk. But the people of the Towers who share her talents need her in this time of chaos.

Darkover Landfall. A lost ship of Terran origin lands on a planet lit by a dim red sun. The colonists and crew are divided between those who want to stay and those who want to leave. Then the Ghost Wind blows and the powers of Darkover claim them.

Hundred Kingdoms series. Continuous border conflicts create a multitude of small, belligerent kingdoms.

Two to Conquer. Bard di Asturien and Varzil the Good are opponents. Terran Pul Harrell is the exact duplicate of Varzil's enemy.

The Heirs of Hammerfell.

Renunciates series. Two orders of women, the priestesses of Avarra and the warriors of the Sisterhood of the Sword, set themselves apart from the patriarchal feudal nature of Darkover during the Ages of Chaos and the time of the Hundred Kingdoms.

The Shattered Chain.

Thendara House.

City of Sorcery.

Against the Terrans—First Age series. "After the Hastur Wars, the Hundred Kingdoms are consolidated into the Seven Domains, and ruled by a hereditary aristocracy of seven families, called the Comyn, allegedly descended from the legendary Hastur, Lord of Light. It is during this era that the Terran Empire rediscovers Darkover."

Rediscovery. Written with Mercedes Lackey, this is science fiction rather than fantasy.

The Spell Sword.

The Forbidden Tower. Four defied the powers of the matrix guardians, forming an "unnatural alliance" and building the Forbidden Tower.

Star of Danger.

The Winds of Darkover.

Against the Terrans—Second Age series. After the initial shock of recontact begins to wear off, the younger and less traditional elements of Darkovan society begin a real exchange of knowledge with the Terrans, teaching them Darkovan matrix technology and learning Terran science and technology.

The Bloody Sun.

The Heritage of Hastur.

The Planet Savers.

Sharra's Exile.

The World Wreckers.

Exile's Song.

The Shadow Matrix. Margaret has the Alton Gift, one of the most dangerous and strongest types of *laran,* but she needs to learn how to control it because an unseen enemy has been tampering with her telepathic channels. She is in love with Mikhail Lanart-Hastur, and they both are drawn to the ruins of an ancient tower, where they travel back in time.

Time Travel • Romance.

Marion Zimmer Bradley's Darkover is a collection of stories. The popularity of Darkover has taken it into the realm of shared worlds (see Chapter 15).

Science Fantasy • Shared Worlds.

Eisenstein, Phyllis

Alaric the Minstrel series. Orphaned Alaric can teleport.

Teleportation • Music.

Born to Exile.

In the Red Lord's Reach.

Fancher, Jane S.

Dance of the Rings series.

Politics • Magic.

Ring of Lightning. Darius Rhomandi defied the tyrannical priesthood to find another source of the magical leythium and lead a group of his followers to found the new city of Rhomatum. Three hundred years later, three of his descendants must overcome their mistrust, jealousy, and opposing political views to save Rhomatum from its ancient enemy and internal political unrest.

Ring of Intrigue. The Rhomandi dynasty is threatened with the sudden death of the ringmaster of Rhomatum, who was responsible for channeling and controlling the magical leythium that fuels the city. Three brothers struggle to save the city created by their ancestor, Deymorin trying to resurrect long fallow defenses, Nekaenor attempting to bring order to a shocked city, and Mikhyel following a convoluted trail that takes him to the heart of the leythium web itself.

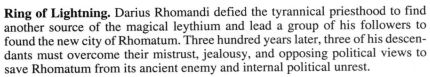
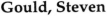

Gould, Steven

Ⓨ Jumper. A young man discovers he has the ability to teleport.

Contemporary Fantasy • Teleportation.

Greeno, Gayle

Ghatti's Tale series. Bondmate pairs consist of a human Seeker linked telepathically to truth-reading, cat-like ghatti, who contribute to keeping order in the world. Reminiscent of Lackey's Valdemar books.

Cats.

Finders Seekers.

Mind-Speaker's Call.

Exile's Return.

Harper, Tara K.

Ⓨ Wolfwalker. Dion is a healer who must kill to survive. Her telepathic bond with her wolf companion is useful when she undertakes a quest to find her brother.

Telepathy • Wolves.

Ⓨ Shadow Leader. Dion is captured on the way home and forced to fight in the arena.

Ⓨ Storm Runner. Features the final battle against the neighboring land to free their wolves and wolfwalkers from enslavement.

Huff, Tanya

Quarter series.

Music • Assassins • Necromancy.

Sing the Four Quarters. Bards can sing elementals invoking the magic kigh of air, earth, water, and fire.

Fifth Quarter. Bannon and Vree, a brother and sister team of assassins, trip a magical trap that allows their target to steal Bannon's body. If he is to survive, he must share Vree's body as they try to reclaim his own from Gyhard.

No Quarter. Former imperial assassin Vree is housing both her own and Gyhard's kigh, or spirits, in her body. In an attempt to find him a body they have traveled to Shkoder, where bards sing the four quarters, communicating with the kigh of earth, air, water, and fire. Vree and Maggie, an apprentice Healer who can sing the fifth quarter, set out on a quest to find and stop Kars, who kills and then animates the dead, causing great disruption in the kigh.

King, Stephen

Firestarter. A young girl who is pyrokinetic (having the ability to start fires with her mind), possibly as the result of government experiments done on her parents, flees from the agents of a terrifying government conspiracy.

Pyrokinesis.

Lackey, Mercedes

🆈🅰 World of Valdemar series. Valdemar, a world where telepathy is used to help ensure justice, and an elite group chosen for their unique aptitudes forms an intimately empathic connection with horse-like companions, has been so popular it has become a shared world series (see Chapter 15). World of Valdemar features several series:

Heralds of Valdemar trilogy.

Horses • Telepathy.

Arrows of the Queen. Once a runaway, Talia has been chosen by the Companion Rolan to be trained as a herald and one of the queen's own elite guard.

Arrow's Flight. When Talia goes to Ancar's realm to investigate his suitability as a husband for Princess Elspeth, she discovers that an evil and ancient sorcery is loose that may destroy Valdemar unless she can send a warning to the queen in time.

Arrow's Fall. Now a full herald, Talia rides forth to patrol the kingdom and dispense herald justice throughout the land.

The Queen's Own is the title of the omnibus edition.

Vows and Honor series.

Oathbound.

Oathbreakers.

🆈🅰 Last Herald Mage series.

Homosexuality.

Magic's Pawn. Vanyel wants to be a bard, but he was born with near-legendary abilities to work both herald and mage magic. Because if left untrained his talent could be a menace, he is sent to live with his aunt, Savil.

Magic's Promise. Vanyel and his Companion Vfandes are drawn into a magical holocaust in a neighboring kingdom, as wild magic takes its toll on Valdemar.

Magic's Price. Valdemar is besieged on all fronts: the king is dying, the neighboring kingdom of Karse is at war with them, and forbidden magic is being used against them. Vanyel, the most powerful herald mage ever known, is the primary target of the evil that is poisoning the land.

YA Mage Winds series.

Winds of Fate. Elspeth, herald and heir to the throne, must find a mentor to awaken her mage abilities so she can fight against the menace creeping forth from the Uncleansed Lands.

Winds of Change. Elspeth has arrived at the Vale of the Tayledras Clan to learn from the Hawkbrother Adepts, but the Vale is attacked by a mysterious Dark Adept, plunging Elspeth into a maelstrom of war and sorcery.

Winds of Fury.

YA Mage Storms series. (Set on Valdemar but not part of one of the interior series.)

Storm Warning. The Companions may have to reveal long-hidden secrets as Valdemar and Karse ally to combat the monarch of the Eastern Empire, whose magical tactics may be beyond any known sorcery.

Storm Rising. Mysterious mage-storms are wreaking havoc, inundating both Valdemar and Karse with earthquakes, monsoons, and ice storms, not to mention venomous magical creatures. The ruler of Karse, High Priestess Solaris, confirms the worst fears of the heralds: if the cause of the storms can't be found, their entire world will end in a magical holocaust.

By the Sword.

Lackey, Mercedes, and Larry Dixon
YA Mage Wars series. This is a prequel to the World of Valdemar, consisting of the following books.

Magic • Telepathy • Horses • Gryphons • Shared Worlds.

Black Gryphon. A magical Cataclysm destroys the strongholds of two of the most powerful mages in the world. Urtho, the creator of the gryphons, is killed and his forces go into exile. The harshness of the times turns Skandranon Rashkae, the black gryphon, to white.

White Gryphon. The residents of the city White Gryphon, having finally achieved a sense of security, find it shattered when a fleet of the mysterious Black Kings appears in their harbor.

Silver Gryphon. The people of White Gryphon have trained an elite guard force called the Silver Gryphons to protect their city. Silverbade, daughter of Amberdrake the Healer, has joined the Silver Gryphons. She is eventually paired with Tadrith, son of Skandranon, to man a remote guardpost. Suddenly all their magic disappears.

Owlflight is not a part of Mage Wars, but takes place shortly after *Storm Breaking*.

See Chapter 15, "Shared Worlds," for more books set in Valdemar.

McCaffrey, Anne

🅐 Pern series. Dragon riders communicate telepathically with fire-breathing, world-saving, telekinetic flying steeds. McCaffrey supports her contention that her series is science fiction with evidence from her novels involving the dragons of Pern, but many of her readers consider it fantasy and themselves fantasy readers. The sequence is not always clear: the Dragonriders of Pern trilogy and the Harperhall of Pern series take place in the same time frame, but one was written for adults and one for teens. McCaffrey's readers care not about that distinction, reading every Pern book they can get their hands on. The Pern books were not published in chronological order, and in fact the elements of time travel that are included cloud the sequence issue further. The books are listed here in the order that McCaffrey uses on her Web site at http://members.aol.com/dragnhld/ (accessed Dec. 1, 1998).

Dragons • Music • Science Fantasy.

Dragonsdawn. The colonists on Pern thought they had found paradise until a deadly spore called Thread started falling, threatening them with annihilation. Pern's most talented geneticists start to work on a solution, then discover that the tiny flying lizards indigenous to Pern have a unique way of fighting Thread.

Moreta, Dragonlady of Pern. The pleasant anticipation of waiting for Moreta's dragon Queen Orlith to clutch (give birth to baby dragons) is shattered when a mysterious plague strikes. So many die that the dragonriders may not be able to char enough Thread out of the sky to save the land.

Nerilka's Story. Appalled by her father's refusal to help the other holds beset by plague, Nerilka packs up medicines and supplies and runs away to Ruatha Hold to help stem the epidemic.

Dragonflight. After a long interval, Thread has returned to Pern, where the strength of the Weyrs has been weakened by the reluctance of the holds to support them through the years that Thread did not fall. Without enough riders and dragons, Pern is facing great peril, and Lessa, Weyrwoman of Benden, hatches a daring and dangerous plan that may be the salvation of the planet.

Dragonquest. The Oldtimers are breeding dissent, and pesky fire lizards are stirring up trouble as the Weyrs continue to fight Thread to ensure the future safety of Pern.

The White Dragon. As dragons go, Ruth is a runt, but that doesn't matter to Lord Jaxom, who has an extraordinarily strong bond with the white dragon. Training in secret, they find themselves in trouble, but they are also in a position to avert a major disaster.

The Renegades of Pern. Some of the people on Pern are holdless, living outside the safety and protection of solid rock. Some of them are outlaws, and the worst are Lady Thella's renegades, preying on the holdless as they evade dragonrider patrols. Aramina's family has lost their hold, but she has a telepathic ability that makes her a prime target for the renegades.

All the Weyrs of Pern. After the discovery of the original colonists' artificial intelligence in the ruins of the original settlement, formulating a plan for annihilating the threat of Thread may be possible.

Chronicles of Pern: First Fall. This is a collection of short stories about the early years of settlement on Pern.

The Dolphins of Pern. When the colonists first arrived on Pern, they brought intelligent dolphins with them, but lost contact during the struggle for survival when Thread began to fall. Now that the threat of Thread may be over T'lion, Readis, and the "ship fish" begin to revive the bond.

Dragonseye. No Thread had fallen on Pern for over 200 years, and the only thing to remind the people is the presence of the dragons. One holder doesn't even believe in Thread. As signs appear heralding a Thread fall, the Weyrleaders, Holders, and Craftmasters try to come up with a way to preserve knowledge of the dangers for future generations.

The Masterharper of Pern. Born in Harper Hall, Robinton is a prodigy. Fax of High Reaches Hold hates harpers in general and Robinton in particular, wanting to keep his lands free of the learning that harpers bring. Robinton, believing the teaching songs, knows that harpers are essential to the survival of Pern because Thread will fall again, and the people must be prepared.

Dragonsong. Menolly wants to sing but her father thinks it's disgraceful, so she feels she has no choice but to run away.

Younger Readers.

Dragonsinger. At the Harper Hall, Menolly strives for acceptance so she can fulfill her ambition to sing.

Younger Readers.

 **Dragondrums.** Piemur's fate changes when his voice does. 1980 Balrog Award Winner.

Younger Readers.

The Girl Who Heard Dragons is a short story collection that does include a Pern novella, but also has several other SF stories in it.

Dragons • Science Fantasy • Time Travel • Short Stories.

Nye, Jody Lynn

The Dragonlover's Guide to Pern, Second Edition, by Jody Lynn Nye (Del Rey, 1997), is a guide to the people, places, and creatures of Pern.

Murphy, Pat

 The Falling Woman. Elizabeth Butleris an archaeologist who has the ability to see history. When she finds an ancient Mayan woman who can see the future, her life changes, in this 1987 Nebula Award-Winning Novel.

Literary Fantasy • Archaeology.

Norton, Andre

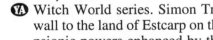 Witch World series. Simon Tregarthe finds himself transported from Cornwall to the land of Estcarp on the planet Witch World, where the natives have psionic powers enhanced by the use of jewels. The series was started in the early 1960s and remains popular.

Parallel Worlds • Telepathy • Shapeshifting • Shared Worlds.

Witch World.

Web of the Witch.

World Year of the Unicorn.

Three Against the Witch World.

Warlock of the Witch World.

Sorceress of the Witch World.

YA Witch World books set in the lands of Arvon and High Halleck, across the sea from Estcarp, feature characters who can shapeshift.

> **Year of the Unicorn.**
>
> **The Crystal Gryphon.**
>
> **Spell of the Witch World.**
>
> **The Jargoon Pard.**
>
> **Gryphon in Glory.**
>
> **Gryphon's Eyrie** (co-written with A. C. Crispin).

YA Other books by Norton set in the Witch World:

> **Horn Crown.**
>
> **Trey of Swords.**
>
> **Zarsthor's Bane.**
>
> **Lore of the Witch World.**
>
> **'Ware Hawk.**
>
> **Were-Wrath.**
>
> **Serpent's Tooth.**
>
> **The Gate of the Cat.**

The popularity of this series has created spin-offs in shared world series (listed in Chapter 15).

Pierce, Tamora

Immortals series. Daine communicates empathically with a wolf pack and has the ability to shift into an animal shape.

> *Shapeshifting • Younger Readers.*

YA **Wild Magic.** Daine thinks what she has is a knack with animals, not real magic. When she discovers she has the ability to sense the presence of dangerous immortal creatures appearing all over the land, she knows she must learn to use her magic to save the kingdom.

YA **Wolf-Speaker.**

YA **Emperor Mage.**

YA **Realms of the Gods.**

Simmons, Dan

> **The Hollow Man.** Telepath Jeremy Bremen is thrust into a nightmare cacophony of others' inner voices when his beloved wife, Gail, the only other telepath he knows, dies a torturous death from cancer. As he flees across the country trying to escape the torrent of others' thoughts, he encounters a mobster and a truly horrifying woman who is the embodiment of evil. They both want to kill him.
>
> *Dark Fantasy • Telepathy.*

Springer, Nancy

YA **The Hex Witch of Seldom.** A girl discovers she has second sight.

> *Younger Readers.*

West, Michelle

 Hunter's Oath. The people of Breodanir worship the Hunter god, a god unknown in the rest of the world. The Hunter born are blessed and cursed with a psionic ability that enables them to see out of the eyes of their dog packs. Because their obsession with the hunt leaves them little room for dealing with day-to-day reality, at age eight they are bound to a commoner huntbrother. The bond is so deep that a huntbrother cannot survive the death of his Hunter. The Hunters are responsible for the well-being of all in Breodanir. Without the annual Sacred Hunt, famine would visit the land and decimate the population. The Sacred Hunt does exact a price, though: in it the participants become the prey of the Hunter god, and at least one becomes the ultimate sacrifice each year. Stephen, a young thief in the King's City, is captured and taken to Elseth to serve as huntbrother to Gilliam. Their lives entwine as they grow to maturity, and Stephen finds he has been placed under a "wyrd" that brings strange beings and deadly situations into their lives.

Gods • Telepathy • Dogs.

 Hunter's Death. Stephen and Gilliam journey to an ancient city once ruled by the Lord of Hell himself, in an attempt to stop him from imposing his rule on the world.

Wieler, Diana

 Ranvan series.

Ranvan: The Defender.

Ranvan: A Worthy Opponent.

Ranvan: Magic Nation. Rhan is off to study cinema, television, stage, and radio at Southern Alberta Institute of Technology, where he finds he has a true gift for one-camera video that is enhanced by flashes of precognition. As a video knight he meets new people, runs into someone from his past, and becomes enmeshed in a skinhead murder conspiracy.

Gaming • Dreams • Precognition.

Shapeshifters

Shapeshifters have the ability to take on a different form, usually that of an animal. Shapeshifting tales seem to have a preponderance of Southwestern settings, but they can occur anywhere. In addition to simply shifting into the form of an animal, or from animal to human, some shapeshifters are animals having the natures of both aspects. Werewolves are common in romantic fantasy (Chapter 18) and dark fantasy (Chapter 16). They are also included in this chapter in the section on supernatural beings.

Kindl, Patrice

 Owl in Love. Raised on spiders and mice by parents who recognized her owlness at birth, Owl, who has the ability to shift into her avian form and fly, is now in love with one of her high school teachers. She is also troubled by a seemingly deranged owl that has moved into the neighborhood. 1995 Mythopoeic Award Winner.

Younger Readers • Owls.

Murphy, Shirley Rousseau

Ⓨ Catswold Portal. When she is thrust through a dimensional portal, Melissa takes the form of a cat.

Cats • Parallel Worlds.

Roberson, Jennifer

Cheysuli series. A race of humans has the ability to communicate psionically with animals whom they can shapeshift into. A prophecy shapes the lives of a family.

Telepathy • Multiracial Beings.

Shapechangers. The Cheysuli are a race of magical shapeshifting warriors. They were allies of the king and champions of the realm until a princess ran away with a Cheysuli liege man, starting a war of annihilation against the Cheysuli race. Alix, daughter of the princess and the liege man, struggles to master the magic in her blood and accept her place in an ancient prophecy.

The Song of Homana. The magical race of the Cheysuli has been forced to flee the land of Homana, but now Prince Carillon is returning from exile with his Cheysuli shapechanging liege men.

Legacy of the Sword. The populace is afraid of Prince Donal, who is being trained as the first Cheysuli in generations to assume the throne.

Track of the White Wolf. Niall, Prince of Homana, must undertake a journey across war-torn lands to claim his bride.

A Pride of Princes. If Homana and Cheysuli are to survive, Niall's sons, Brennan, Hart, and Corin, must all follow the paths for which they are fated.

Daughter of the Lion. Corin's twin sister Keelyalone has the power to shapeshift into any form, but that may not save her from the many traps that have been set for her.

Flight of the Raven. Aidan, son of Brennan, is visited by a mysterious being, who sends him on a quest to find a series of golden links. At the same time, Ihlinis sorcery is used against him.

A Tapestry of Lions. Kellin, heir to Homana's throne, refuses to fulfill his part of the Prophecy of the Firstborn.

Immortality

The prospect of living forever is a theme that is considered more frequently in science fiction than in fantasy, but occasionally there is a book that puts immortality in the fantasy realm. The Highlander series (Chapter 15) is a shared world series dealing with immortality. Many vampire dark fantasy and horror novels also touch on the immortality aspect.

Babbitt, Natalie

Ⓨ Tuck Everlasting. Is the gift of eternal life a blessing or a curse?

Younger Readers.

Duncan, Lois

Locked in Time. Nore finds out a terrible secret about her new stepmother and stepbrothers.

Dreams.

Eddings, David, and Leigh Eddings

Belgarath the Sorcerer. The character Belgarath, an immortal, appears throughout the Eddings's series, but this volume is primarily about him.

Grimwood, Ken

Replay. Forced to live his life over and over and over again, Jeff Winston (in a story much like the Bill Murray film *Groundhog Day)* repeats the same years again and again, but with the knowledge of how he has done it the times before. 1988 World Fantasy Award Winner.

Supernatural Beings

The supernatural plays a big part in fantasy. Many supernatural beings are more commonly found in horror novels, but the elements of scariness and terror found in horror are not present in fantasy. Paranormal beings can be the embodiment of good or evil, or be very ordinary. Examples of supernatural beings are angels, vampires, werewolves, and fairy tale-like fairies.

Cooper, Susan

The Boggart. This tale of a mysterious spirit longing to return to Scotland is of more interest to children than to young adults, despite being a YALSA-L Fantasy List nominee.

Crowther, Peter, ed.

Heaven Sent: 18 Glorious Tales of the Angels. (DAW, 1995). Includes eighteen stories by Charles de Lint, John Brunner, Ed Gorman, and others. Uses "the angel image to present a strong, diverse collection of afterlife sagas. Some paint frightening scenarios; others are humorous or reflective. All use the angel image and idea to create many intriguing images and situations."—*Midwest Book Review.*

Angels • Short Stories.

Dedman, Stephen

The Art of Arrow Cutting. When he receives a key from a woman who later is found dead, a photographer becomes the target of three supernatural beings out of Japanese mythology.

Japan • Myths • Demons • Magic • Contemporary Fantasy.

Murphy, Pat

Nadya (annotated in Chapter 16).

Werewolves • Westerns • Historical Fantasy.

Scarborough, Elizabeth Ann

The Godmother. Felicity Fortune, a modern-day fairy godmother, comes to the aid of Rose Samson, a Seattle social worker who is involved in several cases that are reminiscent of tales from the Brothers Grimm.

Godmother's Apprentice.

Fairy Tales • Godmothers • Contemporary Fantasy.

Shinn, Sharon

Samaria series.

Angels • Technology • Music.

Archangel. In the land of Samaria, Gabriel needs a wife to sing beside him, but Rachael, the woman selected by an oracle, doesn't seem to be exactly what he wanted.

Jovah's Angel. Set 150 years after *Archangel,* in this story some things in Samaria have changed.

NEW **The Alleluia Files.** A mortal woman and an angel form an uneasy alliance to find out the truth about Jovah.

D's Picks

Bradley, Marion Zimmer. Darkover series. (p. 125)

Gould, Steven. *Jumper.* (p. 127)

Grimwood, Ken. *Replay.* (p. 135)

Huff, Tanya. Quarter series. (p. 128)

Kindl, Patrice. *Owl in Love.* (p. 133)

Murphy, Pat. *The Falling Woman.* (p. 131)

Chapter 13

Graphic Novels

Sometimes described as overgrown comics, graphic novels feature stories set to artwork. Usually the violence is also graphic. Art Speigelman's *Maus* and *Maus II* depict mice in the roles of Jews during the Holocaust. These works may be the best-known graphic novels in schools and libraries. Reviews of graphic novels are hard to come by. Occasionally *VOYA* reviews a few. *VOYA* does feature a column in its pages, written by Kat Kan, that deals with graphic novels and teens. *Publishers Weekly* calls this subgenre trade comics rather than graphic novels, but generally reviews non-fantasy graphic novels. Many are restricted for sale to those over the age of eighteen.

Fortunately there are now bibliographic guides to these books. *Graphic Novels* by D. Aviva Rothschild (Libraries Unlimited, 1995), a self-proclaimed graphic novel evangelist, provides an enthusiastic look at this area with astute reviews along with important bibliographic information. Her chapter on fantasy lists forty-nine titles, some of which are series with detailed reviews. Steve Weiner's *100 Graphic Novels for Public Libraries* was published in 1996 by Kitchen Sink Press. Weiner, the graphic novel reviewer for *Library Journal*, includes advice on shelving, display, and preservation of graphic novels and comics as well as a bibliography of recommended titles.

Barr, Mike W., and Brian Bolland

Camelot 3000. King Arthur is brought into the future.

Arthurian Legend • Futuristic Fantasy.

Gaiman, Neal

Sandman series.

Dreams.

Preludes & Nocturnes.

The Doll's House.

Dream Country.

Season of Mists.

A Game of You.

Fables & Reflections.

Brief Lives.

Sandman: World's End. Stephen King provides a terrific introduction to this outstanding entry in Gaiman's deservedly popular series. Using the device of stories within stories, sometimes within other stories, Gaiman presents the reader with a rewarding panoply of adventure and fantasy. The old trope of travelers being stranded at an inn and telling their stories has some interesting new facets. Included are a tale of a fairy sent as ambassador to a corrupt country where the secular and religious have dangerously merged, the tale of a young sailor's adventures, a story of a young man destined to be the youngest president of the United States, and a story of a land where death is the cornerstone of life and disposing of the bodies a high art. The Sandman series is the cream of the crop of original graphic novels.

McCaffrey, Anne

🅈🄰 Dragonflight (Eclipse Graphic Novels). Lela Dowling, Cynthia Martin, and Fred Von Tobel, illustrators. This is a good adaptation of McCaffrey's novel. The vivid illustrations add to this tale of a young woman who rides the queen dragon and through intelligent thought and observation figures out how to save the planet after four centuries free of the peril of Thread. It is hoped that readers of this graphic novel will be enticed into reading the excellent text version of this series.

Dragons • Time Travel.

Moore, Alan, and Dave Gibbons

Watchmen. This is a story of superheroes and their fall from grace.

The Paranormal.

Nocenti, Ann

🅈🄰 Someplace Strange (Epic Comics). John Bolton, illustrator. In classic fantasy tradition, two quarreling brothers are transported to a nightmare world, where they meet Zebra, a punk artist. Her anger looses a horrifying evil being. The brothers discover what is really important.

Parallel Worlds • Dreams.

Pini, Wendy, and Richard Pini

Elfquest series. This series of high fantasy stories featuring magic and a band of elves known as the Wolfriders has spawned regular text novels. This is arguably the best fantasy graphic novel series because of its combination of high fantasy and colorful artwork. Cutter, leader of the Wolfriders, must lead his band from their homeland after it is destroyed by humans. Cutter's destiny is to unite the tribes of elves, facing humans, trolls, and the other clans.

Wolves • Elves • Epic.

Speigelman, Art

 **Maus: A Survivor's Tale Volumes I & II.** The Holocaust as animal fantasy. "The very haunting story of Vladek Spiegelman and his story of the Nazi death camps of World War II. Set in two volumes, Vladek recounts his history of pre-WWII Germany and his trials and tribulations before, during, and after the Holocaust. Art chronicles his father's history and the current events that surrounded his interviews with his father. Volume One was considered so powerful, that it won the Pulitzer Prize. As with almost all holocaust stories, this is a very powerful, and often painful reminder of our past. While graphic in areas, this story is one that everybody should read at least once."—Nathan Sundance Herald.

Holocaust • Mice.

Talbot, Bryan

 The Tale of One Bad Rat. The best graphic novel with a social conscience since *Maus.* The artwork evolves with the story of Helen, a young woman who finds homelessness preferable to life with a sexually abusive father. The story is set in England. Helen is introduced in a tube station, where she is the prey of weirdoes and criminals. After being befriended by some other homeless teens, she moves into a squat with them. Her one true friend is her pet rat. After a tragedy, Helen ends up in the area where Beatrix Potter wrote and illustrated her beloved children's stories and finds new friends, a new life, and a job, and faces her problems. Grittily realistic, *The Tale of One Bad Rat* conveys the inner damage inflicted on Helen in a concise and empathetic manner. The illustrations really expand our view of her inner landscape.

Child Abuse • Rats • Runaways.

Tolkien, J. R. R.

 The Hobbit (Ballantine). David Wenzel, illustrator. When a beloved classic is adapted into a visual format it can never match the rich beauty imagined by the reader, but all the same Wenzel does a good job of interpreting Tolkien's descriptions. In a way this reminded me of Julius Lester's *Othello,* an exquisite retelling of Shakespeare's classic tale. In both cases the original is not and cannot be improved upon, but perhaps the adaptation makes the story more accessible to those who otherwise would have missed an essential read. As adaptations go, this is an excellent one.

Quest • Elves.

D's Picks

Gaiman, Neal. *Sandman: World's End.* (p. 138)

Speigelman, Art. *Maus: A Survivor's Tale.* (p. 139)

Talbot, Bryan. *The Tale of One Bad Rat.* (p. 139)

Chapter 14

Celebrity Characters

Real and imaginary people are alive and well in the pages of fantasy literature. The characters of fiction and other forms of literature take on historical reality in a fantasy world rich in literary allusion. Some of their creators join their characters. The following books make the reader draw on whatever allusions a lifetime of reading has provided.

Anderson, Poul

 A Midsummer Tempest. 1975 Mythopoeic Award Winner.

Shakespeare • Parallel Worlds.

Bova, Ben

Triumph. Joseph Stalin and Franklin Delano Roosevelt are featured in this alternate history tale.

World War II • Joseph Stalin • Franklin Delano Roosevelt • Alternate History.

Davidson, Avram

The Phoenix and the Mirror. This story casts Virgil as a wizard.

Virgil • Magic • Alternate History.

de Camp, L. Sprague, and Fletcher Pratt

The Compleat Enchanter: The Magical Misadventures of Harold Shea (collective title for: *The Incompleat Enchanter, The Castle of Iron: A Science Fantasy Adventure*, and *The Wall of Serpents*). Contains adventures in the worlds created in literature, including Spenser's *Faerie Queene*.

Parallel Worlds.

Farmer, Philip José

Riverworld series.

 To Your Scattered Bodies Go. 1972 Hugo Award Winner. Reborn on a world with a huge central river, Sir Richard Francis Burton and Alice Hargreaves, the real-life model for Alice in Wonderland, are on a quest to discover the end of the river.

The Fabulous Riverboat.

The Dark Design. "Everyone who ever died from Karl Marx to Tom Mix to Joan of Arc wakes up the day after death on the banks of a giant river."—Jacket copy.

The Magic Labyrinth.

Gods of Riverworld. The author joins with the characters, from Mark Twain to everyone who ever died.

Gemmell, David

Dark Prince. In a parallel universe, the evil King Philip of Macedon kidnaps a four-year-old Alexander into his reality.

Alexander the Great.

Kerr, Katharine, ed.

Weird Tales from Shakespeare. (DAW, 1994). Includes "Playbill," by Bill Daniel; "An Augmentation of Dust," by Diana L. Paxson; "Aweary of the Sun," by Gregory Feeley; "The Will," by Barbara Denz; "The Tragedy of K1," by Jack Oakley; "Ancient Magics, Ancient Hope," by Josepha Sherman; "Queen Lyr," by Mark Kreighbaum; "It Comes from Nothing," by Barry N. Malzberg; "The Tragedy of Gertrude, Queen of Denmark," by Kate Daniel; "Alas, My Bleedin," by Dennis L. McKiernan; and "The Muse Afire," by Laura Resnick.

Shakespeare • Short Stories.

Maguire, Gregory

Wicked: The Life and Times of the Wicked Witch of the West. Could it be that Elphaba has been given a bum rap in Oz?

Witches • Oz • Parallel Worlds.

Myers, John Myers

Silverlock. This is an ignored and woefully neglected classic. The picaresque hero's adventures are in the worlds of great Western literature. The reader's delightful challenge is to identify stories, characters, and allusions.

Parallel Worlds • Literature.

Powers, Tim

The Anubis Gates. Samuel Coleridge pops up in this tale of a modern-day scholar's time travel foray into the seventeenth century.

Time Travel • Alternate History.

Rucker, Rudy

The Hollow Earth.

Alternate History.

Swanwick, Michael

Jack Faust. Yet again *Faustus* is reworked, this time giving him access to twentieth-century knowledge in exchange for his soul.

Dealings with the Devil.

Weis, Margaret, ed.

Fantastic Alice. (Ace, 1995). Several fantasy authors provided short stories featuring Lewis Carroll's Alice. Included are "Something to Grin About," by Lawrence Watt-Evans; "The Rabbit Within," by Gary A. Braunbeck; "Epithalamium," by Roger Zelazny; "A Common Night," by Bruce Holland Rogers; "Cocoons," by Robin Wayne Bailey; "Hollywood Squares," by Lawrence Schimel; "Another Alice Universe," by Janet Asimov; "And with Finesse," by Janet Pack; "Alice's Adventures in the Underground Railroad," by Tobin Larson; "Muchness," by Jody Lynn Nye; "Transformation and the Postmodern Identity Crisis," by Lisa Mason; "Teapot," by Jane M. Lindskold; "Who Killed Humpty Dumpty?" by Mickey Zucker Reichert; "Wonderland Express," by Connie Hirsch; "Waiting for the Elevator," by Kevin T. Stein; "Conundrums to Guess," by Peter Crowther; and "A Pig's Tale," by Esther M. Friesner.

Short Stories • Alice in Wonderland • Parallel Worlds.

Williams, Tad

Caliban's Hour. Twenty years after the events that unfolded in Shakespeare's *The Tempest*, Caliban seeks his revenge on Miranda.

Shakespeare • Alternate History.

D's Picks

Bova, Ben. *Triumph.* (p. 141)

Chapter 15

Shared Worlds

Shared world novels are set in a world conceived and developed by one author but used by other authors in their books. Sometimes they arise from a novel or series so beloved that it achieves a life of its own, such as Norton's Witch World and Bradley's Darkover. Some shared worlds are created when a group of like-minded authors want to work together, as in the case of the Trillium series, in which Andre Norton, Julian May, and Mary Zimmer Bradley co-authored the first volume, then each built on it with their own titles. Shared worlds do not necessarily evolve from other books. They can have their genesis in television or movies or in games, either computerized or not.

The introduction of shared world stories, in which an imaginary world is created by an editor, author, or group and is then used as a background by several authors, has resulted in the publication of several series. As in any set of works created by committee, there is bound to be some variation in quality, but the following series have been popular ("relentlessly popular," noted one reviewer). The stories belong in the category of magic-and-adventure.

The shared worlds seem to be particularly popular in series based on role-playing games, movies, television shows, and even computer games. A growing trend in shared world universes has been for the setting and characters to appear in several different venues: novels, graphic novels, comics, games, and on the Internet.

Shared World Series

Bard's Tale

This series is based on the computer game.

Gaming • Music • Magic.

Lackey, Mercedes, and Mark Sheperd. **Prison of Souls.**

Lackey, Mercedes, and Josepha Sherman. **Castle of Deception.**

Lackey, Mercedes, and Ru Emerson. **Fortress of Frost and Fire.**

Lisle, Holly, and Aaron Allston. **Wrath of the Princes.** Surviving shipwreck, revolution, and the malevolent magic of a serpent goddess, Kin Underbridge and Halleyne dar Dero have returned to Feyndala, but they aren't safe because the forces of four nations are arrayed against them.

——. **Thunder of the Captains.** The leaders of two mighty nations and other travelers find that the struggle for survival after a shipwreck is far more perilous than international diplomacy. Their survival depends on the honor of an awkward valet and the uncertain magic of two bards in training.

Sheperd, Mark. **Escape from Roksamur.**

Sherman, Josepha. **The Chaos Gate.**

🅨🅐 Bordertown

This quintessential shared world series basically created the urban fantasy subgenre. Some of the titles below are annotated in the urban fantasy section (Chapter 9). Locus called this "the finest of all shared worlds."

Urban Fantasy • Parallel Worlds • Faerie.

Bull, Emma. **Finder.**

Shetterly, Will. **Elsewhere.**

——. **NeverNever.**

Windling, Terri, and Delia Sherman, eds. **The Essential Borderland.**

Windling, Terri, and Mark Alan. **Borderland.**

——. **Bordertown.**

——. **Life on the Border.**

Conan series

The world created by Robert E. Howard for his heroic barbarian sword and sorcery hero, Conan, has turned into a shared world universe, with books written by L. Sprague de Camp, Lin Carter, Poul Anderson, Robert Jordan, Ronald Green, John C. Hocking, and others. (For a list of titles see Chapter 3.) Conan has also been the subject of a graphic novel series.

Graphic Novels • Film • Barbarians • Sword and Sorcery.

Darkover series

Marion Zimmer Bradley's Darkover also has proven to be popular enough to work its way into a shared world universe. Bradley's own Darkover novels are listed in Chapter 12. She has edited the following anthologies of stories set in the world she created.

Witches • Parallel Worlds • Telepathy • Women.

Domains of Darkover. (DAW, 1990).

Four Moons of Darkover. (DAW, 1988).

Free Amazons of Darkover. (DAW, 1985).

The Keeper's Price. (DAW, 1980).

Leroni of Darkover. (DAW, 1991).

The Other Side of the Mirror. (DAW, 1987).

Red Sun of Darkover. (DAW, 1987).

Renunciates of Darkover. (DAW, 1991).

Snows of Darkover. (DAW, 1994).

Sword of Chaos. (DAW, 1987).

Towers of Darkover. (DAW, 1993).

Brian Froud's Faerielands

In a unique twist on shared worlds, artist and illustrator Brian Froud created over fifty drawings and paintings that were divided among Charles de Lint, Patricia A. McKillip, Midori Snyder, and Terri Windling. They were all to write their own stories based on the premise that Faerie, "inextricably bound as it is to natural forces, is gravely threatened by the ecological crisis that human beings have brought to our world."—Brian Froud's introduction to *Something Rich and Strange.*

Art • Magic.

de Lint, Charles. **The Wild Wood.**

McKillip, Patricia A. **Something Rich and Strange.**

15

Highlander series

Throughout the ages, immortal Duncan MacCleod has battled the forces of evil. A movie series, a television series, and a book series.

Immortality.

Henderson, Jason. **The Element of Fire.**

Holder, Nancy. **Measure of a Man.**

Lettow, Donna. **Zealot: A Novel.**

McConnell, Ashley. **Scimitar.**

Neason, Rebecca. **The Path: A Novel.**

Roberson, Jennifer. **Scotland the Brave.**

Magic series

Larry Niven created a universe of magic in *The Magic Goes Away.* Niven then edited two illustrated volumes. Originally published in the late 1970s and early 1980s, they were reprinted in 1993.

Magic.

The Magic May Return. Includes stories by Fred Saberhagen, Dean Ing, Steven Barnes, Poul Anderson, and Mildred Downey Boxon.

More Magic. Includes stories by Larry Niven, Bob Shaw, Dian Girard, and Roger Zelazny.

Magic in Ithkar series

Magic in Ithkar. Four volumes edited by Andre Norton and Robert Adams include stories by Lin Carter, George Alec Effinger, Linda Haldeman, R. A. Lafferty, and others.

Magic, the Gathering

At this series' base is the role-playing game, but novels and anthologies have taken off from it much as the Dragonlance books have taken off from Dungeons and Dragons™. Here the setting is the magical world of Dominica, where minotaur and elf are embroiled in a bloody conflict involving foul magic and dirty politics. The following is not a comprehensive list, just examples of titles and authors.

Elves • Alternate Worlds.

Braddock, Hanovi. **Ashes of the Sun.**

Emery, Clayton. **Final Sacrifice.**

Forstchen, William R. **Arena.**

McLaren, Teri. **The Cursed Land. Song of Time.**

Vardeman, Robert E. **Dark Legacy.**

Ice, Kathy, ed.

——. **Distant Planes: An Anthology (Magic, the Gathering).** (HarperPrism, 1996). Includes "Insufficient Evidence," by Michael A. Stackpole; "Festival of Sorrow," by Robert E. Vardeman; "Chef's Surprise," by Sonia Orin Lyris; "Foulmere," by Stonefeather Grubbs; "God Sins," by Keith R. A. DeCandido; "A Monstrous Duty," by Kathleen Dalton-Woodbury; "What Leaf Learned of Goblins," by Hanovi Braddock; "Dual Loyalties," by Glen Vasey; "Distant Armies," by Peter Friend; "Better Mousetrap," by Jane M. Lindskold; "The Face of the Enemy," by Adam-Troy Castro; "Horn Dancer," by Amy Thomson; "Shen Mage-Slayer," by Laura Waterman; "Defender," by Edd Vick; and "The Old Way to Vacar Slab," Michael G. Ryan.

Merovingen Nights series

This series was created by C. J. Cherryh in the novel *Angel with the Sword,* in which Altair Jones saves a man from drowning in one of many canals. Following are anthologies featuring stories by Cherryh, Janet Morris, and Chris Morris.

Alternate Worlds • Women • Adventure.

Festival Moon. (DAW, 1987).

Fever Season. (DAW, 1987).

Endgame. (DAW, 1991).

Troubled Water. (DAW, 1988).

Smuggler's Gold. (DAW, 1988).

Divine Right. (DAW, 1989).

Floodtide. (DAW, 1990).

Myst series

Based on the computer game, it is still to be seen whether the books catch on or not.

Gaming.

Miller, Robin. **The Book of Atrus.**

Seaport of Liavek series

Liavek. Shetterly, Will, and Emma Bull, eds. (Ace, 1985). Includes stories by Gene Wolfe, Steven Brust, Pamela Dean, Jane Yolen, Patricia C. Wrede, Steven Brust, Barry B. Longyear, Alan Moore, Megan Lindholm, and others.

Liavek: The Players of Luck. (Ace, 1986).

Liavek: Wizard's Row. (Ace, 1988).

Liavek: The Spells of Binding. (Ace, 1988).

Liavek: Festival Week. (Ace, 1990).

Serrated Edge series

Created by Mercedes Lackey, Serrated Edge is a shared world urban fantasy involving elves who have formed SERRA, the South Eastern Road Racing Association.

Lackey, Mercedes, and Larry Dixon. **Born to Run.** Mixes hot cars, rock and roll, abused youth, and elves.

> *Music • Car Racing • Child Abuse • Shared Worlds.*

> ———. **Chrome Circle.** Mixes Celtic rock, elves and dragons, and romance.

> *Music • Shared Worlds.*

Lackey, Mercedes, and Holly Lisle. **When the Bough Breaks.** A girl with psi powers could wreak havoc on Faerie if her pain is not relieved.

> *Shared Worlds.*

Lackey, Mercedes, and Mark Sheperd. **Wheels of Fire.** Features a parental kidnapping, a racing car, and an elf to the rescue.

> *Shared Worlds.*

Sheperd, Mark. **Spiritride.** Set in Albuquerque, this story features motorcycles and skateboards.

> *Skateboarding • Shared Worlds.*

> ———. **Elvendude.** Features a prince of Faerie who is raised in our world so he can grow to adulthood and take on the dark elves.

> *Changelings • Shared Worlds.*

Shadowrun series

Not only a shared world series, Shadowrun was originally a popular role-playing game from FASA Corporation. It combines urban and dark fantasy in a dangerous future. A few cover descriptions are quoted to show the diversity and flavor of this world.

> *Gaming • Sword and Sorcery • Urban Fantasy • Dark Fantasy • Elves.*

Charrette, Robert N. **Never Deal with a Dragon.**

> ———. **Choose Your Enemies Carefully.**

> ———. **Find Your Own Truth.**

> ———. **Just Compensation.**

> ———. **Into the Shadows.**

Dowd, Tom. **Night's Pawn.**

——. **Burning Bright.**

Findley, Nigel D. **House of the Sun.**

——. **Lone Wolf.**

——. **2XS.**

——. **Shadow Play.**

Kenson, Stephen. **Technobabel.** "He awoke in a body bag, his brain fried, a black hole where his memory should be. If not for the cool carbon-fiber blade concealed in the bones of his arm, he would've been dead for sure. But Michael Bishop—a.k.a. Babel, messiah of the Matrix—is back in the game."—*Technobabel* cover copy.

"Renraku Computer Systems has defied the accords of the Corporate Court. Now they must decipher the secrets of the otaku—and Babel is the technoshaman reborn for the job. But Netwalking in the shadows of the electron jungle means initiation into deadly magacorporate intrigue—and discovering more about Babel's own team than he fears he should know. As allies become adversaries, Babel breaks through the dreaded black ice security to find a doorway to the future—and signs of a corp war looming on the horizon–one that could destroy the technoworld and beyond . . . forever."—*Technobabel* cover copy.

Koke, Jak. **Dead Air.** Combat bikers in a maze pound each other for points.

Dragon Heart Saga.

——. **Stranger Souls.**

——. **Clockwork Asylum.**

——. **Beyond the Pale.** "In the mission given him by the Dragon Dunkelzahn, Ryan Mercury promises to deliver the magical Dragon Heart safely to the metaplanes, where Theyla and her song are all that defend the earth against the onslaught of the Enemy. But when the protector of the world is swallowed by the Chasm, all hope for the future disappears with her. Now nothing stands between humanity and the greatest scourge the planet have ever known."—Jacket copy.

"The enemy bears unlimited power, all of it evil. With Theyla destroyed, and the metaplanes unprotected, the Enemy's army of flesh-shredding beasts is about to lay waste to the world. As the ultimate battle is waged between the forces of good and evil, Ryan and his dauntless shadowrunners have only two options: total victory or certain death."—*Beyond the Pale* cover.

Kubasik, Christopher. **The Changeling.**

Odom, Mel. **Preying for Keeps.**

——. **Headhunters.** "Somebody aced the dragon Dunkelzahn, and one of the mysterious links to the assassination is flat on his back in slab city: a double agent with two identities—both out of commission. Now he's the most-wanted carcass in Tacoma. Jack Skater's mission? Sleaze past the high-tech funeral security, outwit the Knight Errants, cop the stiff, and keep it on ice long enough to get the answer to the shadowrunners' life-and-death question: what's so hot about a stone-cold corpse?"—*Headhunters* cover.

Pollotta, Nicholas. **Shadowboxer.** A dwarf mercenary is trying to find the meaning of the word "IronHel."

Sargent, Carl, and Marc Gascoigne. **Streets of Blood.**

——. **Noseferatu.**

——. **Black Madonna.**

Smedman, Lisa. **The Lucifer Deck.** In twenty-first-century Seattle, Pita witnesses a corporate mage being murdered by the violent spirit he had just conjured.

——. **Blood Sport.** Mama Grande, who prophesied rivers of blood and an Earth in flames, was murdered by two Yucatan missionaries hiding a secret of the Gods. Leni, ex-Lone Star ranger and possible granddaughter of the deceased, teams up with combat biker Rafael and ventures into the dark heart of Aztlan, where human sacrifice is all the rage.

Smith, Nyx. **Who Hunts the Hunter.**

——. **Striper Assassin.**

——. **Fade to Black.**

——. **Steel Rain.**

Spector, Caroline. **Worlds Without End.**

15

⑯ Starshield series

This series was created by Margaret Weis and Tracy Hickman. The first book of the series is *The Mantle of Kendis-Dai,* originally published with the title *Starshield: Sentinels.* Book 2 is *The Nightsword.* The authors have invited readers to help create the Starshield Universe by participating via a Web site: http://www.starshield.com.

Epic • Magic.

⑯ Sword of Knowledge series

This series was created by C. J. Cherryh. Each novel has a different co-author (listed below).

Alternate Worlds • Women.

Asire, Nancy. **Wizard Spawn.**

Fish, Leslie. **A Dirge for Sabis.**

Lackey, Mercedes. **Reap the Whirlwind.**

Thieves' World-Sanctuary series

Created by Robert Lynn Asprin and Lynn Abbey in 1978, all the books in this series were published between 1979 and 1990. While many shared world series are based on games, a game was created based on the Thieves' World series. A graphic novel series was also created. Among the contributing authors were Lynn Abbey, Poul Anderson, Robert Lynn Asprin, Robin Wayne Bailey, Marion Zimmer Bradley, John Brunner, C. J. Cherryh, Christine DeWeese, David Drake, Diane Duane, Philip José Farmer, Joe Haldeman, Vonda N. McIntyre, Chris Morris, Janet Morris (who has done separate novels on Thieves' World: *Beyond Sanctuary, Beyond Wizard-Wall,* and *Beyond the Veil*), Andrew Offutt, Diana L. Paxson, and A. E. van Vogt. The first six volumes (original paperbacks) were gathered into two volumes by the Science Fiction Book Club (with endpaper maps).

> *Alternate Worlds • Magic • Assassins.*

Volume I, **Sanctuary**, brings together books 1–3: *Thieves' World, Tales from the Vulgar Unicorn,* and *Shadows of Sanctuary.*

Volume II, **Cross Currents**, brings together books 4–6: *Storm Season, The Face of Chaos,* and *Wing of Omen.*

Book 7: **The Dead of Winter.**

Book 8: **Soul of the City.**

Book 9: **Blood Ties.**

Book 10: **Aftermath.**

Book 11: **Uneasy Alliances.**

Book 12: **Stealer's Sky.**

> *Graphic Novels. • Gaming.*

Trillium series

Bradley, Marion Zimmer, Julian May, and Andre Norton. *Black Trillium.* Three grand dames of fantasy writing, three princesses, three quests, three magical talismans; one single tale, cowritten by the three was not enough, so Andre Norton followed up with *Golden Trillium,* Julian May with *Blood Trillium* and *Sky Trillium,* and Marion Zimmer Bradley with *Lady of the Trillium.*

> *Quest • Magic • Women.*

Valdemar series

Mercedes Lackey made the world of Valdemar so fully developed and enticing that others wanted to write stories set there. *Sword of Ice: And Other Tales of Valdemar,* edited by Mercedes Lackey and John Yezeguielian (DAW, 1997), includes eighteen stories by Mickey Zucker Reichert, Larry Dixon, Tanya Huff, Michelle Sagara, and others.

> *Magic • Telepathy • Horses.*

Wild Cards series

Based on a science fiction premise that a virus was transmitted to those of Earth by aliens, this series has the feel of superheroic fantasy, featuring interaction among three sects: Aces, those empowered by the virus; Jokers, those mutated by it; and Nats, those unaffected by it. This world was so popular that it spawned a graphic novel series.

Graphic Novels • Superheroes • Science Fantasy.

The following are edited by George R. R. Martin. While most of the series consists of linked stories not individually attributed to a specific author, three individual novels also are part of the series.

Wild Cards: A Mosaic Novel.

Aces High.

Jokers Wild.

Aces Abroad.

Down and Dirty.

Ace in the Hole.

Dead Man's Hand. John J. Miller and George R. R. Martin are co-authors of this novel, seventh in the series.

One-Eyed Jacks.

15

Jokertown Shuffle.

Double Solitaire. By Melinda Snodgrass. This novel is set in the Wild Card World.

Dealer's Choice.

Turn of the Cards. By Victor Milan. This novel is set in the Wild Card World.

Card Sharks: Wild Cards. (No. 1 of New Cycle series). Includes stories by Roger Zelazny, Melinda Snodgrass, William F. Wu, Laura J. Mixon, Kevin A. Murphy, Victor Milan, Stephen Leigh, and Michael Cassutt.

Marked Cards.

Black Trump.

Witch World series

Andre Norton's Witchworld books are another example of a beloved series being taken up by others to turn its setting into a shared world. Norton's own Witchworld novels are listed in Chapter 12. With A. C. Crispin, she wrote *Songsmith.*

Tales of the Witch World. The following were edited by Andre Norton. They contain short stories by a variety of authors.

——. **Tales of the Witch World 1.**

——. **Tales of the Witch World 2.**

——. **Tales of the Witch World 3.**

——. **Four from the Witch World.**

🔼 **Witch World: The Turning.** This is a subseries of Tales of the Witch World. Norton has co-written some of the books in the subseries. The subseries is set after the Witches of Estcarp caused a massive cataclysm that moved mountains, intending to block an invasion. The disaster crippled their powers and brought chaos and destruction to all of Witch World.

———. **Storms of Victory.** With P. M. Griffin. Contains two tales, one about a young Sulcar woman who uses her newly awakened powers to do battle with an ancient evil, and the other about a Dales Lady who defends her lands from pirates with the help of falconers.

———. **Flight of Vengeance.** With P. M. Griffin and Mary Schaub. "A young healer and a lost borderer find new hope and the means to thwart an ancient evil awakened by the cataclysm."—Jacket copy.

———. **On Wings of Magic.** With Patricia Mathews and Sasha Miller.

🔼 **Secrets of the Witch World.**

———. **The Key of the Keplian.** With Lyn McConchie.

Dungeons and Dragons and Other Role-Playing Game Worlds

The game of Dungeons and Dragons (role playing in a sword-and-sorcery setting) has fostered a considerable body of original paperback publications too numerous to list here. The publisher TSR, now Wizards of the Coast, has had great success marketing books based on its various fantasy role-playing games. The most popular authors are the duo of Margaret Weis and Tracy Hickman. Also extremely popular in hardcover, with users of public libraries, is R. A. Salvatore. Many of these fantasy novels, based on a game, verge on horror, with vampires, werewolves, and other types of shapeshifters playing important roles. Popular authors of these novels include:

Bergstrom, Elaine. Ravenloft series.

Elrod, P. N. Ravenloft series.

Golden, Christie. Ravenloft series.

King, J. Robert. Ravenloft series.

Kirchoff, Mary L. Dragonlance series.

Lowder, James. Ravenloft series.

Parkinson, Dan.

Salvatore, R. A. Forgotten Realms series.

Thurston, Robert.

Weis, Margaret, and Tracy Hickman. Dragonlance series.

Some of the series that fall into this category are:

Al-Qadim (Arabian legend).

Dark Sun (Alternate world).

Defenders of Magic.

🔼 Dragonlance (Epic sword and sorcery).

Dragonlance Chronicles.

Dragonlance Heroes.

Dragonlance Legends.

Dragonlance Meetings Sextet.

Dragonlance Preludes.

Dragonlance Tales.

Dragonlance Villains.

Dragonlance Warriors.

Elven Nations trilogy.

YA Forgotten Realms (Epic sword and sorcery).

GreyHawk (Sword and sorcery).

YA Ravenloft (Gothic horror, dark fantasy).

YA Shadowrun (Urban fantasy).

Novels Based on Role-Playing Games

The following authors have written books that have a fantasy role-playing setting. While not shared world tales, they share a background with them.

15

Cushman, Carolyn

YA **Witch and Wombat.** In this tongue-in-cheek tale, the world is losing its magic, so a witch takes a crew of fantasy virtual-reality gamers on a quest to help bring back the magic.

Parallel Worlds • Witches • Magic.

McKiernan, Dennis L.

YA **Caverns of Socrates.** A group of tournament-winning gamers must win through on their quest or they will never be able to break free of the super computer that now holds them.

Rosenberg, Joel

YA Guardians of the Flame series (annotated in Chapter 3).

The Sleeping Dragon.

The Sword and the Chain.

The Silver Crown.

D's Picks

Cushman, Carolyn. *Witch and Wombat.* (p. 155)

Lackey, Mercedes, and Mark Shepherd. *Wheels of Fire.* (p. 149)

Shetterly, Will. *NeverNever.* (p. 146)

Chapter 16

Dark Fantasy

Defining dark fantasy is as difficult as defining fantasy itself. It is very much linked with horror. Both genres scare or terrify, but in dark fantasy the emphasis is on the magic and often on the conflict between good and evil, while in horror the emphasis is on terrifying the reader. Many titles included in this chapter appear on horror lists; many authors who are known for writing horror have been recipients of major fantasy awards. Many of the books covered here will also appear in the forthcoming horror volume of this series.

Beagle, Peter S.

The Innkeeper's Song. Told from multiple viewpoints, this confusing tale follows many characters, including one who has lost his love to drowning and then, after she dies but is not gone, to a mysterious woman. 1994 Locus Poll Winner.

Giant Bones. Includes six novellas set in the world of *The Innkeeper's Song.*

Bischoff, David

Quoth the Crow. Late professor of the work of Poe, William Blessing returns from the dead to make right a future gone seriously awry.

Blaylock, James P.

All the Bells on Earth. Humans try to beat the forces of evil after the devil tries to claim three souls brokered by a bogus minister.

Bradbury, Ray

① **The October Country.**

① **Something Wicked This Way Comes.** This is a chilling classic.

Brooks, Terry

① **Running with the Demon.** Teenager Nest lives next to a park that she, as women in her family have for generations, protects with her best friend Pick, a sylvan (a tiny twig forest creature). The growing population of feeders, invisible evil creatures, foretells a disastrous future for our world unless Nest can summon the necessary magic to stop the demon that knows the secret of her parentage.

Card, Orson Scott

Lost Boys. A Mormon game designer moves his family to a town where young boys have been disappearing.

Gaming • Religion.

de Lint, Charles

The Dreaming Place. Dreaming can be deadly when an old curse and a search for totem spirits become entwined in this tale of two teenaged cousins.

Friedman, C. S.

Cold Fire trilogy. Ostensibly science fiction, these stories involve people who are plagued by nightmares that come to life.

Black Sun Rising.

When True Night Falls.

Crown of Shadows.

Science Fantasy • Dreams.

Joyce, Graham

⚑ **Requiem.** Recently widowed by a weird tragedy, Tom Webster resigns his teaching position and goes to Jerusalem, where Sharon, an old college friend, lives. In Jerusalem he is haunted by visions of an old Arab woman who seems to be trying to tell him something. He is given a segment of the Dead Sea Scrolls that seems to translate into a very different version of the crucifixion of Christ than that told by Mary Magdalene. Like an onion, layer after layer is peeled away gradually, going deeper and deeper into the heart of Tom's fears. *Requiem* is one of those quiet, dark fantasies that haunts the reader long after the last page is turned. It is so enthralling that it must be finished in one sitting. 1996 August Derleth Award Winner.

Literary Fantasy • Religion.

Klause, Annette Curtis

① **Blood and Chocolate.** Beautiful teenager Vivian Gandillon is lonely at her new high school in Maryland, where she has moved with her mother and the rest of her pack after her father was killed when their group of werewolves was run out of its rural West Virginia home. Without a leader the pack is undirected and at loose ends, a disaster waiting to happen. When humans start turning up dead, savaged by strong teeth, the pack is in peril. The description of changing into a wolf form is conveyed so vividly that one wants to howl. This sexy tale has everything—romance, mystery, and truth—making it a truly outstanding read and one of the best horror novels of the decade. Klause is to werewolves what Rice is to vampires.

Shapeshifting • Werewolves.

The Silver Kiss. This vampire romance pits brother against brother and good against evil.

Vampires.

Lackey, Mercedes

Diana Tregarde series. Diana is a witch detective as well as a romance novelist. (See also Chapter 17.)

Burning Water.

Native Americans.

Children of the Night.

Vampires.

Jinx High.

Lee, Tanith

Blood Opera series. The Scarabae family has some secrets. Is it just immortality or does vampirism play a part?

Dark Dance.

Personal Darkness.

Darkness, I.

The Secret Books of Paradys series. In an alternate world darkness, decadence, danger, and eroticism prevail.

The Book of the Damned.

The Book of the Beast.

The Book of the Dead.

The Book of the Mad.

Leiber, Fritz

Conjure Wife. Behind every great man is a witch. This classic Leiber tale is set in academia, where faculty wives/witches secretly enhance the careers of their husbands and destroy those of rivals. It has thrice been made into a movie.

Film • Witches.

Our Lady of Darkness. This book portrays horror in an urban fantasy world. 1978 World Fantasy Award Winner.

Urban Fantasy.

The Dealings of Daniel Kesserich: A Study of the Mass-Insanity at Smithville This long-lost novella was finally published in 1997. It deals with a woman possibly buried alive, a couple of missing men, and strange happenings in a Lovecraftian world.

MacIntyre, F. Gwynplaine

The Woman Between the Worlds. In London in 1898, a strange invisible woman fleeing a parallel world presents herself at a tattoo parlor, requesting full body tattoo to make her visible. "A stunning dark adventure with the flavor of H. P. Lovecraft, a hint of Edgar Rice Burroughs, and a richness of invention and language."—Charles Ardai (jacket copy).

Tattoos • Parallel Worlds.

Murphy, Pat

Nadya. A young female werewolf is orphaned after her parents are killed in their wolfish guises by her lover. She flees, disguising herself as a boy. On the trail west she meets up with Elizabeth, who was abandoned by her wagon train when her father fell ill. Together the young women head west, finding a child, the sole survivor of the massacred wagon train, and facing various and sundry dangers. Nadya feels a kinship with the Wolf clan of the tribe that assists them when Elizabeth is bitten by a snake, but they push on, facing starvation, thirst, and predators, and make it over the mountains to California, passing the camp of the ill-fated Donner party on the way. In Yerba Buena, Nadya realizes that no matter how much she loves Elizabeth she must give her wild wolfish side the wilderness she needs. She heads to Oregon, where she meets a unique multicultural community. As a western, *Nadya* tells the story of two very different, courageous women who triumph over the travails of the westward trail. As a story of a lone werewolf, it is so powerful that it makes the reader, for a few moments, see the world through lupine senses.

Werewolves • Homosexuality • Westerns.

Pierce, Meredith Ann

🅨🅐 Dark Angel trilogy. Written for children and young adults, this is a dark tale of romance and vampires. Long out of print, this beloved series was reissued in 1998.

The Dark Angel.

A Gathering of Gargoyles.

The Pearl at the Heart of the World.

Vampires.

Powers, Tim

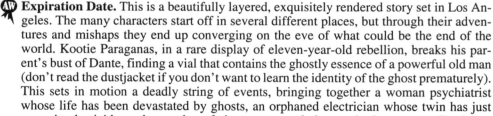

🅐🅦 **Expiration Date.** This is a beautifully layered, exquisitely rendered story set in Los Angeles. The many characters start off in several different places, but through their adventures and mishaps they end up converging on the eve of what could be the end of the world. Kootie Paraganas, in a rare display of eleven-year-old rebellion, breaks his parent's bust of Dante, finding a vial that contains the ghostly essence of a powerful old man (don't read the dustjacket if you don't want to learn the identity of the ghost prematurely). This sets in motion a deadly string of events, bringing together a woman psychiatrist whose life has been devastated by ghosts, an orphaned electrician whose twin has just committed suicide, and a number of ghost eaters and ghosts who have not realized they are dead and still wander the earth in corporeal form. *Expiration Date* is the winner of the 1996 Locus Award for Dark Fantasy.

Contemporary Fantasy • Ghosts • Los Angeles.

🅐🅦 **Last Call.** A gambler discovers that he lost more than he thought in a 1969 poker game involving Tarot cards. Now it is time to pay up. 1993 Locus Poll Winner. World Fantasy Award Winner.

Tarot • Contemporary Fantasy.

Yarbro, Chelsea Quinn

Saint-Germain series. This series emphasizes the vampire's longevity and reveals historical detail of the different eras in which he is involved.

Hotel Transylvania: A Novel of Forbidden Love.

The Palace.

Blood Games.

Path of the Eclipse.

Tempting Fate.

The Saint-Germain Chronicles (linked stories).

Out of the House of Life. Madelaine, Saint-Germain's nineteenth-century French lover, goes on an archaeological expedition to Egypt, where she receives a letter from the count telling of his life in Ancient Egypt.

The Spider Glass.

Darker Jewels. Ferenc Rakoczy, the Count Saint-Germain, is in Russia during the sixteenth-century reign of Ivan the Terrible.

Better in the Dark. Shipwrecked off the coast of Saxony in the year 938, Saint-Germain is held for ransom by Lady Ranegonda and falls in love with her as she faces outlaws and Danes.

Vampire Stories of Chelsea Quinn Yarbro.

Mansions of Darkness (Incan Peru).

Writ in Blood. Saint-Germain is to deliver one last proposal for peace in an attempt to stop World War I from starting.

Vampires.

16

Saint-Germain's lover Atta Olivia Clemens is featured in

A Flame in Byzantium.

Crusader's Torch.

A Candle for D'Artagnan. In seventeenth-century France, Olivia falls in love with D'Artagnan of "Three Musketeers" fame.

Vampires.

Weird Tales

Weird tales are strange stories of the occult and supernatural, often involving satanism and created mythologies.

Koontz, Dean

Phantoms.

Lovecraft, H. P.

"All my tales are based on the fundamental premise that common human laws and emotions have validity or significance in the cosmos-at-large." Lovecraft created an entire mythology, the Cthulhu Mythos, and defined it as "the fundamental lore or legend that this world was inhabited at one time by another race who, in practicing black magic, lost their foothold and were expelled, yet live on outside, ever ready to take possession of this earth again." The publisher Arkham House is named for Lovecraft's fantasy land.

At the Mountains of Madness.

The Dunwich Horror.

The Lurking Fear.

The Shuttered Room.

The Tomb.

Lumley, Brian

Fruiting Bodies and Other Fungi. This is collection of weird tales, including the title story about a fungus that is eating up the houses in a seaside village. The fungus is in turn being eaten away by the sea.

Necroscope series. Nathan Keogh is the Necroscope, a man who can talk with the dead.

Necroscope.

Vamphyri.

The Source.

Deadspeak.

Deadspawn.

Vampire World trilogy. Set in an extradimensional, vampire-inhabited world, this is a sequel to the Necroscope series.

Blood Brothers.

The Last Aerie.

Bloodwars.

Vampires.

D's Picks

Brooks, Terry. *Running with the Demon.* (p. 158)

Klause, Annette Curtis. *Blood and Chocolate.* (p. 158)

Leiber, Fritz. *Conjure Wife.* (p. 159)

Chapter 17

Fantasy Featuring Detection

As the lines between the genres waver and fade, some of the genres combine with delightful results. The clever and witty Lord Darcy series is the archetype. Creatures of dark fantasy—vampires, werewolves, mummies, and witches—frequently are featured in conjunction with detection.

Bacon-Smith, Camille

Eye of the Daemon. An ad promising "cases involving the occult handled with discretion" takes Marnie Simpson to the Philadelphia office of Bradley, Ryan, and Davis, Private Investigators, in search of her missing half brother.

Philadelphia • Private Investigators.

Bowker, David

Yorkshire police detective Vernon Lavergne encounters horrors in this series that combines dark fantasy and detection.

Yorkshire • Police Detectives.

The Death Prayer.

The Butcher of Glastonbury.

Cook, Glen

Garrett, P. I. series.

Private Investigators.

Sweet Silver Blues.

Bitter Gold Hearts.

Cold Copper Tears.

Old Tin Sorrows.

Red Iron Nights.

Dread Brass Shadows.

Petty Pewter Gods.

Deadly Quicksilver Lies.

Davis, Brett

Hair of the Dog. An ex-cop and a reporter are on the hunt for whomever tore out the throats of the researchers who had just announced a cure for lycanthropy.

Police Detectives • Werewolves.

Dedman, Stephen

The Art of Arrow Cutting. When he receives a key from a woman who later is found dead, a photographer becomes the target of three supernatural beings out of Japanese mythology.

Demons • Japan.

Garrett, Randall

Lord Darcy series.

Humor • Amateur Detectives • Magic.

Too Many Magicians.

Murder and Magic.

Lord Darcy Investigates. The preceding titles have been published in an omnibus edition as *Lord Darcy.*

Like Ian Fleming's James Bond, Lord Darcy refused to die with his creator, and the series was continued by Michael Kurland with *Ten Little Wizards* and *A Study in Sorcery.*

Goulart, Ron

The Prisoner of Blackwood Castle. A detective of the Challenge International Detective Agency finds himself in a land of magic.

Private Investigators • Magic.

Green, Simon R.

Hawk & Fisher series.

Hawk & Fisher.

Winner Takes All.

Wolf in the Fold.

Guards Against Dishonor.

The Bones of Heaven.

Hamilton, Laurell K.

Anita Blake series. This is a dark romantic fantasy about Anita Blake, Vampire Hunter, who can reanimate the dead as she seeks answers in this grisly but witty series.

Romance • Vampires • Werewolves • Humor.

Guilty Pleasures. Innocent vampires are being killed and Anita, who hunts those who do not live within the law, is out to find the culprit.

The Laughing Corpse. A murderous zombie is on the loose. Anita did not use a human sacrifice to raise it from the dead, so who did?

Circus of the Damned. Vampire Alejandro wants Anita for a servant, but Jean-Claude, also a vampire, wants her for something else.

The Lunatic Cafe. Anita Blake, vampire slayer and raiser of zombies from the dead, becomes embroiled in a case involving several missing lycanthropes, while at the same time falling in love with junior high school teacher and were-wolf Richard. Jean-Claude, the vampire Master of the City, is out to woo Anita, and creates a situation in which she agrees to date him even though she has become engaged to Richard. The details of lycanthrope society are fascinating, as are the snippets of witch and vampire lore. Tanya Huff's *Blood Price, Blood Trail, Blood Pact,* and *Blood Lines* also feature a strong female protagonist involved with preternatural beings.

 Bloody Bones. Anita is supposed to raise some 300-year-old dead folks in Branson, Missouri, but she finds she must call on Jean-Claude for help when she tries to solve the more recent murders of some teens. 1996 Best SF Romance of the Year Winner.

 Killing Dance. With a price on her head and professional killers on her trail, Anita makes a decision about her love life. Second place, 1997 Best SF Romance of the Year.

Burnt Offerings. An arsonist is targeting vampires.

Hood, Daniel

 Sleuthing sorcerer Liam Rhenford and his dragon familiar keep turning up murders to solve. Unfortunately, inheriting a familiar doesn't make one a wizard.

> *Familiars • Magic.*

Fanuilh.

Wizard's Heir. Liam and Fanuilh are stalking a mad ghost while on the trail of a mystery that has already resulted in one murder.

Beggar's Banquet.

Scales of Justice.

> *Magic • Dragons.*

Huff, Tanya

 Victory Nelson series. Vicki Nelson, former Toronto cop and now a private investigator, solves mysteries featuring the supernatural in conjunction with her ex-partner (now lover) and a vampire romance novelist.

> *Private Investigators • Vampires • Toronto • Romance.*

Blood Price. Ancient forces of chaos have been loosed on Toronto and Henry Fitzroy, vampire bastard son of King Henry VIII, must help Vicki and her former partner Mike find the source of the dark magic, or all their lives will be forfeit.

Blood Trail. Innocent Canadian werewolves are being killed. They turn to Henry Fitzroy for help. He enlists the help of Vicki Nelson, who can detect by daylight.

Blood Lines. A mummy has been sent to the Royal Ontario Museum. When someone unwittingly opens his sarcophagus, he is released to feed on the unwary and grow strong. Vicki alone must try to stop him, because Henry is nearly incapacitated by deadly visions of sunlight.

Blood Pact. When her mother's body disappears from the funeral home, Vicki discovers that something unnatural was behind her mother's death. With Mike and Henry, she investigates, finding that someone at the university is determined to keep Mrs. Nelson on the job—dead or alive!

Blood Debt. Henry's home has been invaded by wraiths who play a deadly nightly game, killing an innocent person each time Henry asks a question that has "no" for the answer.

Hughart, Barry

Master Li series. Set in seventh-century China, this series combines the charm of Robert Van Gulick's Judge Dee mysteries with fantasy and a Holmes-and-Watson ambiance. Aging sage Master Li and Number Ten Ox, his youthful sidekick, solve crimes with wit and hilarity.

China • Alternate History.

 Bridge of Birds: A Novel of Ancient China That Never Was. 1985 World Fantasy Award Winner. 1986 Mythopoeic Award Winner.

The Story of the Stone. Master Li and Number Ten Ox are called upon to investigate the brutal slaying of a monk and the theft of a seemingly inconsequential manuscript from the library of a monastery in the Valley of Sorrows.

Eight Skilled Gentlemen.

Lackey, Mercedes

Ⓨ Diana Tregarde series.

Burning Water.

Children of the Night.

Jinx High. Diana is a romance writer as well as a witch and detective (see also Chapter 16). She helps the police with investigations involving the supernatural.

Vampires • Romance.

Sacred Ground. Jennifer Talldeer is a private investigator and a shaman. She must work in both our world and the spirit world to solve a case that has placed Native Americans under suspicion.

Native Americans • Private Investigators.

Four & Twenty Blackbirds. Constable Tal Rufen becomes obsessed with solving the mysterious murders/suicides that are happening in Alanda.

Alternate Worlds • Magic.

Lethem, Jonathan

 Gun, with Occasional Music. This "noirish" winner of the 1995 Crawford Award is set in a world where news broadcasts are considered to be too depressing, so instead of an announcer, music indicates recent events.

Private Investigators • Science Fantasy • Futuristic Fantasy • Noir.

MacAvoy, R. A.

Tea with the Black Dragon. A 2000-year-old Chinese Imperial dragon in his human form helps in the search for a missing systems analyst.

Technology • Dragons.

Twisting the Rope. This sequel to *Tea with the Black Dragon* finds the dragon in his human guise as musician Mayland Long, embroiled in the mystery surrounding the death of an obnoxious member of Martha Macnamara's Irish band.

Music • Dragons.

Murphy, Shirley Rousseau

Joe Grey, cat detective series.

Cats.

Cat on the Edge. When he is witness to a murder, the feline detective who can understand, speak, and read human language and emotions finds his talents come with a price.

Cat Under Fire. Joe Grey and his feline flame Dulcie try to clear an innocent young man accused of murder and arson.

Cat Raise the Dead. Residents of a senior citizens' home are being tormented by a kidnapper, and Joe Grey is roped into helping them.

Rosenberg, Joel

🅈🄰 D'Shai series.

Performers • Alternate Worlds.

D'Shai.

Hour of the Octopus. Kami Dan'Shir is the first known detective in the very structured world of D'Shai, where he formerly belonged to a troupe of traveling acrobats.

Scott, Melissa, and Lisa Barnett

🅈🄰 **Point of Hopes.** Out-of-work soldier Philip Eslingen is drawn into pointsman (policeman) Nicolas Rathe's investigation into the disappearance of dozens of children from the royal city. On a world where astrology is a science, it may hold the only clues for finding the missing in time. The medieval-like setting and elements of fantasy, mystery, and astrology make this an appealing read.

Astrology • Alternate Worlds • Police Detectives.

Wolfe, Gene

Free Live Free. This involves a private detective in a modern setting of fantasy and science fiction.

Science Fantasy • Private Investigators • Contemporary Fantasy.

Pandora by Holly Hollander. When teen Holly Hollander finds an antique box with "Pandora" on it, criminologist Aladdin Blue is drawn into a murder investigation.

Myths.

Wrede, Patricia C.

🅈🄰 **Mairelon the Magician.** Kim, a guttersnipe, knows that there is something not quite right about a new magician who has appeared in the streets. Little does she know that their lives will become enmeshed.

Magic • Alternate History.

🅐 Magician's Ward. Kim, former street thief, is currently the ward of Lord Merrill, a.k.a. Mairelon the Magician. Kim is appalled when Mairelon's mother decides Kim must take her place in London society just when they are in the midst of trying to find out why their library was the target of a bungled burglary. The ordinary magic workers from the back streets have disappeared, allegedly hired by a mysterious individual. Also, someone is flinging around bizarre magic that has unpredictable results.

Romance • Magicians • Alternate History.

Zambreno, Mary Frances

🅐 Untitled series. In a world with a strong Lord Darcy flavor, Jerymyn, a young wizard to be, and his familiar, Delia, solve mysteries entwined in magic. A young adult series enjoyed by adult readers.

Younger Readers • Alternate Worlds • Familiars.

A Plague of Sorcerers.

Journeyman Wizard.

D's Picks

Garrett, Randall. Lord Darcy series. (p. 164)

Hamilton, Laurell K. *The Lunatic Cafe.* (p. 164)

Huff, Tanya. *Blood Lines.* (p. 165)

Wrede, Patricia C. *Magician's Ward.* (p. 168)

Zambreno, Mary Frances. *A Plague of Sorcerers.* (p. 168)

Chapter 18

Romantic Fantasy

A major trend in the romance genre in the 1990s has been the infusion of fantasy. Time travel, supernatural beings, Faerie, and other fantasy tropes have been showing up liberally in romance novels. The combination of the genres is a delight to those who love both. This type is so popular that it has its own award, the Sapphire Award; a bibliography, *Enchanted Journeys Beyond the Imagination,* by Susan W. Bontly and Carol J. Sheridan (Blue Diamond Publications, 1996); and a monthly print newsletter, *The Alternative Reality Romance Connection.* A monthly online newsletter, *Science Fiction Romance,* at http://members. aol.com/sfreditor/index.htm (accessed Dec. 1, 1998) not only covers the combination of romance and science fiction but also with fantasy and the paranormal as well.

Romance is often a major element in many subgenres of fantasy. Many sword and sorcery books, particularly epics, have a strong element of romance. Romance also appears in many stories and books fitting into the fairy tale category. It is not at all uncommon to find it in fantasy involving alternate universes, parallel worlds, and in fact throughout the genre.

Ashe, Rebecca

Masque of the Swan. Never having thought of herself as attractive, orphan Caralisa is surprised by her popularity when she attends holiday revels with a mysterious masked man who purports to be the legendary Count of Samothrace. This interesting combination of Greek mythology and "The Phantom of the Opera" provides some entertainment, but the romance between the characters never ignites the reader's imagination.

Fairy Tales.

Carroll, Susan

The Bride Finder. Anatole St. Leger, the scion of a family gifted with strange powers, sends the "Bride Finder" to bring him back a sturdy, plain, horse-loving wife. The Bride Finder has always found the right spouses for the St. Legers, and those who marry one not so chosen are doomed. Rev. Fitzleger, the current Bride Finder, brings back sensible, tiny, book-loving, red-haired Madeline, who grows to love this lord who frightens all others. A lively combination of fantasy, the supernatural, and captivating romance.

Psionic Powers • Alternate History.

Deveraux, Jude

Knight in Shining Armor. Tears at a crypt bring a medieval knight to the twentieth century.

Time Travel.

Gabaldon, Diana

Outlander series.

Time Travel.

Outlander. A British nurse, a veteran of World War II on holiday in Scotland with her husband, walks between some standing stones and finds herself in the eighteenth century, where she falls in love and finds that her husband's ancestor is her deadliest enemy.

Dragonfly in Amber.

Voyager.

Drums of Autumn.

Krinard, Susan

Prince of Dreams. While searching for her missing cousin, Diana Ransom enters the world of a handsome vampire.

Vampires.

Prince of Wolves. While seeking to solve the mystery of her parents' deaths, Joelle meets a mysterious French-Canadian high in the remote Canadian Rockies who harbors a wolfish secret.

Werewolves.

Prince of Shadows. Wolf researcher Alexandra finds that the mysterious man she is so fascinated with is more than he first appears to be and could be suspected of a grisly murder.

Vampires • Wolves.

Twice a Hero. Mackenzie goes to an ancient Mayan ruin to try to fulfill her grandfather's dying wish to right a wrong. She finds herself traveling in time and finding love and adventure in the steamy jungle.

Time Travel.

Krinard, Susan, Maggie Shayne, Lisa Higdon, and Amye Liz Saunders

Bewitched. These four novellas feature magic, from a cat who transforms into a woman, to witchcraft, to love spells.

Cats • Witches • Magic.

Resnick, Laura

In Legend Born. A group of five comes together, forging an alliance against the hedonistic Valdani, who have forced the Sileria mountain clans into slavery.

Shayne, Maggie

Annie's Hero. In a heroic but deadly act, a young father loses his life and memory of the present when he becomes a paranormal knight fighting the evil Dark Knights.

Heroes.

Fairytale. Is the power of Faerie needed for Adam to find his own true love?

Faerie.

Forever Enchanted. Bridin takes up life on our world after Tristan steals Bridin's throne, and Tristan follows her here.

Parallel Worlds.

Born in Twilight. Angelica's dreams of being a nun are shattered when she is turned into a vampire. She becomes pregnant by Jameson, who himself did not want to become a vampire.

Vampires.

Stuart, Anne, Chelsea Quinn Yarbro, and Maggie Shayne

Strangers in the Night. Three vampiric romance novellas are included: *Dark Journey, Catching Dreams,* and *Beyond Twilight.*

Vampires.

Wrede, Patricia C.

🆈🅰 Magician's Ward. A delightfully wry variation on regency romance, this book is annotated in Chapter 17.

Wrede, Patricia C., and Caroline Stevermer

🆈🅰 Sorcery and Cecelia. This epistolary novel set in Regency London features two girls beset by magic.

D's Picks

Chapter 19

Short Stories

The short form of fiction has a long and rich tradition in the fantasy genre. The major awards have categories for short fiction, and qualification for membership in the Science Fiction and Fantasy Writers of America can be earned by publication of short stories.

Anthologies are of particular importance because they showcase a broad range of styles and types. Many anthologies offer insightful essays, background information, and informative commentary on trends and authors.

Anthologies

Collins, Nancy A., Edward E. Kramer, and Martin H. Greenberg, eds.

Dark Love. (Roc, 1996). This is dark fantasy combining horror and erotica, in stories by Stephen King, Ramsey Campbell, Douglas Winter, Robert Weinberg, Kathryn Ptacek, and Lucy Taylor.

Cramer, Kathryn, and Peter D. Pautz, eds.

🎗 **The Architecture of Fear.** (Arbor House, 1987). 1988 World Fantasy Award Winner.

Crowther, Peter, ed.

Narrow Houses. (Warner Books, 1994). Combines dark fantasy and horror.

Datlow, Ellen, ed.

Little Deaths. (Dell, 1996). This World Fantasy Award-winning anthology of erotic dark fantasy and horror includes stories by Lucy Taylor, Harry Crews, Nicholas Royle, Joel Lane, Clive Barker, Joyce Carol Oates, Ruth Rendell, Kathe Koja, Pat Cadigan, Doug Clegg, and Dan Simmons.

A Whisper of Blood. (Ace, 1995).

Datlow, Ellen, and Terri Windling, eds.

Black Thorn, White Rose. (Avon, 1995).

Snow White, Blood Red. (Avon, 1993). (This book is annotated in Chapter 5, "Fairy Tales.")

Dziemianowicz, Stefan, Robert Weinberg, and Martin H. Greenberg, eds.

Famous Fantastic Mysteries: 30 Great Tales of Fantasy and Horror from the Classic Pulp Magazines Famous Fantastic Mysteries & Fantastic Novels. (Grammercy, 1991).

Etchison, Dennis, ed.

Metahorror. (Donald M. Grant, 1992). Contains award-winning dark fantasy and horror by Peter Straub, David Morrell, Whitley Streiber, Ramsey Campbell, Thomas Tessier, Joyce Carol Oates, and fifteen other writers.

Friesner, Esther, ed.

Chicks in Chainmail. (Pocket, 1995). This wildly popular humorous anthology features swordswomen and other formidable females.

Did You Say Chicks? (Baen, 1998). Contains short stories of sword-wielding warrior women by Elizabeth Moon, Jody Lynn Nye, Margaret Ball, Harry Turtledove, Esther Friesner, and others.

Gilliam, Richard, Martin H. Greenberg, and Edward E. Kramer, eds.

Grails: Quests, Visitations and Other Occurrences. (New American Library, 1994). Stories by Andre Norton, Jane Yolen, Gene Wolfe, Marion Zimmer Bradley, Alan Dean Foster, Orson Scott Card, Mercedes Lackey, Neil Gaiman, Gene Wolfe, Janny Wurts, Diana L. Paxson, and others explore the past and the future of legendary grails.

Grant, Charles L., ed.

Final Shadows. (Doubleday, 1991). Thirty-six dark fantasy story writers such as Michael Bishop, Graham Masterton, Tanith Lee, Bill Pronzini, Dennis Etchison, and David Morrell contributed to this volume.

Greenberg, Martin H., ed.

After the King: Stories in Honor of J. R. R. Tolkien. (Tor, 1994). Includes stories by Mike Resnick, Terry Pratchett, Dennis L. McKiernan, Stephen R. Donaldson, Peter S. Beagle, Poul Anderson, Andre Norton, Robert Silverberg, Jane Yolen, Poul and Karen Anderson, Charles de Lint, Emma Bull, Judith Tarr, Patricia A. McKillip, John Brunner, Barry N. Malzberg, Gregory Benford, and others.

Griffith, Nicola, and Stephen Pagel, eds.

Bending the Landscape: Fantasy. (White Wolf Publishing, 1997). Includes gay and lesbian fantasy by Mark Shepherd, Holly Wade Matter, Kim Antieau, Mark W. Tiedemann, Simon Sheppard, J. A. Salmonson, Don Bassingthwaite, Ellen Kushner, Tanya Huff, Robin Wayne Bailey, and others.

Hartwell, David G., ed.

Christmas Forever. (Tor, 1993). Contains fantasy and science fiction stories with a holiday flavor by Charles de Lint, Roger Zelazny, Patricia A. McKillip, Jack McDevitt, Joan Aiken, Catherine Asaro, Dave Wolverton, and others.

Hayden, Patrick Nielsen, ed.

 Starlight 1. (Tor, 1996). Winner of the World Fantasy Award for Best Anthology. Includes original stories by Michael Swanwick, Andy Duncan, Jane Yolen, Gregory Feeley, Robert Reed, Susanna Clarke, Susan Palwick, Martha Soukup, Carter Scholz, John M. Ford, Mark Kreighbaum, and Maureen F. McHugh.

Kushner, Ellen, Donald G. Keller, and Delia Sherman, eds.

The Horns of Elfland. (New American Library, 1997). Includes stories with a musical theme.

Lurie, Alison, ed.

The Book of Modern Fairy Tales. (Oxford University Press, 1993). Includes 150 years of fairy tales. The stories and the years they originally appeared are listed in Chapter 5.

Scarborough, Elizabeth Ann, and Martin H. Greenberg, eds.

Warrior Princesses. (DAW, 1998). These are stories of unusual women who are not content to sit quietly by even though they have been born into lives of privilege. The stories are by Anne McCaffrey, Jane Yolen, Elizabeth Moon, and others.

Silverberg, Robert, ed.

The Fantasy Hall of Fame: The Definitive Collection of the Best Modern Fantasy Chosen by the Members of the Science Fiction and Fantasy Writers of America. (HarperPrism, 1998). Contains thirty stories first published between 1939 and 1990, selected by the membership of the Science Fiction and Fantasy Writers of America. The voting criteria are explained and the ranking of the stories is listed.

The top fifteen vote-getting stories are

"The Lottery," by Shirley Jackson

"Jeffty Is Five," by Harlan Ellison

"Unicorn Variations," by Roger Zelazny

"Bears Discover Fire," by Terry Bisson

"That Hell-Bound Train," by Robert Bloch

"Come Lady Death," by Peter S. Beagle

"Basileus," by Robert Silverberg

"The Golem," by Avram Davidson

"Buffalo Gals, Won't You Come Out Tonight," by Ursula K. Le Guin

"Her Smoke Rose Up Forever," by James Tiptree, Jr. (not included in the anthology)

"The Loom of Darkness," by Jack Vance

"The Drowned Giant," by J. G. Ballard

"The Detective of Dreams," by Gene Wolfe

"The Jaguar Hunter," by Lucius Shepard

"The Compleat Werewolf," by Anthony Boucher.

An additional sixteen stories were runners-up, and are included in the book:

"Trouble with Water," by H. L. Gold

"Nothing in the Rules," by L. Sprague de Camp

"Fruit of Knowledge," by C. L. Moore

"Tlon, Uqbar, Orbis Tertius," by Jorge Luis Borges

"The Small Assassin," by Ray Bradbury

"Our Fair City," by Robert A. Heinlein

"There Shall Be No Darkness," by James Blish

"The Man Who Sold Rope to the Gnoles," by Margaret St. Clair

"The Silken-Swift," by Theodore Sturgeon

"Operation Afreet," by Poul Anderson

"The Bazaar of the Bizarre," by Fritz Leiber

"Narrow Valley," by R. A. Lafferty

"Faith of Our Fathers," by Philip K. Dick

"The Ghost of a Model T," by Clifford D. Simak

"The Demoness," by Tanith Lee

"Tower of Babylon," by Ted Chiang.

Williams, A. Susan, and Richard Glyn Jones, eds.

The Penguin Book of Modern Fantasy by Women. (Penguin USA, 1997). World Fantasy Award Winner. Introduction by Joanna Russ. Contains thirty-eight stories written since 1941: "The Demon Lover," by Elizabeth Bowen; "The Tooth," by Shirley Jackson; "The Lake of the Gone Forever," by Leigh Brackett; "The Old Man," by Daphne du Maurier; "My Flannel Knickers," by Leonora Carrington; "The Anything Box," by Zenna Henderson; "Miss Pinkerton's Apocalypse," by Muriel Spark; "A Bright Green Field," by Anna Kavan; "The Ship Who Sang," by Anne McCaffrey; "Marmalade Wine," by Joan Aiken; "The Fall of Frenchy Steiner," by Hilary Bailey; "Cynosure," by Kit Reed; "The Wall," by Josephine Saxton; "The Foot," by Christine Brooke-Rose; "Baby, You Were Great," by Kate Wilhelm; "The Second Inquisition," by Joanna Russ; "Murder, 1986," by P. D. James; "The Milk of Paradise," by James Tiptree, Jr.; "When It Happens," by Margaret Atwood; "Angel, All Innocence," by Fay Weldon; "Night-Side," by Joyce Carol Oates; "Fireflood," by Vonda N. McIntyre; "Wives," by Lisa Tuttle; "Red as Blood," by Tanith Lee; "Sur," by Ursula K. Le Guin; "Peter and the Wolf," by Angela Carter; "The

Pits Beneath the World," by Mary Gentle; "Two Sheep," by Janet Frame; "Relics," by Zoe Fairbairns; "The Evening and the Morning and the Night," by Octavia E. Butler; "(Learning About) Machine Sex," by Candas Jane Dorsey; "Prodigal Pudding," by Suniti Namjoshi; "Boobs," by Suzy Mckee Charnas; "If the Word Was to the Wise," by Carol Emshwiller; "Trial by Teaspoon," by Lynda Rajan; "In the Green Shade of a Bee-Loud Glade," by L. A. Hall; "Death in the Egg," by Ann Oakley; and "Kay and Phil," by Lucy Sussex.

Anthology Series

The Best of Marion Zimmer Bradley's Fantasy Magazine, nos. 1–2. Warner Books, 1994-1995. Edited by Marion Zimmer Bradley.

Catfantastic nos., 1–4. DAW, 1991– . Edited by Andre Norton and Martin H. Greenberg.

Full Spectrum, nos.1–5. Bantam, 1988–1995. Editors included Lou Aronica, Amy Stout, Betsy Mitchell, Shawna McCarthy, Tom Dupree, Janna Silverstein, and Jennifer Hershey. Fantasy, science fiction, and horror stories were included.

Nebula Awards: SFWA's Choices for the Best Science Fiction and Fantasy of the Year. Harcourt Brace, 1966– . No. 32, 1998. This annual anthology includes short pieces and excerpts of nominations for the year as well as essays. Editors have included Pamela Sargent, James Morrow, George Zebrowski, Michael Bishop, Jack Dann, Poul Anderson, Ursula K. Le Guin, James Blish, Lloyd Biggle, Jr., James Gunn, Kate Wilhelm, Joe Haldeman, Brian Aldiss, Roger Zelazny, Clifford D. Simak, Isaac Asimov, Jerry Pournelle, Marta Randall, Robert Silverberg, Samuel R. Delany, Gordon R. Dickson, Frederik Pohl, Frank Herbert, and Damon Knight.

Sword and Sorceress. DAW, 1984– . Edited by Marion Zimmer Bradley. The thirteenth annual volume was published in 1996. Features women in heroic fantasy.

Xanadu, nos.1–3. Tor, 1994–1995. Edited by Jane Yolen. Includes original fantasy stories.

Year's Best Fantasy. St. Martin's Press, 1988–1989. Edited by Ellen Datlow and Terri Windling. Name changed to *Year's Best Fantasy and Horror.*

Year's Best Fantasy and Horror. St. Martin's Press, 1990– . Edited by Ellen Datlow and Terri Windling. The tenth annual collection was published in 1997, the numbering continuing from the previous title, *Year's Best Fantasy.*

Year's Best Fantasy Stories. DAW, 1974–1988. Lin Carter edited the first six volumes and Arthur W. Saha the last eight.

19

Collections

Aldiss, Brian. *Common Clay, Or 20 Odd Tales.* St. Martin's Press, 1996.

Bear, Greg. *Bear's Fantasies.* Wildside Press, 1992.

Blaylock, James P. *Lord Kelvin's Machine.* Arkham House, 1992.

Bloch, Robert. *The Early Fears.* Fedogan & Bremer, 1994.

AW Cady, Jack. *The Sons of Noah and Other Stories.* Broken Room Press, 1992. World Fantasy Award Winner.

AW Campbell, Ramsey. *Alone with the Horrors.* Arkham House, 1993. Campbell's short fiction from 1961 to 1991 is included. 1994 World Fantasy Award Winner.

Chappell, Fred. *More Shapes Than One.* St. Martin's Press, 1991.

Crowley, John. *Antiquities.* Incunabula, 1993.

de Lint, Charles. *Dreams Underfoot.* Tor, 1993.

———. *Spiritwalk.* Tor, 1992.

———. *The Ivory and the Horn.* Tor, 1995.

Denton, Bradley. *The Calvin Coolidge Home for Dead Comedians and a Conflagration Artist.* Wildside Press, 1994.

AW Emshwiller, Carol. *The Start of the End of It All and Other Stories.* Mercury House, 1991. 1991 World Fantasy Award Winner.

Gaiman, Neil. *Angels & Visitations: A Miscellany.* Dream Haven, 1993.

Goldstein, Lisa. *Travelers in Magic.* Tor, 1994.

Holdstock, Robert. *The Bone Forest.* Avon Nova, 1992.

AW Jones, Gwyneth. *Seven Tales and a Fable.* Edgewood Press, 1993. 1996 World Fantasy Award Winner.

Kessel, John. *Meeting in Infinity.* Arkham House, 1992.

Kilworth, Garry. *Hogfoot Right and Bird-Hands.* Edgewood Press, 1993.

Kipling, Rudyard. *Kipling's Fantasy Stories.* Tor, 1992.

Lafferty, R. A. *Lafferty in Orbit.* Broken Mirrors Press, 1991.

Lamsley, Terry. *Under the Crust.* Wendigo, 1993.

AW Lethem, Jonathan. *The Wall of the Sky, the Wall of the Eye.* Harcourt Brace, 1996. World Fantasy Award for Best Collection.

Ligotti, Thomas. *Grimscribe: His Lives and Works.* Jove, 1994.

Morris, Kenneth. *The Dragon Path: Collected Stories of Kenneth Morris.* Tor, 1995. This collection of stories is based on the mythology of several different cultures.

Oates, Joyce Carol. *Haunted: Tales of the Grotesque.* Penguin/Dutton, 1994.

Shepard, Lucius. *The Ends of the Earth.* Arkham House, 1991. 1992 World Fantasy Award Winner.

Waldrop, Howard. *Night of the Cooters: More Neat Stories.* Ace, 1993.

Wolfe, Gene. *Storeys from the Old Hotel.* Tor, 1992. This story collection showcases over thirty stories, including a Liavek shared-world tale, an alternate history story, some dark fantasy, and a broad spectrum of short works. 1989 World Fantasy Award Winner.

Wurts, Janny. *That Way Lies Camelot.* HarperPrism, 1996. This is a collection of stories set in the most magical of settings, featuring magic in many forms.

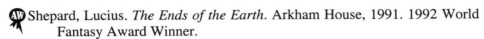

19

Chapter 20

Resources

The resources listed here are for the purpose of broadening the reader's knowledge of the genre. They include secondary materials, organizations, and awards.

Bibliographies and Biographies

Ashley, Michael. *Who's Who in Horror and Fantasy Fiction.* Elm Tree Books, 1977. Includes annotations and critical bio-bibliography for 400 authors. Additional sections: "Chronology," c. 2000 B.C.E. –1977; "An index to key stories and books"; "Selected weird fiction anthologies," annotated; "Weird and horror fiction magazines," annotated; "Awards," August Derleth Fantasy Award and World Fantasy Award.

Ashley, Michael, and William G. Contento. *The Supernatural Index: A Listing of Fantasy, Supernatural, Occult, Weird, and Horror Anthologies.* Greenwood Publishing Group, 1995. Indexes more than 21,000 stories by more than 7,700 authors in more than 2,100 anthologies.

Barron, Neil. *Fantasy Literature.* Garland, 1990. This is a scholarly historical treatment of the genre.

Barron, Neil, ed. *What Fantastic Fiction Do I Read Next? A Reader's Guide to Recent Fantasy, Horror and Science Fiction.* Gale, 1998. Noncritical, this guide lists books released in the specified time span of 1989–1997. Indexes characters, settings, and key worlds.

Bloom, Harold, ed. *Classic Fantasy Writers.* Chelsea House, 1994.

————. *Modern Fantasy Writers*. Chelsea House, 1995.

Bontly, Susan W., and Carol J. Sheridan. *Enchanted Journeys Beyond the Imagination, Vols. 1 and 2: An Annotated Bibliography of Fantasy, Futuristic, Supernatural, and Time Travel Romances*. Blue Diamond Publications, 1996. Bontly and Sheridan have identified romance books that fall into the science fiction, fantasy, and supernatural areas. They have managed to categorize this diverse and unusual but wildly popular area with panache. They list time travel romances written by more than 90 authors, identifying times and destinations, grouping the books by American West, American Revolution/Frontier, America, Contemporary, Europe, Old South/Civil War, Regency England, and an area for the time travel romances that don't fit elsewhere. Other classifications include fantasy (myth and legend), futuristic (categorized by Earth-related, other worlds, and UFOs), and supernatural romance (with angels, ghosts, vampires, magic), and more. This unique bibliography is a boon to reader's advisors, both in libraries and bookstores, offering access to some of the most popular subgenres of romance fiction. Readers of these genres will be delighted to find old favorites and discover new ones. The bibliography includes listings of pseudonyms and listings by category and series. An author/title index is included.

Burgess, Michael. *Reference Guide to Science Fiction, Fantasy, and Horror*. Libraries Unlimited, 1992.

Cawthorn, James, and Michael Moorcock. *Fantasy: The 100 Best Books*. Carroll & Graf, 1991.

Hall, Hal W., ed. *Science Fiction and Fantasy Reference Index, 1985–1991: An International Author and Subject Index to History and Criticism*. Libraries Unlimited, 1993.

————. *Science Fiction and Fantasy Reference Index, 1992–1995: An International Subject and Author Index to History and Criticism*. Libraries Unlimited, 1997. These volumes provide definitive listings of secondary materials.

MacRae, Cathi Dunn. *Presenting Young Adult Fantasy Fiction* (Twayne's United States Authors Series, No. 699). Twayne, 1998. *VOYA* editor MacRae used teen consultants in writing about subgenres with particular appeal to young adults. It features in-depth biographical and critical information on authors Terry Brooks, Barbara Hambly, Jane Yolen, and Meredith Ann Pierce.

Perret, Patti. *The Faces of Fantasy*. Tor, 1996. Renowned photographer Perret offers fantasy lovers a treat in this visual feast of beloved authors. Photographed in various locales and settings, each portrait searches for an inner vision of the more than 100 writers featured. Terri Windling provides a fascinating historical overview of fantasy fiction in the introduction.

Pringle, David. *Modern Fantasy: The Hundred Best Novels. An English Language Selection, 1946–1987*. Peter Bedrick Books, 1989.

Pringle, David, ed. *St. James Guide to Fantasy Writers*. St. James Press, 1996.

Rovin, Jeff. *The Fantasy Almanac.* Dutton, 1979. Includes alphabetical definitions of authors, characters, mythological and supernatural beings and beasts, places, and the like in mythology, folklore, fairy tales, literature, comic strips, motion pictures, and television. Illustrated.

Searles, Baird, Beth Meacham, and Michael Franklin. *A Reader's Guide to Fantasy.* Facts on File, 1982. Bibliography and criticism are provided for over 160 authors. An introduction for neophytes is included.

Tymn, Marshall B., Kenneth J. Zahorski, and Robert H. Boyer. *Fantasy Literature: A Core Collection and Reference Guide.* Bowker, 1979. The core collection, more than 240 works, is an alphabetical and critically annotated selection of adult fantasy, although much of the material is suitable for all ages. There is an extensive introductory essay. The listings of "Fantasy Scholarship," periodicals, societies, and organizations are briefly annotated.

Waggoner, Diana. *The Hills of Faraway: A Guide to Fantasy.* Atheneum, 1978. This is an eclectic selection of 996 titles, critically annotated, of interest to adults. There is an extensive and critical introductory essay. An appendix, "Subgenres of Fantasy," lists titles (numbered as in the annotated list) by type: magic, mythic fantasy, Faerie, ghost fantasy, horror fantasy, sentimental fantasy, magic time travel, travels from one universe to another, science fantasy, fairy-story fantasy, toy tales, animal fantasy, worlds of enchantment, new histories, and new universes.

Encyclopedia

Clute, John, and John Grant. *The Encyclopedia of Fantasy.* St. Martin's Press, 1997. The first, only, and definitive encyclopedia of fantasy, this is a "must have" for every serious fantasy collection. All academic and public libraries should have it, as should most high school libraries. It has over a million words in 4,000 entries. Everything you ever wanted to know about fantasy from the dawn of time to 1995 is included. Not only covering the written word, it also takes on movies, television, art, and live performances that are fantasy based. Awards, conventions, themes, and motifs are listed.

Guides and Atlases

These delightful books will enchant all fans of fantasy, and many of science fiction, because they describe and map the lands that readers' imaginations have made real.

Anthony, Piers, and Jody Lynn Nye. *Piers Anthony's Visual Guide to Xanth.* Avon Books, 1989. This book takes a look at the geography, locations, flora, and fauna of the magical land of Xanth.

Barlowe, Wayne Douglas. *Barlowe's Guide to Fantasy.* HarperPrism, 1996. Fifty fantasy creatures and characters are brought to life by illustrator Wayne Barlowe, very much in the manner of a naturalist's studies. Essential facts about each creature include language, weaponry, dietary customs, and, if applicable, favorite prey.

Holdstock, Robert, and Malcolm Edwards. *Lost Realms.* Illustrations by John Avon, Bill Donohoe, Godfrey Dowson, Dick French, Mark Harrison, Michael Johnson, Pauline Martin, David O'Connor, Colleen Payne, Scitex 350, and Carolyn Scrace. Limpsfield, England: Dragon's World, 1984. With reference to history, legend, and use in fiction, describes places familiar to readers of fantasy: islands, continents, cities, undersea worlds, and the underworld. Places as diverse as Avalon, Middle Earth, Lemuria, Mu, Troy, Shambhala, Eldorado, Atlantis, Plutonia, Pellucidar, Tuonela, Yggdrasil, and Faerie (Land of Youth) are included. The color illustrations are vivid. The bibliography lists some fiction.

Jordan, Robert, and Teresa Patterson. *The World of Robert Jordan's The Wheel of Time.* Tor, 1997. This is a guide to the popular bestselling series. It serves as an atlas, with maps of the world, the Seanchan Empire, the nations of the Covenant of the Ten Nations, and historical maps of the nations as they were when Artur Paendrag Tanreall began his rise to fame. It also includes illustrations of landscapes, objects of power, and the central characters.

Manguel, Alberto, and Gianni Guadalupi. *The Dictionary of Imaginary Places.* Illustrated by Graham Greenfield. Maps and charts by James Cook. Macmillan, 1980. Clearly this is a labor of love. Imaginary places (countries, castles, islands, whatever) from all types of literature and films are described in straight gazetteer style, complete with information on the inhabitants, flora and fauna, and social customs. The source work is cited. There are 150 maps and 100 illustrations. The scope is international and, of course, encompasses much more than genre fiction. There is an index of authors and titles. This is not simply a reference book, but may be read with delight for its own sake. The authors invite additional citations for a supplement or revised edition.

Nye, Jody Lynn. *The Dragonlover's Guide to Pern, Second Edition.* Del Rey, 1997. This is a guide to the people, places, and creatures of Pern.

Post, J. B., comp. *An Atlas of Fantasy.* Rev. ed. Ballantine, 1979. This is much improved in map reproduction from the first edition (Mirage Press, 1973), with some changes. Following is a selection from the contents; many are for works cited in this guide. They are listed in order of sequence in the atlas.

Baum, L. Frank, "Oz and Environs."

Burroughs, Edgar Rice, "The Worlds of . . ." Barsoom [Mars], Pal-Ul-Don (Tarzan series), Land of the Ant Men (Tarzan series), Onthar and Thenar

(Tarzan series), The Lost Empire (Tarzan series), Amtor (Venus series), Pellucidar (Hollow Earth-Pellucidar series), The Moon (*The Moon Maid*); Poloda and Umos (*Beyond the Furthest Star*); Caspak and Caprona (*The Land That Time Forgot*), Wild Island.

Cabell, James Branch, "Poictesme."

Howard, Robert E., "Hyperborian Age" (Conan series).

Tolkien, J. R. R., "The Worlds . . ." Middle Earth (*Lord of the Rings*), Gondor and Mordor (*Lord of the Rings*), Thror's Map (*The Hobbit*), Wilderland (*The Hobbit*), Beleriand (*The Silmarillion*).

Eddison, E. R., "The Three Kingdoms and Ouroboros Country": Ouroboros Country (*The Worm Ouroboros*); The Three Kingdoms (*Mistress of Mistresses*); The Campaign in North Rerek and the Meszrian Border (*Mistress of Mistresses*).

Sleigh, Bernard, "Fairyland" (*Ancient Mappe of Fairyland*).

Lewis, C. S., "Narnia."

Myers, John Myers, "Commonwealth" (*Silverlock*).

Hamilton, Edmond, "The Worlds of Captain Future" (*Captain Future*, a pulp magazine, thirteen maps).

Brackett, Leigh, "Leigh Brackett's Mars."

Smith, Clark Ashton, "Hyperborea" (*Hyperborea*), Zothique.

Norton, Andre, "The Witch World."

Le Guin, Ursula K., "Earthsea" (*A Wizard of Earthsea*).

Zelazny, Roger, "Dilfar and Environs" (*Warlocks and Warriors*).

Moorcock, Michael, "The Young Kingdoms" (Elric series).

Vance, Jack, *The Dying Earth.*

Leiber, Fritz, "Lankhmar in the Land of Nehwon" (Fafhrd and the Grey Mouse series).

Alexander, Lloyd, "Prydain" (three maps).

Carter, Lin, "Lemuria."

Bradbury, Ray, "Mars" ("The Million Year Picnic").

Campbell, J. Ramsey, "The Severn Valley at Brichester" (*The Inhabitant of the Lake*).

Herbert, Frank, *Dune.*

Kuttner, Henry, "Atlantis" (Elek series).

Jakes, John, "Tyros" (Brak series).

Dain, Alex, "Kanthos, Sulmannon, and Anzor" (*Banc of Kanthos*).

Kurtz, Katherine, "Gwynedd and Its Neighbors" (Deryni series).

McCaffrey, Anne, "Pern" (The Dragonriders of Pern series).

Fraser, George MacDonald, "The Duchy of Strackanz" (*Royal Flash*).

Lovecraft, H. P., "The Worlds of H. P. Lovecraft," Dreamworld, Arkham.

Adams, Richard, "The Beklan Empire" (*Shardik*).

Brackett, Leigh, "The Worlds of Eric John Stark" (*The Ginger Star, The Hounds of Skaith, The Reavers of Skaith*).

Brooks, Terry, "The Four Lands" (*The Sword of Shannara*).

Donaldson, Stephen R., "The Land" (The Chronicles of Thomas Covenant the Unbeliever).

History and Criticism

In addition to the following works, material on fantasy can be found among some histories and criticisms of science fiction.

Attebery, Brian. *Strategies of Fantasy*. Indiana University Press, 1992.

Boyer, Robert H., and Kenneth J. Zahorski, eds. *Fantasists on Fantasy: A Collection of Critical Reflections*. Avon, 1984. Includes essays by George MacDonald, G. K. Chesterton, H. P. Lovecraft, Sir Herbert Reed, James Thurber, J. R. R. Tolkien, August Derleth, C. S. Lewis, Felix Martí-Ibáñez, Peter S. Beagle, Lloyd Alexander, Andre Norton, Jane Langton, Ursula K. Le Guin, Mollie Hunter, Katherine Kurtz, Michael Moorcock, and Susan Cooper.

Brooke-Rose, Christine. *A Rhetoric of the Unreal: Studies in Narrative and Structure, Especially of the Fantastic*. Cambridge University Press, 1981. Includes references to science fiction and horror as well as fantasy.

Carter, Lin. *Imaginary Worlds: The Art of Fantasy*. Ballantine, 1973. Covers high and low fantasy, fairy tales, folklore, Arthurian legend, and horror. Discusses 341 authors.

de Camp, L. Sprague. *Literary Swordsmen and Sorcerers: The Makers of Heroic Fantasy*. Arkham House, 1976. The key authors discussed are William Morris, Lord Dunsany, H. P. Lovecraft, E. R. Eddison, Robert E. Howard, Fletcher Pratt, Clark Ashton Smith, J. R. R. Tolkien, and T. H. White.

Filmer, Kath, ed. *Twentieth Century Fantasist's Essays on Culture, Society and Belief in Twentieth-century Mythopoeic Literature*. St. Martin's Press, 1992.

Hall, Hal W., ed. *Science Fiction and Fantasy Reference Index, 1985-1991 An International Author and Subject Index to History and Criticism*. Libraries Unlimited, 1993.

Hillegas, Mark R., ed. *Shadows of Imagination: The Fantasies of C. S. Lewis, J. R. R. Tolkien, and Charles Williams.* Southern Illinois University Press, 1969. Contains twelve essays.

Irwin, W. R. *The Game of the Impossible: A Rhetoric of Fantasy.* University of Illinois Press, 1976. Includes an essay defining fantasy and the fantastic in English literature from 1880 to the early 1970s.

Le Guin, Ursula K. *The Language of the Night: Essays on Fantasy and Science Fiction.* HarperCollins, 1992. Includes writings on the writing and reading of fantasy and science fiction—an eloquent statement.

Magill, Frank N., ed. *Survey of Modern Fantasy Literature.* 5 vols. Salem Press, 1983.

Manlove, C. N. *Modern Fantasy: Five Studies.* Cambridge University Press, 1975. The authors discussed are Charles Kingsley, George MacDonald, C. S. Lewis, J. R. R. Tolkien, and Mervyn Peake.

Rabkin, Eric S. *The Fantastic in Literature.* Princeton University Press, 1976. Discusses the fantastic in many types of literature, including fairy tales, detective fiction, horror fiction, and science fiction.

Rottensteiner, Franz. *The Fantasy Book: An Illustrated History from Dracula to Tolkien.* Collier Books, 1978. Includes 202 illustrations, 40 in color, from books of fantasy, the pulps, and motion pictures. A good part relates to a chapter on ghosts and horror. There is a section on "The International Contribution." The bibliography is excellent, with many foreign citations.

Schlobin, Roger C., ed. *The Aesthetics of Fantasy, Literature and Art.* London: Harvester Press, 1982. Essays by Gary K. Wolfe, C. N. Manlove, W. R. Irwin, Kenneth J. Zahorski, Robert H. Boyer, and others are included.

Sobczak, A. J., and T. A. Shippey, eds. *Magill's Guide to Science Fiction and Fantasy Literature.* 4 vols. Salem Press, 1996.

    Volume 1: *The Absolute at Large–Dragonsbane*
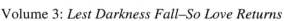

    Volume 2: *Dream–The Lensman Series*

    Volume 3: *Lest Darkness Fall–So Love Returns*

    Volume 4: *Software and Wetware–Zotz!*

Journals

Locus
P.O. Box 13305
Oakland, CA 94661

Published monthly, *Locus* lists all SF and fantasy published in English. Seven accomplished reviewers not only discuss book-length fiction but also review short stories. Author interviews, news of events and personalities, bibliographies, and the highly respected Locus *Poll* also make this very useful.

New York Review of Science Fiction
Dragon Press
P.O. Box 570
Pleasantville, NY 10570
Web site: http://ebbs.english.vt.edu/olp/nyrsf/nyrsf.html
(accessed Dec. 1, 1998)

A monthly scholarly looking publication, *New York Review of Science Fiction* publishes reviews for fantasy, science fiction, and horror that "reveal the strengths and weaknesses of good books." They also publish articles and essays related to science fiction, fantasy, and horror.

Realms of Fantasy
11305 Sunset Hills Rd.
Reston, VA 20190

Published bimonthly, this journal includes reviews of books, television, and games. Features include discussions of the genre by esteemed authors of fantasy, including Terri Windling and Jane Yolen. Many of its readers purchase it for the short stories by new and established authors.

Science Fiction Chronicle
P. O. Box 022730
Brooklyn, NY 11202-0056

Monthly publication of reviews and science fiction and fantasy news. It is also a good source for up-to-date information on awards.

Online Resources

All online site hyperlinks are checked regularly and updated at http://www.sff.net/ people/dherald/. (All sites listed here were accessed November 30, 1998, unless otherwise noted.)

Ace Books from Putnam Berkley: http://www.penguinputnam.com/catalog/fiction/books/browse_cat6_pg1.html (accessed Nov. 30, 1998). Select Science Fiction/Fantasy from the Category pull-down menu and click on search. It will take you to the listings by title.

Avon Eos: http://www.avonbooks.com/avon/sf. html.

Baen: http://206.9.140.78/.

Bantam Spectra: http://www.bdd.com/forum/bddforum.cgi/scifi/.

Del Rey: http://www.randomhouse.com/delrey/.

E-Scape: The Digital Journal of Speculative Fiction: http://www.interink. com/current/index.html.

Fantasy Booklist: http://www.mcs.com/~finn/home.html.

Fantasy Finder: http://www.hoh.se/fantasyfinder.

Feminist Science Fiction, Fantasy, & Utopia: http://www.wenet.net/~lquilter/ femsf/.

Future Fantasy Bookstore: http://futfan.com/. Includes lists and links to sample chapters.

Infinity Plus: The Science Fiction and Fantasy Homepage: http://www.users. zetnet.co.uk/iplus/. Contains novel excerpts, short stories, reviews, and interviews with authors.

Ingram's Fantasy A-List: http://www.ingrambook.com/Surf/product_info/ category_info/category_files/fa.htm.

International Association for the Fantastic in the Arts: http://ebbs.english. vt.edu/iafa/iafa.home.html.

Internet Speculative Fiction Database: http://www.sfsite.com/isfdb/sfdbase.html.

Just Imagine: http://www.abc.nl/abc/first/justjan/.This is a bookstore from the Netherlands listing science fiction and fantasy.

Los Angeles Public Library Readers Advisory Fantasy Lists: http://www. colapublib.org//advisory/fantasy/index.html.

NESFA Press: http://www.nesfa.org/press/.

Omni Magazine: SF, Fantasy, Horror: http://www.omnimag.com/fiction/ index.html.

Orbit: http://www.orbitbooks.co.uk/#top. This is useful for a look at British science fiction and fantasy publishing.

Penguin Putnam including DAW, Ace, and Roc: http://www.penguinputnam. com/catalog/index.htm.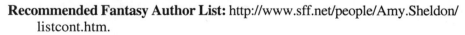

Reader's Robot Fantasy Page: http://www.tnrdlib.bc.ca/fa-menu.html.

Recommended Fantasy Author List: http://www.sff.net/people/Amy.Sheldon/ listcont.htm.

Science Fiction and Fantasy Themed Reviews: http://www.serve.com/ sfreview/.

Science Fiction Book Club: http://www.sfbc.com:9001/mybookclub/ craftycreatures/bookclubs/sfc/Splash.htm.

Science Fiction Weekly: http://www.scifi.com/sfw/.

SF Site: The Home Page for Science Fiction and Fantasy: http://www.sfsite.com/. It includes lots of reviews and tons of information and is a nicely designed site.

Sidewise Awards for Alternate History: http://www.skatecity.com/ah/sidewise/.

The Locus Index: Science Fiction, Fantasy, & Horror: 1984-1997: http://www.sff. net/locus/0start.html. Indexes the magazine, including lists of all books received for review. This is probably the most comprehensive listing of science fiction, fantasy, and horror published for the period since 1984.

Tor: http://www.tor.com/.

Tristom Cook's Internet Top 100 Science Fiction and Fantasy List: http://www. clark.net/pub/iz/Books/Top100/top100list.txt.

University of Michigan Science Fiction and Fantasy Page: http://www.umich. Edu/~umfandsf/.

Voyager from HarperCollins UK: http://www.fireandwater.com/imprints/index.htm.

White Wolf: http://www.white-wolf.com/Fiction/Fiction.html.

Wildside List of SF and Fantasy authors pages: http://www.wildsidepress.com/.

Publishers

Ace is one of the three science fiction and fantasy imprints of Putnam Penguin.

Arbor House is known for its fine anthologies.

Arkham House was founded to publish the works of H. P. Lovecraft, and still publishes works in the weird tales tradition.

Avon Eos is the new imprint for science fiction and fantasy replacing Avon's defunct **Aspect** imprint. The Web site lists whether a title is science fiction or fantasy.

Baen is a leader in publishing science fiction and fantasy.

Ballantine is the venerable granddaddy of fantasy publishing and is closely linked with the development of the genre. Ballantine now publishes fantasy under the Del Rey imprint.

Bantam/Doubleday/Dell publishes an occasional fantasy title under one of the three main imprints, but most of the fantasy they publish is under the Spectra imprint.

Carroll & Graf publishes an occasional fantasy title.

DAW was started by Donald A. Wolheim, and is now a fantasy and science fiction imprint of Penguin Putnam.

Del Rey is an imprint of Random House that publishes fantasy and science fiction.

Gollancz is a British publisher that publishes Terry Pratchett and others.

HarperCollins publishes a great deal of fantasy in Great Britain, including the authors J.R.R. Tolkien, David Eddings, and R. A. Salvatore.

HarperPrism is the fantasy and science fiction imprint of HarperCollins in America.

Headline is a British publisher of fantasy and science fiction.

Knopf published the Philip Pullman series, His Dark Materials.

Morrow publishes an occasional fantasy title.

NESFA Press of the New England Science Fiction Association publishes a small number of out-of-print classics as well as works by honored guests at the Boskone convention.

Orb (an imprint of Tor) publishes fantasy and science fiction in trade paperback editions.

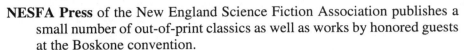

Orbit is a British imprint of Little Brown. It publishes L. E. Modesitt, Alan Dean Foster, and others.

Penguin Putnam publishes fantasy under the **Ace**, **DAW**, and **Roc** imprints.

Roc is one of the imprints of Penguin Putnam. It publishes several fantasy novels each year.

Science Fiction Book Club is where many fans get their information about new titles. The club often publishes omnibus editions and is also a source for paperback originals in hardcover.

Simon & Schuster publishes an occasional fantasy title.

Spectra is the fantasy and science fiction imprint of Bantam/Doubleday/Dell.

St. Martin's Press is the parent company of Tor, and publishes a limited number of fantasy titles.

Tor was selected ten years in a row as favorite publisher in the Locus Poll. It arguably publishes more fantasy and science fiction than any other publisher. Looking at the Tor catalog is a must for good collection development in fantasy.

TSR is the game company that made a big splash with DragonLance. It is now an imprint of Wizards of the Coast.

Underwood-Miller is a small publisher that has published Jack Vance and others.

Viking has published fantasy in the past, but currently **Ace**, **DAW**, and **Roc**, sister imprints in the Penguin Putnam family, are publishing the fantasy titles.

White Wolf publishes cutting edge fantasy. It is a game company.

Wizards of the Coast is the new owner of TSR and its bestselling DragonLance series.

Mark V. Ziesing is a bookseller who also sometimes publishes. He has been nominated to the Locus Poll in his capacity as a publisher.

Organizations and Conventions

The British Fantasy Society (BFS) was established in 1971 and sponsors the annual FantasyCon. They have a Web site at: http://www.geocities.com/SoHo/6859/index.htm (accessed Nov 30, 1998). FantasyCon XXII was held in 1998 in Birmingham. BFS also provides a list of recommended books, consisting of novels and anthologies nominated for the British Fantasy Awards.

The Mythopoeic Society is devoted to the study, discussion, and enjoyment of myth and fantasy literature. They hold an annual conference called Mythcon. The twenty-ninth annual conference was held in Wheaton, Illinois, in 1998 and honored C. S. Lewis. The Mythopoeic Society maintains a Web site at: http://www.mythsoc.org/ (accessed Nov 30, 1998). The address of the corresponding secretary as of 1998 is:

> Edith Crowe, Corresponding Secretary
> The Mythopoeic Society
> P.O. Box 320486
> San Francisco, CA 94132-0486
> E-mail: ecrowe@email.sjsu.edu

Science Fiction & Fantasy Writers of America was founded in 1965 by Damon Knight, who also served as the first president. Originally the Science Fiction Writers of America, the name was changed to include "fantasy" in 1992, better reflecting the entwining and close relationship of the two genres. Membership is only open to writers of published science fiction or fantasy.

The Tolkien Society maintains a Web site at: http://www.tolkiensociety.org/ (accessed Nov 30, 1998). The society was founded in 1969 to further interest in the works of J. R. R. Tolkien.

The **World Fantasy Convention** had no Web site as of Dec. 9, 1998, but the organizers of each year's convention usually do. The 1998 Worldcon was in Monterey, California. Future conventions are slated for Corpus Christi, Texas, in 2000 and Montreal, Quebec, Canada, in 2001.

The twenty-fifth World Fantasy Convention is slated to be held in Providence, Rhode, Island, in 1999. Information is posted at http://world.std.com/~sbarsky/mcfi/wfc (accessed Nov 30, 1998).

> World Fantasy Convention 1999
> PO Box 1010
> Framingham, MA 01701-1010
> USA

Attendance at the convention is limited to 1,000 people, but supporting memberships are also available. Members make nominations for the World Fantasy Awards, but a panel of judges makes the final decisions.

Awards

The best, most up-to-date information on awards can be found on the World Wide Web at ISFDB Awards Listings http://www.sfsite.com/isfdb/award.html or Award Web http://www.city-net.com/~lmann/awards/ (accessed Nov 30, 1998).

The awards listed are of particular interest to fantasy readers.

Fantasy Awards

Balrog Award

The Balrog Award, named after a Tolkien character, was awarded from 1979 to 1985 by the International Fantasy Gamers Society. The winners in the best novel category are listed here.

1979   Tom Reamy. *Blind Voices.*

1980   Anne McCaffrey. *Dragondrums.*

1981   Stephen R. Donaldson. *The Wounded Land.*

1982   Katherine Kurtz. *Camber the Heretic.*

1983   Stephen R. Donaldson. *The One Tree.*

1984   George R. R. Martin. *Armageddon Rag.*

1985   David Brin. *The Practice Effect.*

William L. Crawford Memorial Award

A panel of judges gives this award for the best first fantasy published during the calendar year at the International Association for the Fantastic in the Arts annual convention.

1985   Charles de Lint. *Moonheart.*

1986   Nancy Willard. *Things Invisible to See.*

1987   Judith Tarr. The Hound and the Falcon trilogy.

1988   Elizabeth Marshall Thomas. *Reindeer Moon.*

1989   Michaela Roessner. *Walkabout Woman.*

1990   Jeanne Larsen. *Silk Road.*

1991   Michael Scott Rohan. The Winter of the World trilogy.

1992   Greer Ilene Gilman. *Moonwise.*

1993   Susan Palwick. *Flying in Place.*

1994   Judith Katz. *Running Fiercely Toward a High Thin Sound.*

1995   Jonathan Lethem. *Gun, With Occasional Music.*

1996   Sharon Shinn. *The Shape-Changer's Wife.*

1997   Chitra Banerjee Divakaruni. *The Mistress of Spices.*

August Derleth Award

The British Fantasy Award, often referred to as the August Derleth Award, is selected by members of the British Fantasy Society and attendees of the annual FantasyCon. The close relationship between fantasy and horror is indicated by the number of horror novels awarded this fantasy prize. Several of the books that have received this award are covered in the horror volume of this series rather than in *Fluent in Fantasy*.

1973   Michael Moorcock. *The Knight of the Swords.*

1974   Michael Moorcock. *The King of the Swords.*

1975   Poul Anderson. *Hrolf Kraki's Saga.*

1976   Michael Moorcock. *The Hollow Lands.*

1977   Gordon R. Dickson. *The Dragon and the George.*

1978   Piers Anthony. *A Spell for Chameleon.*

1979   Stephen R. Donaldson. The Chronicles of Thomas Covenant, the Unbeliever.

1980   Tanith Lee. *Death's Master.*

1981   Ramsey Campbell. *To Wake the Dead.*

1982   Stephen King. *Cujo.*

1983   Gene Wolfe. *The Sword of the Lictor.*

1984   Peter Straub. *Floating Dragon.*

1985   T. E. D. Klein. *The Ceremonies.*

1986   Bob Shaw. *The Ragged Astronauts.*

1987   Stephen King. *It.*

1988   Ramsey Campbell. *The Influence.*

1990   Dan Simmons. *Carrion Comfort.*

1991   Ramsey Campbell. *Midnight Sun.*

1992   Jonathan Carroll. *Outside the Dog Museum.*

1993   Graham Joyce. *Dark Sister.*

1994   Ramsey Campbell. *The Long Lost.*

1995   Michael Marshall Smith. *Only Forward.*

1996   Graham Joyce. *Requiem.*

1997   Graham Joyce. *The Tooth Fairy.*

Gandalf Award

The Gandalf Award, named after Tolkien's wizard, was administered by the Worldcon and sponsored by Lin Carter and S. A. G. A (The Swordsmen and Sorcerers Guild of America, Ltd.). It was only awarded for book-length fantasy in 1978 and 1979. A grand master award was presented from 1973 to 1980 and the winners were

1973   J. R. R. Tolkien.

1974   Fritz Leiber.

1975   L. Sprague de Camp.

1976   Andre Norton.

1977   Poul Anderson.

1978   Ursula K. Le Guin.

1979   Ray Bradbury.

1980   C. L. Moore.

Locus Poll Awards

Readers of *Locus* are annually given a chance to select their favorites in a magazine poll. Because *Locus* is to science fiction, fantasy, and horror what *Billboard* is to music and *Variety* to acting, the poll really reflects what serious readers of fantasy like. The poll has been taken annually since 1971. Ballots are only accepted from subscribers and the results are published in the July or August issue. An online resource listing nominees, winners and results can be found at http://www.sff.net/locus/poll/index.html.

Poll results are given in the categories of SF novel, fantasy novel, horror/dark fantasy novel, first novel, novella, novelette, short story, collection, anthology, nonfiction, art book, editor, magazine, book publisher, and artist. In 1994 and 1990 dark fantasy was not listed as part of the horror catagory. Horror was first a category in 1989. Even though the poll has been conducted since 1971, the best fantasy novel category first appeared in 1980. Prior to that, fantasy was included in the "novel" category.

Winners of the Locus Poll are

1978   J. R. R. Tolkien. *The Silmarillion.*

1979   No award.

1980   Patricia A. McKillip. *Harpist in the Wind.*

1981   Robert Silverberg. *Lord Valentine's Castle.*

1982   Gene Wolfe. *The Claw of the Conciliator.*

1983   Gene Wolfe. *The Sword of the Lictor.*

1984   Marion Zimmer Bradley. *The Mists of Avalon.*

1985   Robert A. Heinlein. *Job: A Comedy of Justice.*

1986   Roger Zelazny. *Trumps of Doom.*

1987   Gene Wolfe. *Soldier of the Mist.*

20

1988   Orson Scott Card. *Seventh Son.*

1989   Orson Scott Card. *Red Prophet.*

1990   Orson Scott Card. *Prentice Alvin.*

1991   Ursula K. Le Guin. *Tehanu: The Last Book of Earthsea.*

1992   Sheri S. Tepper. *Beauty.*

1993   Tim Powers. *Last Call.*

1994   Peter S. Beagle. *The Innkeeper's Song.*

1995   Michael Bishop. *Brittle Innings.*

1996   Orson Scott Card. *Alvin Journeyman.*

1997   George R. R. Martin, *A Game of Thrones;* Sean Russell, *Sea Without a Shore.*

1998   Tim Powers. *Earthquake Weather.*

Locus Poll of All-Time Favorite Fantasy Books

This poll was conducted in 1987. It would be fascinating to see the results if it were conducted now.

1.   *The Lord of the Rings Trilogy.* J. R. R. Tolkien.

2.   *The Hobbit.* J. R. R. Tolkien.

3.   *A Wizard of Earthsea.* Ursula K. Le Guin.

4.   *The Shadow of the Torturer.* Gene Wolfe.

5.   *The Last Unicorn.* Peter S. Beagle.

6.   *The Once and Future King.* T. H. White.

7.   *Nine Princes in Amber.* Roger Zelazny.

8.   *The Chronicles of Thomas Covenant, the Unbeliever.* Stephen R. Donaldson.

9.   *Dragonflight.* Anne McCaffrey.

10.   *Little, Big.* John Crowley.

11.   *Alice in Wonderland.* Lewis Carroll.

12.   *The Gormenghast Trilogy.* Mervyn Peake.

13.   *The Riddlemaster of Hed.* Patricia A. McKillip.

14.   *The Incompleat Enchanter.* Fletcher Pratt and L. Sprague de Camp.

15.   *Watership Down.* Richard Adams.

16.   *The Dying Earth.* Jack Vance.

17.   *Glory Road.* Robert A. Heinlein.

18.   *A Spell for Chameleon.* Piers Anthony.

19.   *Dracula.* Bram Stoker.

20.   *The Wizard of Oz.* L. Frank Baum.

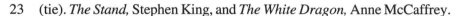

21.   *Silverlock.* John Myers Myers.

22.   *Something Wicked This Way Comes.* Ray Bradbury.

23   (tie). *The Stand,* Stephen King, and *The White Dragon,* Anne McCaffrey.

25.   *Lord Valentine's Castle.* Robert Silverberg.

26.   *The Chronicles of Narnia.* C. S. Lewis.

27.   *The Shining.* Stephen King.

28.   *Conjure Wife.* Fritz Leiber.

29.   (Tie). *Deryni Rising*, Katherine Kurtz, and *The Worm Ouroboros*, E. R. Eddison.

31.   *Witch World.* Andre Norton.

32.   *Salem's Lot.* Stephen King.

33.   *A Wrinkle in Time.* Madeleine L'Engle.

Mythopoeic Award

The Mythopoeic Award is awarded at the annual Mythcon. Winners are chosen by a committee of Mythopoeic Society members. In 1992 the society divided the fantasy award into categories of fantasy for children and for adults.

1971   Mary Stewart. *The Crystal Cave.*

1972   Joy Chant. *Red Moon and Black Mountain.*

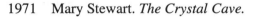

1973   Evangeline Walton. *The Song of Rhiannon.*

1974   Mary Stewart. *The Hollow Hills.*

1975   Poul Anderson. *A Midsummer Tempest.*

1981   J. R. R. Tolkien. *Unfinished Tales.*

1982   John Crowley. *Little, Big.*

1983   Carol Kendall. *The Firelings.*

1984   Joy Chant. *When Voiha Wakes.*

1985   Jane Yolen. *Cards of Grief.*

1986   Barry Hughart. *Bridge of Birds.*

1987   Peter S. Beagle. *The Folk of the Air.*

1988   Orson Scott Card. *Seventh Son.*

1989   Michael Bishop. *Unicorn Mountain.*

1990   Tim Powers. *The Stress of Her Regard.*

1991   Ellen Kushner. *Thomas the Rhymer.*

20

Adult Book Award:

1992   Eleanor Arnason. *A Woman of the Iron People.*

1993   Jane Yolen. *Briar Rose.*

1994   Delia Sherman. *The Porcelain Dove.*

1995   Patricia A. McKillip. *Something Rich and Strange.*

1996   Elizabeth Hand. *Waking the Moon.*

1997   Terri Windling. *The Wood Wife.*

1998   A. S. Byatt. *The Djinn in the Nightingale's Eye.*

Children's Book Award:

1992   Salman Rushdie. *Haroun and the Sea of Stories.*

1993   Debra Doyle and James D. Macdonald. *Knight's Wyrd.*

1994   Suzy McKee Charnas. *The Kingdom of Kevin Malone.*

1995   Patrice Kindl. *Owl in Love.*

1996   Diana Wynne Jones. *The Crown of Dalemark.*

1997   (Combined with adult literature award). Windling, *The Wood Wife.*

1998   Jane Yolen. *Young Merlin Trilogy.*

Sidewise Awards

"The Sidewise Awards for Alternate History were conceived in late 1995 to honor the best 'genre' publications of the year. The award takes its name from Murray Leinster's 1934 short story "Sidewise in Time," in which a strange storm causes portions of Earth to swap places with their analogs from other timelines. The first Sidewise Awards were announced in summer 1996."—Sidewise Award Web site, http://www.skate-city.com/ah/sidewise/.

1995   Paul J. McAuley. *Pasquale's Angel.*

1996   Stephen Baxter. *Voyage.*

1997   Harry Turtledove. *How Few Remain.*

World Fantasy Award

Members of the annual World Fantasy Convention may make nominations, but the winners are selected by a panel.

1975   Patricia A. McKillip. *The Forgotten Beasts of Eld.*

1976   Richard Matheson. *Bid Time Return.*

1977   William Kotzwinkle. *Dr. Rat.*

1978   Fritz Leiber. *Our Lady of Darkness.*

1979   Michael Moorcock. *Gloriana.*

1980   Elizabeth A. Lynn. *Watchtower.*

1981   Gene Wolfe. *The Shadow of the Torturer.*

1982   John Crowley. *Little, Big.*

1983   Michael Shea. *Nifft the Lean.*

1984   John M. Ford. *The Dragon Waiting.*

1985   (Tie). Robert Holdstock, *Mythago Wood,* and Barry Hughart, *Bridge of Birds.*

1986   Dan Simmons. *Song of Kali.*

1987   Patrick Suskind. *Perfume.*

1988   Ken Grimwood. *Replay.*

1989   Peter Straub. *Koko.*

1990   Jack Vance. *Lyonesse: Madouc.*

1991   (Tie). James Morrow, *Only Begotten Daughter,* and Ellen Kushner, *Thomas the Rhymer.*

1992   Robert R. McCammon. *Boy's Life.*

1993   Tim Powers. *Last Call.*

1994   Lewis Shiner. *Glimpses.*

1995   James Morrow. *Towing Jehovah.*

1996   Christopher Priest. *The Prestige.*

1997   Rachel Pollack. *Godmother Night.*

1998   Jeffrey Ford. *The Physiognomy.*

World Fantasy Life Achievement Award

Winners of this award are listed in Chapter 2 (see pp. 12-13.) It is presented annually at the World Fantasy Convention.

SF and Fantasy Awards

Fantasy novels are often nominated for and sometimes win awards that are labeled as science fiction or speculative fiction. The following awards can be presented for works of fantasy, but are just as likely to be awarded to works of science fiction.

Compton Crook Award. Awarded by the Baltimore Science Fiction Society for the best first novel of science fiction (including fantasy).

Philip K. Dick Award. Awarded to a science fiction or fantasy book published in paperback. It is administered by the Philadelphia SF society.

Hugo Awards are nominated for and voted on by the membership of the World Science Fiction Convention. One of the most prestigious awards, this is a reflection of fan opinion.

Nebula Awards are awarded by the Science Fiction and Fantasy Writers of America. Membership in SFWA is only open to published authors in the field, making this prestigious award an award of peers that reflects high literary merit.

Prix Aurora Award is given for the best in Canadian science fiction and fantasy.

The SFWA Hall of Fame (The Grand Masters). Many winners of the Grand Master Award, presented by the Science Fiction and Fantasy Writers of America, are known for their fantasy or have written both fantasy and science fiction.

1974	Robert Heinlein (deceased).
1975	Jack Williamson.
1976	Clifford D. Simak (deceased).
1978	L. Sprague de Camp.
1981	Fritz Leiber (deceased).
1983	Andre Norton.
1985	Arthur C. Clarke.
1986	Isaac Asimov (deceased).
1987	Alfred Bester (deceased).
1988	Ray Bradbury.
1990	Lester del Rey (deceased).
1992	Frederik Pohl.
1994	Damon Knight.
1995	A. E. van Vogt.
1998	Robert A. Heinlein, C. L. Moore, Hal Clement, and Frederik Pohl.

Sapphire Award is given for the Best SF Romance of the Year. It is sponsored by the SF Romance Newsletter. They have a Web site at http://members.aol.com/sfreditor/bestsfr.htm.

James Tiptree, Jr. Award. Named for Alice Sheldon, who wrote under this male pseudonym, this award is presented for science fiction and fantasy that looks at gender in a different way. The James Tiptree, Jr. Award is "given to the work of science fiction or fantasy published in one year which best explores or expands gender roles."—James Tiptree, Jr. Award Web site.

The Vocabulary of Fantasy
or Common Conventions

Speaking the language of fantasy readers can be very helpful for reader's advisors. The terms listed here may provide some insight into the genre.

Alchemy. A form of magic akin to chemistry.

Amulet. A small object worn or carried as a charm to protect against hostile magic.

Atlantis. A lost continent reputed to have been a land of enlightenment and magic.

Avalon. A land from Arthurian legend that exists in out world and out of it at the same time.

Bards. Individuals who play music and tell stories, often teaching through their tales. Often they are travelers roaming from place to place. Harpers are their equivalent in Anne McCaffrey's books.

Basilisks. Reptiles who can kill with their gaze.

Changelings. Children of Faerie who are left in the place of an abducted human child.

Charm. A written or sung spell. Also sometimes used as a synonym for amulet or talisman.

Chimera. Beasts made up of combinations of other animals.

Cockatrice. Synonym for basilisk.

Cold iron. An element that stops magic, particularly Faerie magic. It also stops werewolves and many denizens of the supernatural world.

Daemons or **Demons.** Creatures that sometimes bedevil the characters, sometimes are summoned as the result of magic to perform a task. In Pullman's His Dark Design series, they are companions who appear when someone is born and cannot live after their companions' deaths.

Dark Lord. The bad guy.

Dark Tower. A terrifying place, often difficult to enter and labyrinthine inside. Sometimes the interior space is larger than the exterior.

Doppelganger. A double or duplicate of a person. Sometimes an evil twin.

Dragons. Creatures that breathe fire, fly, and guard huge hordes of precious jewelry, gems, gold, and silver.

Dryads. Tree nymphs or forest spirits.

Dwarves. Creatures that are much the opposite of elves, frequently bearded and gruff. Miners and gem collectors. They are associated with darkness and earth.

Elves. Often residents of Faerie, these beings are usually tall and slender, although in some cases they are diminutive. They have pointed ears (think skinny Vulcans) They are frequently vindictive, neither forgetting nor forgiving a slight. They are associated with air and light.

Enchanters. See Wizards.

Faerie. A realm very close to Earth whose inhabitants are usually called elves. Elves have a proclivity for entering into sexual relationships with humans. Time, in Faerie, moves at a different rate, so a night spent there can equal several years in our world.

Glamour. A spell or enchantment that confuses the sense of sight. A glamour can make someone, someplace, or something appear totally different than it really is.

Goblins. Evil and sometime mischievous creatures.

Grimoires. Books of magic, sometimes like recipe books for casting spells.

Gryphon. Creature with an eagle's head and wings on the body of a lion.

Halflings. People who were born to a mixed human and elfin couple.

Harpies. Foul smelling, part bird, part woman, evil creatures.

Hobbits. Diminutive, home loving creatures with hairy toes, created by Tolkien.

Labyrinths. Structures that play a role in many fantasies, usually those of Celtic origin. Walking the labyrinth is a way of invoking magic, often of an ecologically healing type. They are maze-like constructs, sometimes underground.

Mabinogion. A collection of Welsh legends that provides a background for Celtic fantasy.

Mages. See Wizards.

Manticore. Sphinx-like creature with a human head on a lion's body, with the addition of a scorpion's tail and scary teeth.

Middle Earth. Tolkien's world.

Narnia. The world created by C. S. Lewis.

Necromancy. The area of magic that deals with communicating with or raising the dead to turn them into zombies.

Oracles. Beings who are consulted to give advice, which is almost always ambiguous.

Orcs. These can be boar-headed and boorish, evil creatures. Like many disgustingly evil creatures, they are often mentioned but not described physically.

Pentagram. A mark made on the ground or floor, used while the mage is invoking magic. Frequently the magic worker must stay within the undisturbed lines, while at other times, especially when summoning a demon or an elemental, the pentagram serves to keep the demon or elemental confined.

Rowan. A type of tree, the wood of which possesses magical abilities and protects from evil.

Runes. An invented alphabet, often of a spiky nature so that it can be used to scratch spells into rock. Runes are often used for producing a written form of magic on various surfaces, sometimes even in the form of tattoos on flesh.

Shire. Where the Hobbits live in Middle Earth.

Sidhe. Another name for the residents of Faerie.

Sorcerers. See Wizards.

Talisman. An object with magical significance, often a necklace, that traps magical essences or spirits.

Tarot cards. Cards used for divination, for fortune telling.

Three daughters or three sons. The youngest traditionally succeeds to the parents, responsibilities, but more recent variations have tried to change this convention.

Unicorns. Animals that will go only to virgins. They hold the power of healing and purification in their horns.

Unseelie Court. The congregation of Faerie's royalty.

Weird Tales. Lovecraftian type stories, Cthulhu mythos, Elder gods stories.

Witches. See Wizards.

Wizards, sorcerers, mages, enchanters, and witches. Practitioners of magic or sorcery; good, evil or indifferent casters of spells.

Wyverns. Dragon-like creatures that are smaller than dragons and lacking in intelligence. Sometimes they have scorpion-like tails.

The YALSA-BK Best Fantasy for YA List

The members of YALSA-BK, an Internet group composed mainly of librarians serving young adults, young adults themselves, and writers, discussed young adult literature and came up with the following list of recommended titles for young adults. As usual when discussing the fantasy genre, there was disagreement about which titles were really fantasy and which should be eliminated because they were science fiction. There was also disagreement about the age level of some of the titles. All titles chosen are those that members consider important for young adult readers. They are arranged in alphabetical order by title within place categories that were determined by the number of nominations. The numbers indicate the position of popularity, with *1* being the most popular. Matt Loy was the organizer of the project. It is published here with his permission and with permission of The Young Adult Library Services Association, advisory of the American Library Association.

1 Dark Is Rising series/Susan Cooper.
   Time Fantasy Quartet (*A Wrinkle in Time*, etc.)/Madeleine L'Engle.

2 Lord of the Rings trilogy/J. R. R. Tolkien.

3 *Giver*/Lois Lowry.

4 *Golden Compass*/Philip Pullman.
   Sabriel/Garth Nix.

5 Chronicles of Narnia/C. S. Lewis.
   Chronicles of Prydain/Lloyd Alexander.
   Earthsea Tetrology/Ursula K. Le Guin.

6 *Beauty*/Robin McKinley.
   Oz series/L. Frank Baum.
   Princess Bride/William Goldman.

7 *Blood and Chocolate*/Annette Curtis Klause.
   Blue Sword/Robin McKinley.
   Dark Angel/Meredith Ann Pierce.

   Enchanted Forest Chronicles/Patricia C. Wrede.
   Watership Down/Richard Adams.

8 *Ella Enchanted*/Gail Carson Levine.
   Owl in Love/Patrice Kindl.
   Tuck Everlasting/Natalie Babbit.

9 *Fire and Hemlock*/Diana Wynne Jones.
   Hero and the Crown/Robin McKinley.
   Hobbit/J. R. R. Tolkien.
   Mists of Avalon/Marion Zimmer Bradley.
   Pern series/Anne McCaffrey.
   Redwall series/Brian Jacques.
   Song of the Lioness Quartet/Tamora Pierce.

10 *Boggart*/Susan Cooper.
    Ear, the Eye, and the Arm /Nancy Farmer.
    Last Unicorn/Peter S. Beagle.
    Woman in the Wall/Patrice Kindl.

11   *Borrowers*/Mary Norton.

China Garden/Liz Berry.

Dragon's Bait/Vivian Vande Velde.

Howl's Moving Castle/Diana Wynne Jones.

Magic Circle/Donna Jo Napoli.

Rose Daughter/Robin McKinley.

Silver Kiss/Annette Curtis Klause.

Tam Lin/Pamela Dean.

Weetzie Bat/Francesca Lia Block.

Wheel of Time series/Robert Jordan.

Witch World series/Andre Norton.

Xanth series/Piers Anthony.

12   *Alice in Wonderland* and *Through the Looking-Glass*/Lewis Carroll.

Archangel series/Sharon Shinn.

Archer's Goon/Diana Wynne Jones.

Belgariad series/David Eddings.

Black Unicorn/Tanith Lee.

Briar Rose/Jane Yolen.

Deed of Paksenarrion/Elizabeth Moon.

Deerskin/Robin McKinley.

Dogsbody/Diana Wynne Jones.

Fade/Robert Cormier.

Illustrated Man/Ray Bradbury.

Little Prince/Antoine de Saint-Exupery.

Mairelon the Magician/Patricia C. Wrede.

Martian Chronicles/Ray Bradbury.

Moorchild/Eloise McGraw.

Mr. Was/Pete Hautman.

Mrs. Frisby and the Rats of NIMH/Robert C. O'Brien.

Riddle-master of Hed series/Patricia A. McKillip.

Seaward/Susan Cooper.

Something Wicked This Way Comes/Ray Bradbury.

Subtle Knife/Philip Pullman.

Tricksters/Margaret Mahy.

13   Bardic Voices series/Mercedes Lackey.

Chronicles of Amber/Roger Zelazny.

College of Magics/Caroline Stevermer.

Companions of the Night/Vivian Vande Velde.

Deryni series/Katherine Kurtz.

Dragonbone Chair/Tad Williams.

Dragon Pit series/Jane Yolen.

Enchantress from the Stars/Sylvia Louise Engdhal.

Eva/Peter Dickinson.

Fionavar Tapestry series/Guy Gavriel Kay.

Gulliver's Travels/Jonathan Swift.

Incarnations of Immortality series/Piers Anthony.

Jumper/Steven Gould.

Magician's Ward/Patricia C. Wrede.

Mallorean series/David Eddings.

Mennyms/Sylvia Waugh.

Outlander series/Diana Gabaldon.

People series/Zenna Henderson.

Perelandra trilogy/C. S. Lewis.

Playing Beatie Bow/Ruth Park.

Riftwar Saga/Raymond E. Feist.

Running out of Time/Margaret Peterson Haddix.

Screwtape Letters/C. S. Lewis.

Servant of the Empire/Raymond E. Feist, Janny Wurts.

Seventh Son/Orson Scott Card.

Shadow/Joyce Sweeney.

Shannara series/Terry Brooks.

Tales from the Brothers Grimm and the Sisters Weird/Vivian Vande Velde.

Tea with the Black Dragon/R. A. MacAvoy.

Thief/Megan Whalen Turner.

Westmark trilogy/Lloyd Alexander.

Wizardry series/Diane Duane.

Woman Who Loved Reindeer/Meredith Ann Pierce.

Zel/Donna Jo Napoli.

14 *A Chance Child*/Jill Paton Walsh.

A String in the Harp/Nancy Bond.

A Wind in Cairo/Judith Tarr.

Beauty/Sheri S. Tepper.

Belgarath the Sorcerer/David Eddings, Leigh Eddings.

Chimes of Alyafaleyn/Grace Chetwin.

Circle of Magic Quartet/Tamora Pierce.

Damiano/R. A. MacAvoy.

Dhalgren/Samuel R. Delaney.

Dither Farm/Sid Hite.

Dragon Prince/Melanie Rawn.

Dream of the Stone/Christina Askounis.

Dreams Underfoot/Charles de Lint.

Ghatti's Tale series/Gayle Green.

Gibbons Decline and Fall/Sherri S. Tepper.

Guinevere series/Persia Woolley.

Halfblood series (*Elvenbane, Elvenblood*)/Mercedes Lackey, Andre Norton.

Holding Wonder/Zenna Henderson.

Hounds of the Morrigan/Pat O'Shea.

Immortals Quartet/Tamora Pierce.

King's Dragon/Kate Elliott.

Letters from Atlantis/Robert Silverberg.

Long Night Dance/Betsy James.

Mage Winds series/Mercedes Lackey.

Magic and the Healing/Nick O'Donohoe.

Moonheart/Charles de Lint.

Myth series/Robert Asprin.

Mythago Wood/Robert Holdstock.

Nightingale/Kara Dalkey.

October Moon/Michael Scott.

Once and Future King/T. H. White.

Pigs Don't Fly/Mary Brown.

Polgara the Sorceress/David Eddings, Leigh Eddings.

Princess and the Goblin/George MacDonald.

Remarkable Journey of Prince Jen/Lloyd Alexander.

Sleep of Stone/Louise Cooper.

Spiritwalk/Charles de Lint.

Sword of Truth series/Terry Goodkind.

Tailchaser's Song/Tad Williams.

The City, Not Long After/Pat Murphy.

Tigana/Guy Gavriel Kay.

Time and Again/Jack Finney.

Time Machine/H. G. Wells.

Tough Guide to Fantasyland/Diana Wynne Jones.

True Game series/Sherri S. Tepper.

Wildside/Steven Gould.

Appendix C

Recommended Core Collection

The following includes books currently in print that should be in every well-stocked public library fantasy collection. Because so much of fantasy appears in series form, selected authors have only partial listings of titles. Series that are consistently excellent throughout are listed in their entirety, while others only have one or a few listed. The date following each title is the original publication date, and the dates following the publisher names are publication dates for particular releases. When both hardcover and paperback versions are in print, publication information has been included for only one edition of each even though some of the titles are available in multiple editions. Listing all the English-language publishers and ISBNs of the four Tolkien titles included on this list alone would take up two full pages. Different ISBNs exist for mass market paperbacks, trade paperbacks, hardcover, boxed sets, deluxe editions, omnibus editions, and variously illustrated editions. It is always advisable to check a current *Books in Print* for up-to-date publication information.

Anderson, Poul.
> *Three Hearts and Three Lions.* (1961). Baen Books, 1993. ISBN 0671721860 (paperback).

Anthony, Piers. Incarnations of Immortality series.
> *On a Pale Horse.* (1983). Ballantine Books, 1989. ISBN 0345338588 (paperback).
> *Bearing an Hourglass.* (1984). Ballantine Books, 1991. ISBN 0345313151 (paperback).
> *With a Tangled Skein.* (1985). Ballantine Books, 1990. ISBN 0345318854 (paperback).

Anthony, Piers. Xanth series (1977–).
> *A Spell for Chameleon.* (1977). Ballantine Books, 1977. ISBN 0345347536 (paperback).
> *The Source of Magic.* (1979). Ballantine Books, 1977. ISBN 0345350588 (paperback).
> *Castle Roogna.* (1979). Ballantine Books, 1977. ISBN 0345350480 (paperback).

Beagle, Peter S.
> *The Last Unicorn.* (1968). NAL/Dutton, 1990. ISBN 0451450523 (paperback).

Bear, Greg.
> *Songs of Earth and Power.* (1992). Revised omnibus edition of *The Infinity Concerto* (1984) and *The Serpent Mage* (1986). Tor Books, 1996. ISBN 0812536037 (paperback).

Bradley, Marion Zimmer. Darkover series (1962–).

> *The Forbidden Tower.* (1977). Severn House, 1994. ISBN 0727845896 (hardcover).
>
> *The Heritage of Hastur.* (1975). DAW Books, 1989. ISBN 0886774136 (paperback).
>
> *Sharra's Exile.* (1981). DAW Books, 1988. ISBN 0886773091 (paperback).
>
> *The Mists of Avalon.* (1983). Del Rey, 1987. ISBN 0345350499 (paperback).

Brooks, Terry.

> *Magic Kingdom for Sale—Sold!* (1986). Ballantine Books, 1990. ISBN 0345317580 (paperback).
>
> *The Sword of Shannara.* Ballantine Books, 1995. ISBN 0345314255 (paperback).

Brust, Steven. Vlad Taltos series.

> *Jhereg.* (1983). Ace Books, 1987. ISBN 0441385540 (paperback).
>
> *Yendi.* (1984). Ace Books, 1987. ISBN 0441944604 (paperback).
>
> *Teckla.* (1986). Ace Books, 1987. ISBN 0441799779 (paperback).

Card, Orson Scott. Chronicles of Alvin Maker. (1987–98).

> *Seventh Son.* (1987). Tor Books, 1993. ISBN 0812533054 (paperback).
>
> *Red Prophet.* (1988). Tor Books, 1996. ISBN 0812524268 (paperback).
>
> *Prentice Alvin.* (1989). Tor Books, 1989. ISBN 0812502124 (paperback).
>
> *Alvin Journeyman.* (1995). Tor Books, 1996. ISBN 0812509234 (paperback).
>
> *Heartfire.* (1998). Tor Books, 1998. ISBN 0312850549 (hardcover).

Cooper, Susan.

> The Dark Is Rising Sequence. (1965–77). Simon & Schuster, 1987. ISBN 0020425651 (paperback, boxed set).
>
> *Over Sea, Under Stone.* (1965). Simon & Schuster, 1989. ISBN 0020427859 (paperback).
>
> *The Dark Is Rising.* (1973). Simon & Schuster, 1986. ISBN 0689710879 (paperback).
>
> *Greenwitch.* (1974). Simon & Schuster, 1986. ISBN 0689710887 (paperback).
>
> *The Grey King.* (1975). Simon & Schuster, 1986. ISBN 0689710895 (paperback).
>
> *Silver on the Tree.* (1977). Simon & Schuster, 1986. ISBN 0689711522 (paperback).

de Lint, Charles.

> *Jack of Kinrowan.* (1987–90). Tor Books, 1995. ISBN 0812538986 (paperback, omnibus).

Dickson, Gordon R.
> *The Dragon and the George.* (1976). Ballantine Books, 1976. ISBN 0345350502 (paperback).

Eddings, David.
> *Pawn of Prophecy.* (1982). Ballantine Books, 1990. ISBN 0345335511 (paperback).

Feist Raymond E.
> *Magician.* (1982). Voyager (UK) 1993. ISBN: 0-586-21783-5 (paperback). This title is now available in two volumes.
> *Magician: Apprentice.* Bantam Spectra, 1994. ISBN 0553564943 (paperback).
> *Magician: Master.* Bantam Spectra, 1994. ISBN 0553564935 (paperback).

Gabaldon, Diana.
> *Outlander.* (1991). Delta, 1998. ISBN 0385319959 (paperback). Delacorte, 1991. ISBN 0385302304. (hardcover).

Gentle, Mary.
> *Rats and Gargoyles.* (1991). Roc, 1991. ISBN 0451451066 (hardcover). New American Library, 1992. ISBN 0451451732 (paperback).

Goldstein, Lisa.
> *The Red Magician.* (1982). Tor Books, 1995. ISBN 0312890079 (paperback).
> *Walking the Labyrinth.* (1996). Tor Books, 1998. ISBN 0312859686 (paperback).

Goodkind, Terry. Sword of Truth series. (1994–).
> *Wizard's First Rule. (*1994). Tor Books, 1994. ISBN 0312857055 (hardcover). Tor Books, 1995. ISBN 0812548051 (paperback).
> *Stone of Tears.* (1995). Tor Books, 1995. ISBN 0312857063 (hardcover). Tor Books, 1996. ISBN 0812548094 (paperback).
> *Blood of the Fold.* (1996). Tor Books, 1996. ISBN 0312890524 (hardcover). Tor Books, 1997. ISBN 0812551478 (paperback).
> *Temple of the Winds.* (1997). Tor Books, 1997. ISBN 0312890532 (hardcover). Tor Books, 1998. ISBN 0812551486 (paperback).

Grimwood, Ken.
> *Replay.* (1987). William Morrow, 1998. ISBN 068816112X (paperback).

Hughart, Barry.
> *Bridge of Birds: A Novel of Ancient China That Never Was.* (1984). Ballantine Books, 1990. ISBN 0345321383 (paperback).

Jacques, Brian.
> *Redwall.* (1986). Ace Books, 1998. ISBN 0441005489 (paperback).

Jones, Diana Wynne.
> *Howl's Moving Castle.* (1986). Greenwillow, 1986. ISBN 0688062334 (Library binding).

Jordan, Robert.

> The Wheel of Time series. Tor Books, 1993. ISBN 0812538366 (paperback first 3 volumes, boxed set). Tor Books, 1997. ISBN 0812540115 (paperback second 3 volumes, boxed set).
>
> *The Eye of the World.* (1990). Tor Books, 1993. ISBN 0812511816 (paperback).
>
> *The Great Hunt.* (1990). Tor Books, 1992. ISBN 0812517725 (paperback).
>
> *The Dragon Reborn.* (1991). Tor Books, 1993. ISBN 0812513711 (paperback).
>
> *The Shadow Rising.* (1992). Tor Books, 1993. ISBN 0812513738 (paperback). Tor Books., 1992. ISBN 0312854315 (hardcover).
>
> *The Fires of Heaven.* (1993). Tor Books, 1994. ISBN 0812550307 (paperback).
>
> *Lord of Chaos.* (1994). Tor Books, 1995. ISBN 0812513754 (paperback). Tor Books, 1994. ISBN 0312854285. (hardcover).
>
> *Crown of Swords.* (1996). Tor Books, 1996. ISBN 0312857675 (hardcover). Tor Books, 1997. ISBN 0812550285. (paperback).
>
> *The Path of Daggers. (*1998). Tor Books, 1998. ISBN 0312857691 (hardcover).

Kay, Guy Gavriel.

> *Tigana.* (1990). Viking, 1999. ISBN 0670833339 (hardcover). New American Library, 1994. ISBN 0451451155 (paperback).

King, Stephen, and Peter Straub.

> *The Talisman.* (1984). Viking, 1984. ISBN 0670691992 (hardcover). Berkley, 1991. ISBN 0425105334 (paperback).

Klause, Annette Curtis.

> *Blood and Chocolate.* (1997). Bantam Books, 1997. ISBN 0385323050 (hardcover).

Kushner, Ellen.

> *Thomas the Rhymer.* (1990). Tor Books, 1991. ISBN 0812514459 (paperback).

Lackey, Mercedes. Heralds of Valdemar trilogy. (1987–88).

> *Arrows of the Queen.* (1987). DAW Books, 1996. ISBN 0886773784 (paperback).
>
> *Arrow's Flight.* (1987). DAW Books, 1987. ISBN 0886773776 (paperback).
>
> *Arrow's Fall.* (1988). DAW Books, 1996. ISBN 0886774004 (paperback).

Le Guin, Ursula K.

> *The Lathe of Heaven.* (1971). Avon Books, 1997. ISBN 0380791854 (paperback).
>
> The Earthsea tetrology. (1968–90).
>
> *A Wizard of Earthsea* (1968). Atheneum, 1991. ISBN 0689317204 (hardcover, library binding). Bantam Spectra, 1984. ISBN 0553262505 (paperback).

The Tombs of Atuan. (1971). Bantam Spectra, 1984. ISBN 0553273310 (paperback). Atheneum, 1991. ISBN 0689316844 (hardcover, library binding).

The Farthest Shore (1972). Bantam Spectra, 1984. ISBN 0553268473 (paperback). Atheneum, 1991. ISBN 0689316836 (hardcover, library binding).

Tehanu. (1990). Atheneum, 1991. ISBN 0689315953 (hardcover, library binding). Bantam Spectra, 1991. ISBN: 0553288733 (paperback)

Leiber, Fritz.

*Conjure Wife. (*1953). Tor Books, 1993. ISBN 0812512960 (paperback).

Lethem, Jonathan.

Gun, With Occasional Music. (1994). Tor Books, 1995. ISBN 0312858787 (paperback).

Lewis, C. S.

The Chronicles of Narnia. (1950–1956). HarperCollins Juvenile Books, 1994. ISBN 0060244887 (hardcover, boxed set). HarperCollins Juvenile Books, 1994. ISBN 0064471195 (paperback, boxed set).

The Magician's Nephew. (1955). HarperCollins Juvenile Books, 1994. ISBN 0064471101 (paperback). HarperCollins Juvenile Books, 1994. ISBN 0060234970 (hardcover).

The Lion, the Witch and the Wardrobe. (1950). HarperCollins Juvenile Books, 1994. ISBN 0064471047 (paperback). HarperCollins Juvenile Books, 1997. ISBN 0060277246 (hardcover).

The Horse and His Boy. (1954). HarperCollins Juvenile Books, 1994. ISBN 0064471063 (paperback). HarperCollins Juvenile Books, 1994. ISBN 0060234881 (hardcover).

Prince Caspian. (1951). HarperCollins Juvenile Books, 1994. ISBN 0064471055 (paperback). HarperCollins Juvenile Books, 1994. ISBN 0060234830 (hardcover).

Voyage of the Dawn Treader. HarperCollins Juvenile Books. 1994. ISBN 0064471071 (paperback). HarperCollins Juvenile Books, 1994. ISBN 0060234865 (hardcover).

The Silver Chair. HarperCollins Juvenile Books, 1994. ISBN 0064471098 (paperback). HarperCollins Juvenile Books, 1994. ISBN 0060234954 (hardcover).

The Last Battle. HarperCollins Juvenile Books, 1994. ISBN 0060234938 (hardcover). HarperCollins Juvenile Books, 1994. ISBN 006447108X (paperback).

Lovecraft, H. P.

At the Mountains of Madness. (1964). Ballantine Books, 1990. ISBN 0345329457 (paperback).

Caffrey, Anne. Pern series. (1968–).

Dragonflight. (1968). Ballantine Books, 1997. ISBN 0345419367 (paperback).

Dragonquest. (1971). Ballantine Books, 1990. ISBN 0345335082
(paperback).
The White Dragon. (1978). Ballantine Books, 1994. ISBN 0345341678
(paperback).

McKillip, Patricia A.

The Forgotten Beasts of Eld. (1984). Harcourt Brace, 1996. ISBN
0152008691 (paperback).
The Hed trilogy. (1976--79).
Riddlemaster of Hed. (1976). Del Rey, 1989. ISBN 0345331044
(paperback).
Heir of Sea and Fire. (1977). (Currently not in print in the U.S.) Futura
Orbit (UK), 1981. ISBN 0708880509 (paperback).
Harpist in the Wind. (1979). Del Rey, 1989. ISBN 0345324404
(paperback).

McKinley, Robin.

Beauty. (1978). HarperTrophy, 1993. ISBN 0064404773 (paperback).

Moon, Elizabeth.

The Deed of Paksenarrion. (1988). Baen Books, 1992. ISBN 0671721046
(paperback, omnibus).
Sheepfarmer's Daughter. (1988). Baen Books, 1995. ISBN 0671654160
(paperback).
Divided Allegiance. (1988). Baen Books, 1988. ISBN 0671697862
(paperback).
Oath of Gold. (1988). Baen Books, 1990. ISBN 0671697986 (paperback).

Murphy, Pat.

The Falling Woman. (1986). Tor Books, 1993. ISBN 0312854064
(paperback).

Nix, Garth.

Sabriel. (1996). HarperCollins, 1996. ISBN 0060273224 (hardcover).
HarperTrophy, 1997. ISBN 0064471837 (paperback).

Norton, Andre, and Mercedes Lackey. The Halfblood Chronicles.

The Elvenbane. (1991). Tor Books, 1993. ISBN 081251175 (paperback).
Elvenblood. (1995). Tor Books, 1996. ISBN 0812563190 (paperback).

Powers, Tim.

Expiration Date. (1995). Tor Books, 1996. ISBN 0812555171 (paperback).

Pratchett, Terry. Discworld series. (1983–).

Small Gods. (1992). Harper, 1994. ISBN 0061092177 (paperback).
Lords and Ladies. (1992). Harper, 1996. ISBN 0061056928 (paperback)
Wyrd Sisters. (1988). New American Library, 1996. ISBN 045145012
(paperback).
Reaper Man. (1991). New American Library, 1992. ISBN 045145
(paperback).

Pullman, Philip. His Dark Materials. (1995–).

    The Golden Compass. (1995). Alfred A. Knopf, 1996. ISBN 0679879242
        (hardcover). Alfred A. Knopf, 1998. ISBN 0679893105 (paperback).

    The Subtle Knife. (1997). Alfred A. Knopf, 1997. ISBN 0679879250
        (hardcover). Del Rey, 1998. ISBN 0345413369 (paperback).

Shetterly, Will.

    Dogland. (1997). Tor Books, 1997. ISBN 0312851715 (hardcover). Tor
        Books, 1998. ISBN 0312866054 (paperback).

    Elsewhere. (1991). Tor Books, 1992. ISBN 0812520033 (paperback).

Springer, Nancy.

    Larque on the Wing. (1994). Avon, 1999. ISBN 0380972344 (paperback).

Stewart, Mary. The Merlin Quartet. (1970–83).

    The Crystal Cave. (1970). Ballantine Books, 1996. ISBN 0449911616
        (paperback).

    The Hollow Hills. (1973). Ballantine Books, 1996. ISBN 044991173X
        (paperback).

    The Last Enchantment. (1979). Ballantine Books, 1996. ISBN 0449911764
        (paperback).

    The Wicked Day. (1983). Ballantine Books, 1996. ISBN 0449911853
        (paperback).

Tepper, Sheri S.

    Beauty. Bantam Spectra, 1992. ISBN 0553295276 (paperback).

Tolkien, J. R. R.

    The Hobbit. (1937). Houghton Mifflin, 1997. Illustrated by Alan Lee. ISBN
        0395873460 (hardcover). Ballantine Books, 1992. ISBN 0345339681
        (mass market paperback).

    The Lord of the Rings. (1954–1955). Houghton Mifflin, 1988. ISBN
        0395489326 (hardcover, boxed set).

    The Fellowship of the Ring. (1954). Ballantine Books, 1989 ISBN
        0345339703 (paperback). Houghton Mifflin, 1988. ISBN 0395489318
        (hardcover). Tolkien (UK), 1997. ISBN 0261103571 (paperback).

    The Two Towers. (1954). Houghton Mifflin, 1988. ISBN 0395489334
        (hardcover). Ballantine Books, 1986. ISBN 0345339711 (paperback).

    The Return of the King. (1955). Ballantine Books, 1993. ISBN 0345339738
        (paperback). Houghton Mifflin, 1988. ISBN 039548930X (hardcover).

Turtledove, Harry.

    Misplaced Legion. (1987). Ballantine Books, 1991. ISBN 0345330676
        (paperback).

Weis, Margaret, and Tracy Hickman. Death Gate Cycle.

    Dragon Wing. (1990). Bantam Spectra, 1990. ISBN 0553286390
        (paperback).

    Elven Star. (1990). Bantam Spectra, 1991. ISBN 0553290983 (paperback).

    Fire Sea. (1991). Bantam Spectra, 1992. ISBN 0553295411 (paperback).

Serpent Mage. (1992). Bantam Spectra 1993. ISBN: 0553561405 (paperback)

The Hand of Chaos. (1993). Bantam Spectra, 1993. ISBN 0553563696 (paperback).

Into the Labyrinth. (1993). Bantam Books, 1994. ISBN 0553567713 (paperback).

Seventh Gate. (1994). Bantam Spectra, 1995. ISBN 055357325X (paperback).

White, T. H.

The Once and Future King. (1958). Ace Books, 1996. ISBN 0441003834 (paperback). Putnam, 1980. ISBN 0399105972 (hardcover).

Williams, Tad. Memory, Sorrow, and Thorn series.

The Dragonbone Chair. (1988). DAW Books, 1994. ISBN 0886773849 (paperback). Hill & Wang Publishing, 1988. ISBN 0809900033 (hardcover).

Stone of Farewell. (1990). DAW Books, 1994. ISBN 0886774802 (paperback).

To Green Angel Tower. (1993). DAW Books, 1994. ISBN 0886775981 (paperback, part 1). DAW Books, 1994. ISBN 0886776066 (paperback, part 2). DAW Books, 1993. ISBN 0886775213 (hardcover).

Windling, Terri.

The Wood Wife. (1996). Tor Books, 1997. ISBN 0812549295 (paperback).

Windling, Terri, and Delia Sherman, eds.

The Essential Borderland. (1998). Tor Books, 1998. ISBN 0312865937 (hardcover).

Wolfe, Gene.

Shadow and Claw (omnibus edition of *The Shadow of the Torturer* [1980] and *The Claw of the Conciliator* [1981]). Tor Books, 1994. ISBN 0312890176 (paperback).

Wrede, Patricia C.

Magician's Ward. Tor Books, 1997. ISBN 0312853696 (hardcover).

Zelazny, Roger. Amber series (first sequence).

Nine Princes in Amber. Avon, 1995. ISBN 0380014300 (paperback). G K Hall & Co, 1998. ISBN 0783884257 (hardcover, large print).

The Guns of Avalon. (Out of print.)

Sign of the Unicorn. Avon, 1999. ISBN 0380008319 (paperback).

The Hand of Oberon. Avon, 1998. ISBN 0380016648 (paperback).

The Courts of Chaos. Avon, 1999. ISBN 0380471752 (paperback).

References

Bloom, Harold. *Classic Fantasy Writers*. Chelsea House, 1994.

Clute, John, and John Grant, eds. *The Encyclopedia of Fantasy*. St. Martin's Press, 1997.

Hartwell, David G., and Kathryn Cramer, eds. *Masterpieces of Fantasy and Enchantment*. St. Martin's Press, 1988.

Lofting, Hugh. *The Story of Dr. Dolittle, Being the History of His Peculiar Life at Home and Astonishing Adventures in Foreign Parts*. Frederich A. Stokes, 1920.

Manlove, C. N. *Modern Fantasy: Five Studies*. Cambridge University Press, 1975.

Perret, Patti. *The Faces of Fantasy*. Tor, 1996.

Shippey, Tom, ed. *The Oxford Book of Fantasy Stories*. Oxford University Press, 1994.

Silverberg, Robert, ed. *The Fantasy Hall of Fame: The Definitive Collection of the Best Modern Fantasy Chosen by the Members of the Science Fiction & Fantasy Writers of America*. HarperPrism, 1998.

Tymn, Marshall B., Kenneth J. Zahorski, and Robert H. Boyer. *Fantasy Literature: A Core Collection and Reference Guide*. R. R. Bowker, 1979.

Author/Title Index

Subject Index